A
Very
Human
President

A Very Human President

BY

Jack Valenti

W·W·NORTON & COMPANY · INC ·
New York

Copyright © 1975 by Jack Valenti

First Edition

Library of Congress Cataloging in Publication Data

Valenti, Jack.
  A very human President.

  1. Johnson, Lyndon Baines, Pres. U. S., 1908–
1973.   2. Valenti, Jack.   I. Title.
E847.V34   1975   973.923'092'4 [B]   75–17701
ISBN 0–393–05552–3

Published simultaneously in Canada
by George J. McLeod Limited, Toronto

Book designed by Jacques Chazaud
Typefaces used are Janson and Caslon Bold
Manufactured by Vail-Ballou Press, Inc.

Printed in the United States of America

1 2 3 4 5 6 7 8 9

To my mother, may God be with her,

and

my father

Contents

Foreword

From my earliest reading, I have always been fascinated with the figure of Achilles. He was so immensely human, a man preeminently noble but led by an excess of his own high nature to flawed action. As the central character in the *Iliad*, he dominates the story even when he is offstage. It is in the sentient Achilles, his courage and his anger, his skill, his pride, his commanding presence that of all literary and mythical creations he stands forth as one most like great captains of mortal history. So it is that I am persuaded that there was much of Achilles in Lyndon Johnson.

There will be a considerable body of literature in many books on the Johnson presidency. Not one of them, as this volume attempts to make clear, will really be definitive on the work President Johnson performed, the deeds he accomplished, the flaws he exhibited, or an accurate and total measure of the man himself.

To the press which examined his actions, and to the public which benefited from his achievements, part of the fascination of Lyndon Johnson is due to the complexity of the man.

I am bound to say that I personally will never look upon his like again in my lifetime for he cannot be duplicated. He was an awesome engine of a man: terrorizing; tender; inexhaustibly energetic; ruthless; loving of land, grass, and water; engulfing; patient; impatient; caring; insightful; devoted to wife, family, and friends; petty; clairvoyant; compassionate; bullying; sensitive; tough; resolute; charming; earthy; courageous; devious; full of humor; brilliantly intelligent; brutal; wise; suspicious; disciplined; crafty; generous. He was all of these and more. He had one goal: to be the greatest president doing the greatest good in the history of the nation. He had one tragedy: a war whose commitments he could not break and whose tenacity he did not perceive.

I think I knew him as well as anyone beyond his wife and family, and I know I did not know all of him. I have tried to put into this book the president I did know and to say that knowledge as truthfully as one can see and tell the truth.

I admired him greatly, and never once wavered in my loyalty to him as a man and leader. But I never reckoned loyalty and love as barriers to the sighting of faults and flaws. No man or woman is without them. Had President Johnson been so, he would not have the barest resemblance to the towering, endlessly mesmerizing figure he surely was.

There is in this book no pursuit of others' stories or comments. I have not interviewed anyone, except my own memory and my written notes. For this book is about the President Johnson *I* knew, worked with, talked with, met with, suffered with, followed, and served. It is about *my* experiences—what I saw, heard, and said—in the White House. Every conversation recounted is firsthand. Every event recorded has me as an eyewitness to the event.

I have given my judgments, but they are plainly labeled. I am not trying to debunk or exalt. This book is an honest account.

Having spent a working lifetime in and around the political arena, as campaign manager, political counselor, and as White House assistant, I have no grand ideas about political leaders. I have learned that in politics the very best of us is apt to be partly right and partly wrong. All public men are flawed, inclined toward error, subject to the vagaries of emotion, pride, infatuation with self that all of us, public and non-public people, learn to live with. There are no infallible heroes, bleached dry of sin, unblemished by lesser notions, with ideals fully intact, and a conscience preserved against the need for contrition.

Thus, when we understand that human beings are our leaders, we can view them with tolerance and forbearance. What we can hope for are leaders who will be right more often than they are wrong, and not inspire within ourselves larger expectations than mortal men are capable of delivering. Perhaps we can be forgiven if we ask them to be wiser than those who give them power, and possessed of character, vision, and caring in such dimension that the tasks they obligate themselves to fulfill will not go unserved by all their skills and all their courage, and that they will bring honor to the duties they have sworn by solemn oath to perform. It is because the public political person is so intensely human that he gives off sparks.

I have worked in two of life's classic fascinations, politics and movies, and while there are dazzling attractions in both areas, it is the political man who most excites me. Since LBJ was the quintessential political being, I suppose that is why I was in thrall continuously to him. I was never bored by him or with him, I was either in a stew or a passion.

If in my life now I find it difficult to caustically criticize presidents who followed and will follow Lyndon Johnson it is because I understand so vividly the difficulties that besiege whomever is president. To criticize, the old cliche goes, is easy. To think, to decide, and then to act, is terribly hard. To put it in the words of President Johnson— "Any damn jackass can kick a barn down, but it takes a pretty good carpenter to build one."

My gratitude goes to Bethlyn Hand, Nancy Scott, and Ruth France who helped me so much in the preparation of this book, and to Thomas Crocker, former Woodrow Wilson Scholar at Princeton, who was so helpful. My thanks, too, to my wife, Mary Margaret, who knew the Johnson family better than I, who worked closely with Majority Leader Johnson and Vice-President Johnson, and who inspected these pages to give them fuller truth.

Jack Valenti
Washington, D.C.

Nothing could overcome his central will or rupture his sense of duty.

PART I

The
Beginning

"**G**et in the second chopper and come to my office as soon as you land. Understand?" Lyndon Johnson, just a few hours into his presidency, the thirty-sixth in a line that began with George Washington, cupped his hands against my ear to shield his words from the deafening roar of two presidential helicopters whirring impatiently in the night air of Andrews Air Force Base outside Washington, D.C.

Air Force One bearing the new president, and the body of the slain John F. Kennedy, had just landed after a flight from Dallas. It was a few minutes after 6:00 P.M., EST, Friday, November 22, 1963.

The trip of eighteen miles by chopper from Andrews to the White House took seven minutes. The memory of that first of many journeys from Andrews to the White House and back is still vivid in my mind. We skimmed low across a flickering chasm of illuminated homes and darting headlights ribboning their ways in dismantled design across Washington. I could have almost reached out and touched the slim tower of the Washington Monument as we passed. Then I saw the ground coming up to meet us.

Across the Ellipse, we dropped quickly and then floated, suspended in the air, as the pilot maneuvered to touch the grassy opening at the South Grounds. (The helicopter landing pad at the White House is but a few short feet from the entrance to the Diplomatic Reception Room, the prime entering area of the south side of the White House.)

This was my first visit to the White House.

I had over the preceding years driven around the White House when I visited Washington. The lines of tourists waiting to visit the public rooms was always so long I was never tempted to try it myself. One day, I thought, I will see if I can arrange some kind of special tour without waiting that interminable length of time. But I never got around to it.

Now I was truly going to get a special tour.

The president's chopper had landed at 6:32 P.M., just a scant minute or so before ours put to ground. The president was still at the entrance to the Diplomatic Reception Room, talking to Under Secretary of State George Ball, and Defense Secretary Robert McNamara. I joined them and we all began to walk, not through the Diplomatic Reception Room, but through the Rose Garden to the walkway that led from the Mansion to the West Wing. We strode to the doorway of the West Wing, but not to the president's Oval Office. I found it strange that the president would not go to his office. I learned later that LBJ had decided not to use JFK's office but for the time being to continue using his vice-presidential suite in the Executive Office Building. That is why we descended the stairs from the West Wing first floor to the basement and through this underfloor to the exit at the West Basement. We walked across the private street dividing the West Wing from the EOB and thence up the elevator to the third floor vice-presidential office.

The vice-presidential office was a three room suite and within minutes it was crowded. The president ensconced himself in the large, high-ceilinged, fireplaced room, comfortably but not luxuriously furnished.

Shortly before 7:00 P.M., I escorted Senator J. William Fulbright, chairman of the Senate Foreign Relations committee, and Ambassador Averell Harriman into the office.

I fidgeted outside, in the middle of what would have appeared to an objective onlooker to be a melange of confusion. No one of the Johnson aides, Marie Fehmer, his secretary; the late Cliff Carter, his chief political agent; Bill Moyers, nor any of the rest, was quite certain of what lay ahead. We were all busy on the phone and trying to assemble what measure of office discipline we could construct. Supervising it all was Walter Jenkins, the number one assistant to the president, a privileged post no one in the Johnson entourage contested, nor chose to. Jenkins, a mild and scholarly man, generous to his colleagues, full of integrity, endlessly at work, sat in the background and, as usual, was on the phone constantly with his notebook in front of him, transcribing conversations as he talked in that swift Gregg shorthand he knew so well.

A bit after 7:00 P.M., the president talked with former President Harry Truman, and at 7:10 he conversed over the phone with former President Dwight Eisenhower. Some moments later he was on the phone to Sargent Shriver, the slain president's brother-in-law.

At about 7:40 the congressional leadership came to call. They were ushered in. I sat quietly inside near the wall of the office, listening to the president importuning them for their help and their counsel.

Some moments after 8:00 P.M., LBJ sat at his desk to have some soup. It was his first "food" since his morning breakfast in Fort Worth.

At 9:27 P.M., the president came out of his office followed by Walter Jenkins and Cliff Carter. He smiled at Marie Fehmer and then he motioned for me to come to him. He put his arm around me and said, "Drive home with me, Jack. You can stay at my house tonight and then we will have a chance to do some talking. Are you ready to leave now?" Well, I thought, I suppose I am ready in view of the fact I was not quite sure precisely why I was even here in the first place.

I fell in beside the president and with Cliff Carter we marched down the hall of the Executive Office Building flanked in front and rear by Secret Service agents. We emerged onto the street separating the West Wing from the EOB and climbed into the big black limousine waiting for us, two Secret Service men in the front seat. The rest of the agents piled into another car in back and we headed toward the Elms, the large dwelling the Johnsons had purchased from Mrs. Perle Mesta.

When we arrived at the circular driveway at the entrance to the home it had all the appearance of a small convention. A security post had been set up at the driveway approach and a legion of agents was literally surrounding the house. When we stopped, agent Rufus Youngblood, the soft-talking southerner who had so courageously flung his body over LBJ's to protect him from whatever might be assaulting him, spoke: "Mr. President, we have not had time to really arrange phone communications here. For the time being, we are operating over your residence phones."

Youngblood also vouchsafed the totally unnecessary information that the phones were taking a helluva beating from the incoming calls. An emergency phone had been put in to take care of the Secret Service communications net and it would be several hours before the presidential communication system could be set up at the Elms. The president nodded, and climbed the step to his front door.

He had left this home as one man and he was returning as very much another.

Mrs. Johnson embraced him warmly, kissing him and hugging him. The president said, "Bird, I would like a bite to eat and could you fix something for the rest?" Mrs. Johnson opened her arms as if to collectively embrace us. "Darling, we have food in the dining room. Come sit down and relax."

First, though, the president wanted to sit in the library. Mrs. Johnson brought him a large glass, chocked with ice and orange juice and the president sprawled in the massive black chair in the library. He sipped his orange juice and then abruptly, though easily and without apparent thought, lifted his glass to a picture of the late Speaker, Sam Rayburn, on the wall, the grim bulldog visage staring at us, the bald pate looming above the stern countenance.

"I salute you, Mr. Speaker, and how I wish you were here now, when I need you." The words were spoken softly. The president was obviously moved by the spark of that moment.

By this time the house was beginning to fill with Johnson people who came to see the new president. Horace Busby, the scholarly Texan who for years was the chief wordsmith for the president, gripped the edge of the president's chair and began to talk to him in low tones. Shortly, the president and all of us moved to the dining room where we ate the first full meal most of us had had in a long time.

The time sped by. About midnight, the president decided to go to bed. He beckoned to Cliff Carter, Moyers, and me and we climbed the stairs to the second-story bedrooms. "Bill," he said to Moyers and Carter, "you and Cliff find a bedroom on the third floor. Put your things up there and then come on down so we can talk." They headed to the third floor and the president took me by the arm. "You stay in this bedroom, Jack," he said. We went inside the bedroom. He sat down on a chair near the doorway.

"I suggest you call Mary Margaret and get some clothes sent up here for you. I also think you ought to get your affairs in order in Houston so you can dispose of your business. I want you to be on my staff at the White House. You can live with me here and at the White House when we finally move there. Meanwhile, you can look for a house so that Mary Margaret and Courtenay can join you." (Indeed, I did live at the White House, occupying a two-room suite on the third floor of the mansion from December 7, 1963 until February 15, 1964, when my family arrived to take up residence in Georgetown. The Johnsons waited fourteen days before moving into the presidential living quarters at the White House.)

That was the way it was. I hesitated a bare moment. I was not certain how to respond. In truth, I had no response. The president had clearly thought this through and he was not giving me any alternative, even if I chose to explore one.

The president rose and I followed him to his bedroom at the end of the hall. He got into his pajamas and lay on the vast bed, triggering the television set into life by remote control. He sat half-upright on the left side of the bed and motioned me to a chair at his side. We watched now the unfolding drama on the TV set, the endlessly probing eye of the camera and narrator's voice recounting just who Lyndon Johnson was, his background, his career, and there were speculative accounts by various commentators on how fit a president he would be.

By this time Moyers and Carter had come in, Carter sitting at the foot of the bed and Moyers sitting on the right side. We watched in silence for some time.

I had picked up a notepad and was doodling when the president began to speak, almost as if he were talking to himself. He mused about what he ought to do and began to tick off people he needed to see and meetings he should construct in the next several days. I scribbled down the essence of what he was saying so I would have a clear view of what he wanted, so it could be done without fret or delay. Within an hour I had scrawled over thirty pages of that notebook. It became my direction-finder the next several days as all that the president had described was put into concrete action.

That night the president had what might be called his first staff meeting. Bill Moyers, Cliff Carter, and I listened more than we talked.

The president seemed relaxed, stretched out on the bed, watching the bright glow of the TV set. He was surrounded by men whom he trusted, and in whose persons he fully knew reposed love and respect and enduring loyalty to him. Here in this bedroom was the man the whole world was inspecting via television, and whose measure was being taken in every chancellery in every capital in every country on all continents. He had spent over thirty years in the political arena. He knew all the tremors and soft spots and the unknowns that infested every cranny of the political jungle. He could catalog a thousand good and bad qualities, achievements, as well as errors made visible by those national leaders whom he knew.

He was mindful of what lay ahead of him, this was evident. There was not what one would call eagerness to greet the next day, but there was studied appraisal of the weights and scales into which a hundred swift decisions must be fitted and he gave no outward sign that he was anxious or worried or hesitant.

It was early morning when finally he signalled he was ready to get some few hours of sleep. Moyers, Carter, and

I, still gripped with an inflexible tension (at least I was), said our goodnights and each took to our beds. I wandered to my bedroom and for an hour I lay awake, trying to assess the capricious wind that had carried me so fast to so strange a place.

For me it all began one sunny day in 1957 in Houston, Texas, the day I met the then majority leader of the United States Senate.

The Lyndon Johnson I met that day was near the summit of his Senate power, a chamber he dominated with confidence and parliamentary skill. He knew every secret of the Senate, he knew its voids and its hesitations as well as he knew the wellsprings of strength and occasional lunges toward that redemption of pledges given and the service to country and state that each member had sworn so solemnly to bestow.

Historians might well certify that in all the history of the Senate there has never been, even in the epiphanies of senatorial legend and myth, a leader who mastered the rules and rubric of that body and who perceived the motives and motivations of its members so well. Johnson as Senate chieftain produced two formulas which more than any others generated success. He never slept when there was work to be done (and often wouldn't let the Senate sleep either) and he always looked beyond the next objective. He searched out alternative actions with the same care other men gave to their families. He steered clear of trivia, which is the indigenous political virus. He had no hobbies except the Senate. He never made trifles serious business nor allowed serious business to be treated as trifles. He played the Senate as a grand master would organize a world's championship chess match, plotting each move several moves in advance. To all this he applied an intellect more capacious and finely tuned than any other contemporary public man. All this demanded (and received) an energy and resolution that bordered on the devout.

All these characteristics were not newly minted. If one probes the early life of Lyndon Johnson there are to be found all these qualities surfacing in him as a young man.

When he first came to Washington in 1931, age twenty-three, as a fledgling congressional secretary to Congressman Robert Kleberg of King Ranch fame, there was an organization called the Little Congress. It was peopled by secretaries and assistants to congressmen. They had their own elected hierarchy. It should come as no surprise to latter-day Johnson watchers that LBJ would, almost immediately on arriving in Washington, be elected as the Speaker of the Little Congress, highest office in that group, and thus celebrated by his young peers as the best among them.

When in 1935 he was appointed by President Franklin Roosevelt to head the National Youth Administration in Texas, at age twenty-six, the now heralded and seemingly inexhaustible Johnson energy embraced his new duties. Within a year, the Texas NYA was held up as a model for other states to emulate. He deployed his forces throughout Texas and there was more bustle evident and more work being done than in any other state.

Here, on examination, the senatorial and presidential Johnson was being formed. Attention to detail, minute and usually overlooked detail, became his hallmark. A mania for perfection, doing the job right the first time was to be his goal. A compassion for the powerless, especially the Mexican-American, formed in him, roots to his past that he never forgot. One can not grow up on the land in Texas, soil that grudgingly gave up a living to those who inhabited it, and not be affected by the ebb and flow of the quality of life. Rain, grass, weather became enor-

mously important. Education, hardbought, difficult, became a holy cause. He felt at home with the drifters, the
farmers, the Mexican-Americans, the blacks, those pressed
to the wall by circumstances and the wiles of the elements,
both beyond their personal control.

If you had asked Johnson what he was most proud of,
he would have listed near the top of his achievements
bringing electricity to the lamplit homes of the hill
country folk. In central Texas, there are dams and rural
electrification that changed the life of farmers for the better and it was Lyndon Johnson who cajoled and importuned both a president and a Congress to make it all effective.

As a young man in his teens he taught as a substitute
teacher in the Cotulla, Texas school, where his students
were Mexican-American children struggling to learn an
alien language, and the impression of that time on his conscience was never to be erased. It is small wonder that in
all his campaigns the one group that never deserted him,
that always stood by him, lauded him and followed him
and believed him were the Spanish-speaking voters of
Texas. It is a piece of strange business that "back East,"
this compact Johnson cadre of supporters, that included
Mexican-Americans and blacks, was little understood.
The so-called oil establishment viewed him with suspicion, and with few exceptions, opposed him bitterly in his
campaign with Coke Stevenson in 1948, fought him as a
vice-presidential candidate in 1960, and never really made
their peace with him.

(In 1964, when the conservative Democratic bloc threatened to fight Senator Ralph Yarborough in the primary by
putting forward a distinguished Texas congressman, Joe
Kilgore, LBJ passed the word that he would, for the first
time, make his choice known in a primary fight. He had
no particular affection for Yarborough who was proved to

be on too many occasions more than obstreperous, but he said to his Texas colleagues, "I want Yarborough back in the Senate. He may not like me and he gives me trouble, but he votes with the people, and that's reason enough to keep him in office." I remember that incident very well for I was the instrument LBJ used to carry the message. Though the conservative wing of the party grumbled, they presented no opponent to Yarborough. The president had his way.)

So it was in 1957 that my first meeting with Lyndon Johnson took place. At that time I had co-founded and with my partner Weldon Weekley directed a thriving advertising agency built from the ground up. We had started with one client and now we were, by Houston standards, the proprietors of one of the region's most successful agencies.

A week before my first meeting with the majority leader, Warren Woodward, one of LBJ's closest lieutenants in Houston, called me. It seemed that the majority leader wanted to meet young men in Houston with whom he was not acquainted. He wanted, said Woodward, to bring more new young men into his friendship, to get to know them, to let them know him. Unlike a good many officeholders who foolishly imagine their electoral destiny to be fixed in time and place, who believe their supporters will never grow old and tired and then one day wake up to find that death and aging have depleted their elite cavalry, Johnson knew that the secret of longevity in office is the constant replenishing of the palace guard. Too often, otherwise intelligent and sanely efficient congressmen and senators forget that political maxim and too late discover young bulls crowding the primaries. By that time their eroded position is too far gone to repair, and the leader, frustrated, angry, unsupported, either falls in the election or sullenly withdraws.

Lyndon Johnson was determined this was not going to happen to him. Each year, he made forays into different parts of the state to recruit new lieutenants, to entice to his banner younger men of wider energy and more committed passions than his older captains. I think it is fair to say that in 1957 the Johnson organization was brimming with health and actively in motion in all of the 254 counties of Texas.

Woodward instructed me carefully, and when I agreed to meet the majority leader, I could imagine Woody putting a check mark beside my name on his little folder and possibly murmuring, "only four more to call today."

At the appointed hour of 5:00 P.M., I presented myself at the Shamrock Hilton Hotel on the southern periphery of the city. In a private room on the third floor, I mingled with about twenty-five of my volunteer friends. They were all young. (I would guess that at thirty-five I was one of the oldest in the room. When the senator prescribed that his recruits be young, he meant young; just be sure they can vote.)

Now we waited, drinking coffee, exchanging small talk. The opulent environments of the Shamrock Hilton seemed a bit overdone, but the day was bright and clear and the room was airy and I was glad to leave my office early. It had been a steadily boring day.

The senator came in. Abruptly. The door opened and he walked in quickly, moving from one young man to the next, saying, "I'm Lyndon Johnson," gripping the hand firmly, eyes full on the face of slightly awestruck young acolytes. I murmured something, I can't remember what; then the senator took a cup of coffee and talked to us. I have not the foggiest recall of what he said. I can only remember the overall impression I had. He prowled the room as he talked. When he put the coffee cup on a small table, he stuck his left hand in his pocket and absently jingled coins. You usually never have to identify natural leaders when they are in a room. You are drawn to them as inexorably as you find heat in a chilled enclosure. There is no guidebook for this kind of animal magnetism. It can scarcely be taught in university cloisters nor can it be found in Dale Carnegie after-working-hours classes. In the street gangs that form in the urban centers, the sociologists tell us that no election is ever held. The leader assumes authority because he is the leader, not necessarily the strongest or the biggest or the bravest, though it is possible all these attributes might be assembled in his person. He leads until he fails or falters or exhibits fear and then he is displaced. One may call it charisma or personality or strength of character or whatever. Lyndon Johnson, in that room with young men made an impression on them and me that lay somewhere between the fascination of watching a great athlete in motion and the half-fear, half-admiration of seeing a panther on a cliffside, silken, silent, ready to spring.

From that day forward I was a Lyndon Johnson man.

I was in the Senate auditorium on July 5, 1960, when LBJ announced his candidacy for the Democratic presidential nomination, just a few short days before the convention would begin. My main memory of that announcement day was watching the Johnson entourage enter the auditorium from a side door. I particularly remember one staff member. She was blond, lovely, almost slight, and she moved easily, gracefully. I learned later her name was Mary Margaret Wiley, secretary to the majority leader. Two years later I married her.

I was there in Los Angeles at the Democratic convention in 1960, working with Jim Rowe and Leonard Marks as one of their aides in trying to flush out delegates to the LBJ cause. We were singularly unsuccessful.

As I sat in front of the TV set on the vice-presidential nominating evening, I heard the JFK choice for second spot. Already this news had been an open secret by early afternoon. It had a stunning impact, not only on the nation, but most emphatically on the Texas delegation, most of whom like me marched on the periphery. I was caught by total surprise. Perhaps that is not as strong as I would like to make it. Mind-boggling would be a better description.

Some years later I came to know the reasons why. It was plain to LBJ that with a Democratic president in the White House the post of majority leader would lose much of its influence and possibilities of power. The chief executive, a Democrat, assuming that JFK won, would call the shots and the majority leader could only be an ally, not a leader.

Moreover, LBJ felt in his gut that he could be the decisive element in a triumphant campaign. The South was restless, fretting under its distaste for northern candidates. LBJ felt that he could speak the language of the southerner, understand his complaints, and draw him toward the Democratic party. If he declined the post and JFK lost, it would be, LBJ thought, due to his own declination of the vice-presidency.

And so all of these factors bore down on him. He accepted the offer of Kennedy to the outrage of his foes and the astonishment of his friends.

Within two weeks of the convention, my phone rang and the familiar voice of LBJ flowed through the wire. "I want you and your agency to handle all the advertising, media selection, and TV production for the Kennedy-Johnson ticket in Texas. Get in touch with Woody Woodward as quickly as possible," he said. "And then arrange to be in Austin for a meeting we will hold in about a week. You'll get clear instructions as to date, time, and place." There was a slight pause, then the voice stern and hard said: "I aim to carry Texas for this ticket. We are not going to lose Texas. A lot will depend on how well you do your job. Is that clear?" Yes, sir, it was clear, and when I had hung up, I plunged into this new assignment.

In truth, the key asset in the Kennedy-Johnson campaign in Texas was Lyndon Johnson and everyone knew it. The battle was on and LBJ was in total command which is to say no one slept or dawdled or hesitated. This was no campaign for timid souls or torpid spirits. It was a twenty-four-hours-a-day assignment. My other clients simply had to accept the fact that I was to vanish from my agency scene except for this one crucial task: Win for the Democratic party in Texas.

Within days every Johnson county leader in each of the 254 Texas counties had his marching orders. The cadres of Johnson forces geared up for the prime political fight of our lives.

There was one obstacle and we all knew it, though many of us decried it. It was the Catholic issue. But if you were an LBJ man, and you were also a thorough-going Protestant, hand-wringing, river-dipping, brush-arbor revival or whatever type, you simply swallowed your prejudices and flung yourself into the fray as if you had conducted novenas all your life. As a Catholic myself, I was one of those in the front lines who bitterly resented the fact that religion was to be the cancer in the camp, but it was, and we had to accept this and overcome it as best we knew how.

Lyndon Johnson had no irritating ambivalence about Catholics, or any other creed. He was an ecumenist before the word gained credence. Before and after being president he could attend a Catholic church, a synagogue, or any one of a number of Protestant services with equal passion and participation. He believed in God, and though brought up in the creed of the Disciples of Christ, proudly and tolerantly watched his wife and daughters bind themselves in the Episcopal faith. He simply detached himself from any dogma, indeed, found rigidly-fixed doctrine as unappetizing in religion as he disavowed it in politics. He recognized the Catholic issue intrusion as the principal thorn to be plucked and he deployed his troops in the field with this common enemy firmly fastened in his sights. (When in his presidency, some gossip scouts published news he was to follow his daughter, Luci, in her conversion to Catholicism, LBJ only smiled. He was as far from conversion to any certain faith as he was beyond being tied to predictions about political behavior in his fellow man. He wanted to be free to choose whatever church he wanted to attend that Sunday. He could get as much cheer and hope from Billy Graham and Reverend George Davis—of the National Christian Church in Washington—as he could get from Father Schneider of Stonewall and Rabbi Schachtel of Houston. In many ways, Lyndon Johnson was truly the most tolerant man I have ever known about other men's religious beliefs.)

But there were rancorous mutterings in east Texas, in the Bible belt that stretched across the central plains and hill country, and in the northern tier of the state to the Panhandle the animus was evident. These discordant sounds plainly marked the depth of the religious discontent that nourished defections to the Republicans. It was going to be close, we all knew that, which, of course, only plunged LBJ deeper and more energetically into the fray.

In September, my agency held the operational reins to a unique confrontation that both LBJ and John Kennedy knew had to take place sooner or later. It was the collision between the presidential candidate and the Texas Protestant leadership. It was decided that our Agincourt would be in Houston.

Kennedy pledged he would confront Protestant ministers, on live television, in which this religious issue so long quivering beneath the surface was now to erupt in the open, and like a live grenade it was to be tossed from one to the other of the opposing forces. No one could predict its outcome and as I delved into the details of putting this show on the air I began to have some anxious misgivings. We pulled the pin on the grenade at 9:00 P.M., September 12, 1960, in the Crystal Ballroom of the Rice Hotel in Houston. Once the cameras began to turn my job was done. The drama was now ready to unfold and it was Kennedy versus the ministers.

The ballroom was packed with Houston ministers, (as we intended it would be) many of whom scowled their hostility, and displayed some of their relish at the opportunity of getting their rhetorical hands on the young papist candidate. If I had dared, I might have gripped some rosary beads myself, but as one of my associates said to me when I suggested the rosary bead ploy, "Right now, Jack, we need longbows and cavalry more than we need prayer." I said nothing, but thought we could use a little of both.

I almost embraced John Kennedy when he finally appeared. (It should be noted that in the pre-TV activities and post-program rejoicing, I never met him or talked to him.) He did something at the outset that was a classic political maneuver. Hundreds of ministers waiting, with only a handful of Kennedy partisans in the audience, the grounds, as it were, in the hands of the enemy, Kennedy suddenly appeared at the door to the ballroom.

No one was with him. He was utterly alone. Not one aide or friend or relative or anyone was near him. He paused only momentarily at the entrance, and then strode, purposefully, easily, with neither nod nor smile, but strangely confident, through the aisleway and across in front of the banked chairs where the ministers sat, and then to the rostrum where he sat alone.

It was a brilliant *tour de force*. Somehow, that act of serenity, the march to the microphone alone with no one to guide or counsel him, set the whole meeting at tilt, and reset the combat scales. I cannot probe the minds of those ministers even now, yet I cannot but believe that they compulsively admired his emboldened entrance, as if he were saying to his doubters, "I am not afraid of you or this confrontation."

The rest is history.

The ministers were totally ineffective in their zeal to dismantle Kennedy's oft-stated belief in separation of church and state. His opening statement which declared his personal convictions about his religion and its bearing on his political life and the ensuing question-and-answer period seemed, to me at least, proof against any more debates. Kennedy had clearly won, even to my LBJ-biased view. News commentaries the next day verified this view. The smell of victory was both lively and evident.

That telecast, imprisoned on tape, was to be used a hundred times in Texas in other cities where it was an absolute imperative that we quash this religious issue before it gunned us down in the polling booths. I was later told that the national Kennedy apparatus used the same tape in dozens of other American cities where this same question of a Catholic in the White House threatened to snap already tautly drawn political threads.

LBJ was delighted and made his pleasure known to me. He knew better than any man the necessity of a clear-cut win in the ministerial confrontation. We had done that, thanks to Kennedy's flawless performance in a dicey forum where it could have easily gone the other way.

On election day, the LBJ-exhorted legions were at work all across the state. It was a massive effort, the most finely honed of any Johnson campaign where the stakes were the highest and the possibility of ruin the most savage.

The result was still too close. The Kennedy-Johnson ticket, with all the planned and executed efficiency of the Johnson organization, carried Texas by a mere 46,233 votes.* But it was a win. Texas was safely in the Democratic column. Lyndon Johnson had performed as he had declared he would. He carried Texas.

* * *

On June 1, 1962, Mary Margaret Wiley and I were married in Houston, and Vice-President Johnson was there to give the bride away.

My wife and I spent much time with the Johnson family. I wrote a number of speeches for LBJ and he and I talked often about political matters, particularly as they concerned Texas. In February 1963 at the invitation of LBJ, we accompanied him to the imauguration of Juan Bosch as president of the Dominican Republic and in June 1963 we were both with him when he represented the United States at the funeral of Pope John XXIII in Rome.

So, I was drawn increasingly closer to the vice-president, sharing his thoughts, giving him counsel and help when he called for it. It was in the fall of 1963 that he called on me again for aid in an adventure that was to be the most cataclysmic in all my life.

The president and the vice-president, in tandem, were to pay a three-day visit to Texas with the two central events to be an appreciation dinner in Houston on No-

---

* This thin sliver of a margin can best be appreciated by comparing it with the 704,619 vote difference in Texas between Johnson and Goldwater in 1964.

vember 21, 1963, for Congressman Albert Thomas, the powerful chairman of the Subcommittee on Independent Offices of the House Appropriations Committee, and a fund-raising dinner in Austin on November 22. I was given command of the Houston visit.

The decision made by the White House seemed politically correct. The fourth largest state in the Union was shifting to the right of center. Texas had always been situated in the middle of the political road, and the Democratic party, while controlled by the moderates and the conservatives, nonetheless was continually vibrated by its vocal and energetic liberal wing. In November, 1963, the move was more to the right. Kennedy was losing ground. It was a strange and formless phasing out of pro-Kennedy feelings and a phasing in of the anti's. The Belden Poll, conducted in Texas, revealed the drop in presidential popularity. Texas, so thinly sliced in the 1960 election, was crucial, even vital, to the president's re-election plans.* It was the judgment of the White House that a tour, first to San Antonio, heavily Catholic, center of the largest Chicano enclave, thence to Houston—and the Thomas dinner—with more voters than any other urban area in Texas, then to Fort Worth and Dallas, there to confront the bastions of conservatism, and the climax at a gigantic statewide fund-raising evening in Austin, the state capital, would hopefully produce an upsurge for the president. The plans were designed not only to give a lift to sagging

---

* On the day of JFK's arrival in Houston, the *Houston Chronicle* front-paged the headline, GOLDWATER COULD BEAT JFK IN TEXAS. The story went on to disclose a statewide survey taken by the *Chronicle* which indicated that if the election were held on this day, Goldwater would garner 1.3 million votes to Kennedy's 1.2 million votes, a 52 percent to 48 percent margin for the Arizona senator. "General disenchantment with the Kennedy administration and an adverse reaction to his civil rights program are the two most frequently mentioned reasons for the President's decline in popularity," said the *Chronicle* story.

Democratic morale, but also to replenish the re-election war chest with badly needed funds.

Vice-President Johnson was ambivalent about these desires. He sensed that the usually brutal conflicts between liberal and conservative in Texas were at more than usual boiling points. When the vice-president sniffed the air, he found it foul. Governor John Connally,* handsome, facile, a spellbinding persuader, extraordinarily popular, was riding the crest of his electoral strength. Connally was in venomous discord with the senior Texas senator, Ralph Yarborough. Between these two resolute men there was a strong, raging feeling of mutual distrust, bordering on hatred. Yarborough, a passionate and lonely figure in Texas politics, felt pressed and cornered by the ever-growing and ever-looming reach of the bold governor. Without the softening influence of more cautious advisers, Yarborough flung aside all entreaties for a truce. He brooded over what he considered slights, which once made visible to him (and sometimes only him) swelled into gargoyle masses, amidst

---

* John Bowden Connally is, in my book, one of the most fascinating and attractive public figures to mount the American political stage. As a young law student at the University of Texas he first came within the Johnson orbit. Younger by several years than LBJ, he was drawn to Johnson, as other young men in later times would be drawn to Connally. They were of a piece, dominating, awesomely energetic, shrewd, and prescient, feeling and sensing where others were oblivious. Connally learned from Lyndon Johnson and he brought Johnson mannerisms and the LBJ approach-to-problems to his own being, attaching them to his personal charm and physical grace and facility to communicate.

Both Connally and LBJ had one spectacular quality which I can confirm is a mighty big asset when testy issues are on the table. It is the ability to command confidence in those around them. Connally, on stream and in movement, disengages doubts from those who hear him, unfastens others' fears, dissolves all hesitancies; in short, he leads.

I would have to count John Connally as one of the two or three ablest men in public life today.

what Yarborough deemed to be dark conspiracies aimed at unseating him. He, too, would be on the ballot in 1964, and he stalked the state searching out his enemies in unlighted passageways. Moreover, because the senator considered Connally to be the confidant and protégé of Lyndon Johnson, it followed naturally he should also mistrust the vice-president with an intensity equal to the distaste he felt for Connally.

It was clear to JFK that a 1964 campaign with the sitting governor and senior senator at each other's jugular would not have happy results in November, 1964. And so the president importuned the vice-president for this visit to Texas. He needed the money for the campaign, that was plain, but he desperately needed to warm up a state so precious to his re-election, and he sought, through Ken O'Donnell, his principal political agent, to mollify Yarborough and enlist Connally. JFK pressed the vice-president for an all-clear signal.

But the vice-president deferred to Connally for final approval on the trip. The brunt of preparation for such an excursion would fall to the governor and therefore the governor must not only approve the visit, but give it total logistical and political support. Connally hesitated. He, too, was not sure of the timing nor the need. He was not so much uneasy about Yarborough as he was about the reception that Kennedy would get, not only in the streets but at the fund-raiser in Austin. Failure was not congenial to Connally. So he waited. Finally, in a private meeting with President Kennedy in Washington, he agreed. The signals were hoisted and the plans were sealed.

At 4:23 P.M. in the lateness of a blue-skied day, on November 21, 1963, the sleek, silver-bellied Boeing 707, Air Force One, the personal plane of the president of the United States, settled confidently on runway 90 of Houston's International Airport, with only an eloquent screech to give evidence of making contact with the concrete strip. The big plane braked quickly and taxied to the open ramp area where a crowd of several thousand waited in anticipatory excitement. Then, it slowed, and stopped, gleaming in the sun, with stately letters in blue that spelled out UNITED STATES OF AMERICA above the long blue striping that went from nose tip to tail assembly, along and through the window line.

Congressman Albert Thomas of Houston and Senator Ralph Yarborough were aboard the president's plane and would disembark with him. And there among the greeting group was the vice-president, whose plane had landed only minutes before.

I checked the security police, and made a last minute reconnaissance of the area to see that the motorcade cars were in place. I nodded to the captain of the police standing beside the open convertible that was to take the president and his wife, and their party to downtown Houston and the Rice Hotel where they were to rest before the dinner that evening.

As we waited for the president and his entourage, I chatted with the vice-president. He seemed calm, poised, unattended by doubt. His was an ambiguous position. His own role in the future was partially clouded. Columnists were dropping vague and disquieting hints that Johnson would be "dumped" from the ticket. At a recent press conference, the president answered this question sharply by making it solidly clear that indeed Lyndon Johnson would be on the ticket with him. But the rumors refused to die.

And yet the vice-president never once allowed his discipline to give way. He never uttered, to my knowledge, one word of criticism about the president or his staff, either privately or publicly. In my conversations with the vice-president, in all my inclusion in gatherings where he was present, at the dinner table I shared on many occasions with him, he invariably referred to the president with respect and affection. I could see, as could others, that it was not easy for this energetic, restless, authoritative man who ruled the Senate with a firmness it had not known for generations, who during the Eisenhower years was the second most influential man in the nation, to become a non-person, as it were, to be becalmed in the background seas and always to comport himself with self-effacing dignity.

I found it true that some members of President Kennedy's official family did not follow their leader's example and sometimes their treatment of the vice-president must have surely stretched his patience to the limits. But John Kennedy gave Lyndon Johnson continuous respect and Johnson responded in kind. They were both political professionals. They knew the rules of the game and they played by them, accepting what had to be, and each in turn doing what he had to do, each measuring and keeping under control personal passions and emotions generated by what some observers concluded was an unnatural arrangement to begin with. And so Lyndon Johnson did his job, as best he could, serving out his days in bleak expectancies.

Now the air of anticipation on the ramp came alive. The door of the presidential jet swiveled open. The stairway was in place. First there was a blank darkness. The doorway, hostile to the sun, shrouded what it had to offer. Then, she was there. When Jacqueline Kennedy came into view, the screams of approval and applause from the crowd was a booming compliment. Mrs. Kennedy was almost always absent on political tours. She chose to make her first 1963 political appearance as the president's wife in a southwestern political setting. She waved hesitantly, a whisper of a smile on her face, and the smile grew wider as the applause soared to higher reaches.

The president was now by her side. He waved, the crowd went wild, youngsters leaping in excited adulation. He waved vigorously, smiling, thoroughly enjoying himself. He took his wife's arm, helped her down the stairs. Mrs. Kennedy came down the steps, slowly but with assurance, her left hand touching the rail slightly. A black cone beret sat far back on her head. The wind at the airport rushed at her, but not once did she employ that wisp of a gesture, the brow-clearing touch of hand to forehead that was so much the mark of Jackie Kennedy.

I blurted out orders to my group of aides. Get to the cars, I shouted, make sure the motorcade is ready to roll. Keep the ceremonial greeting line at attention. Move along. The security police circled the plane. The crowd was pressing against the barricades. Two more aides were dispatched to the crowd line.

The president moved down the receiving line. Mrs. Kennedy was guided by her husband to be first to shake hands and he followed close on her heels. Governor and Mrs. Connally, Senator Yarborough, and Congressman Thomas followed the president.

Later I realized I was so busy watching that I did not shake hands with the president or Mrs. Kennedy. I raced to the motorcade checking the cars. They were ready. Over my shoulder I could see the president "hitting the fence," a presidential ploy I was to become so familiar with. The crowd was almost mad in their enthusiasm. I remembered thinking that this was a cheerful augury to what would come later as the motorcade moved downtown. So far, everything was still working marvelously. Congressman Thomas was elated. He gripped my shoulder, "Great work, Jackson."

Then, it happened. The first foul-up. Senator Yarborough refused to ride with the vice-president. The police officer looked at me helplessly. I was furious at this act of pique by Yarborough, but I had no time to be an arbitrator. We commandeered Albert Thomas's car, seated the senator next to the congressman and placed Vice-President and Mrs. Johnson in another car.* The motorcade was underway. As the cars moved slowly out, circling on the ramp and heading toward the airport exit, I clambered in a Ford and found myself riding with Kenneth O'Donnell.

On the Gulf Freeway stretching toward downtown Houston, ten miles away, there was no place for crowds. They would come later, I hoped, as we made an entry onto the streets leading to the downtown area. O'Donnell was dour, unsmiling. Some months later, when I found myself in the role that O'Donnell was filling that day, I recognized and understood the withheld approval that was inert within O'Donnell. I was an unknown factor. How well did I know my job, how well had I done it, were questions that I imagine flowed unspoken through his mind. Though he had sent advance men in to check and organize, the burden of success lay on the shoulders of the local people. This was our town. We knew what needed to be done, and success or failure depended on us.

Two days earlier I had met with Jerry Bruno who was the chief of the presidential advance squad. He had gone with me to the Sam Houston Coliseum while I pointed

---

* Senator Yarborough, ever suspicious, and irritated because the vice-president had prior claims on Texas patronage, conveyed to Johnson all his own misgivings about Connally. It was Yarborough's judgment that LBJ was the Machiavelli inciting much of the senator's problems in Texas. But even Yarborough partisans were taken aback by the abrupt breach in courtesy that Yarborough displayed at the Houston airport when the presidential motorcade was due to begin. Escorted to an open car to ride with Vice-President and Mrs. Johnson, the senator turned away, refused to enter the car, ignored Mrs. Johnson's warm smile. I quickly got the senator into a car with Congressman Thomas, who looked surprised when I deposited Ralph Yarborough into the seat beside him.

out to him the precise arrangements we had made. We walked through the entire coliseum, Bruno asking questions to which I gave seemingly satisfactory answers. He made no specific suggestions and then flew away to check the other cities. I never saw him again in connection with this event. The advance man on the spot was an affable and effective man named Marty Underwood. Later, I would get to know him as a thorough-going professional. He and I talked constantly in person and on the phone. After a few days, he felt easier in my presence and apparently let me have my head in the arrangements. I had passed approval one afternoon a day before the arrival when Marty gave me a JFK tie-clip. This was the advance man's Legion of Honor. It was a ceremonial embrace worthy of being recorded on film, constructing within me, I suppose, the proper amount of gratitude.

I learned a good deal about advance operations on this particular occasion which I managed to insert in my own tasks as President Johnson's appointments secretary. I counted it of no small importance in my White House operations to rely whenever possible on the local people. I found it maddening when an advance man, possibly surfeited with his own importance, trampled callously on local toes, inciting local outrage over orders given without firsthand knowledge of the political nuances and hidden problems that only knowledgeable local people would understand. I found Marty Underwood specially skilled in the care and feeding of local chiefs. His principal asset which he brought with unfailing good humor to his assignments was a faith in the general intelligence of those who lived in the city being visited, and whose political judgment he respected. He never intruded on me in affairs where I considered outside judgment not to be of substantive value. He never ordered anything done without checking the local effects with me. But Underwood was a

special breed of man. Most advance men are not so prescient, and bungled assignments, bruised feelings, and a
general disheveling of the entire event are predictable
when the advance man views himself as "above the locals."

I was praying that all the elements of a presidential
visit, detailed and endless, were going to fall into place. It
would not be for want of work, for I, and those with me—
particularly my agency staff people—had been toiling for
weeks frustrated by annoyances, the avalanche of details
and lack of communication with Washington as to specifics, such as who was going to ride in what car and in
what position in the motorcade. It was a ritual to be repeated a thousand times later in other times and places, for
the soiled affections of public officials denied their proper
place near the Sun King are apt to be abrasive.

On the ride downtown, O'Donnell was visibly nervous.
I was surprised at that. I had assumed he had been involved in a hundred such enterprises and would be a cool
cat, nerves under harness. But he wasn't. He was plainly
and obviously fidgety. In short, he wasn't sure of anything
and his manner betrayed his doubts.

Now we were off the freeway and within a dozen blocks
of the Rice Hotel, and the crowds were there. God, they
were there. Three, four, and five deep, as we neared the
wide streets of downtown Houston. They were enthusiastic and we could hear their shouts as the presidential
convertible passed them. As the crowds grew thicker and
more friendly, O'Donnell's flat-planed face, so resembling
Jack Palance, began to take on a more cheerful mien. He
peered out the windows, first one side and then the other.
"They're here, aren't they?" he said to no one in particular.

"They damn sure are," I responded, with a clear infer-
ence that I had personally herded them into place with
precision instructions. Finally we turned on Main Street.

On both sides of the wide street there was nothing to see but a great wave of human beings, clinging together, leaping up to see better, screaming, waving, laughing. In front of the Rice Hotel, as the motorcade finally stopped, there were fully 5,000 or more people at the hotel intersection, flooding the side streets and gathering in a fleshy semicircle totally screening off everything.

"What's your estimate?" asked O'Donnell, ever the statistical technician.

"I'd say between 300,000 and 400,000." (the *Houston Post* later called it over 300,000.)

"Be sure the newspapers and TV guys get that figure. Have the chief of police give it to them," he ordered.

I leaped from the car, O'Donnell in my wake. The presidential party had already been taken to the elevators and were on their way to the massive suite which I had badgered the hotel officials into making immaculate.

The hotel lobby was a sea of confusion. I thrust myself through the crowd, using a police officer as my interference. I wedged myself in an elevator with security men. O'Donnell was nowhere to be found, but I was secure in the notion that O'Donnell was not new to crowded hotel lobbies and he could find his own way. I went immediately to the suite of the vice-president, and within seconds was knocking on his door.

The vice-president was in an expansive mood. "Fine reception, Jack," he said, "I think the president will be pleased."

I greeted Mrs. Johnson and my wife, who had arrived before the presidential party. The suite was thronged with friends of the vice-president. I whispered to my wife, "It went well, very well." She smiled and said, "I am so glad."

The vice-president beckoned to me and I followed him into a room adjoining the living room of the suite. There we sat and talked. I watched his face in the half-light of the room. The face was scoured with the lines of thousands of sun-blasted days in his Texas hill country. They lay deep in the neck and the forehead. His was an imposing face, the more impressive when he stretched himself to full height, usually looming over his fellows.

The campaign trip was of vast importance to the vice-president. His pride and his own status was at stake, and would be on the line in the Kennedy re-election march in 1964. LBJ knew that his association with the Kennedy administration had diminished his power in his own home state. In the Houston *Chronicle* this day was a story on page fourteen headlined LBJ IMAGE TARNISHED IN TEXAS. The story said in part:

> In all areas except South Texas there is a recurrent theme: That Johnson is more disliked now than at any time in his long career in public office.
>
> The dislike is attributed directly to his having accepted the vice-presidency, thereby identifying himself as part of the JFK team.

The vice-president held up a large pamphlet. It was the printed program for the Austin dinner which my agency had created and completed in record time. "This is excellent, Jack. You did it right, and you did it on time." He paused, and then said, "Will we have any problems tonight?" What he really meant was whether the local political scene was in shape, would there be any mavericks stirring trouble; in short, had we inserted discipline in the proceedings?

"No, sir, no problems. We are all set. Everything is in readiness. The hall will be full. You saw the greeting the president got today from the crowds. I believe all will go well."

He nodded. Somehow I felt the anxiety he felt. The

tour was committed. It had to keep going. LBJ wanted, with an intensity I had not previously seen, the visits to each city to be paragons of hospitality and warmth. Yet, this was a tour in which his own immense talents were absent from the planning and the implementation. He was depending, for example, on the Albert Thomas organization in Houston and on John Connally people in the other cities. In the Senate and in the tending of his political fences, Johnson dove into every detail. Nothing, no matter how insignificant was beneath his querying hand. He chose to know and be told everything, in splendid and unending specifics. When I got to know him much more intimately I came to understand this ceaseless quest for facts.

The vice-president rose to his feet, shrugged his shoulders into his jacket, and beckoned me to follow him. We went into the large living room where Mrs. Johnson, Mary Margaret, and others were sitting. Abruptly, LBJ turned to me. "Why don't you pack a bag and fly with me to Fort Worth tonight, and then we'll go on to Austin tomorrow night? We'll have a chance to talk." He smiled at Mary Margaret and continued speaking to me though facing her. "You can be back home late tomorrow night or the morning after. That's not taking you away too long, is it?"

I was pleased. The vice-president had divined my thoughts. I did want to go with him and because I had a role in the Austin fund-raising dinner, I catered to the idea of flying with him on his 707 so we could discuss the next night's big event.

Mary Margaret composed a small frown. I knew what she was thinking: "Is this trip necessary?" Our first baby, Courtenay Lynda, was only three weeks old and the prospect of my being gone from Houston, if only for two days, was not congenial to her. But she remained silent.

Neither one of us knew that when I boarded the vice-president's plane late that same evening, with two night's clothing in a small hand valise, I was never to return to my life in Houston.

Now it was time to go to the coliseum for the Albert Thomas dinner. I bade a temporary goodbye to the vice-president and Mrs. Johnson, made arrangements for Mary Margaret to be transported to the dinner, and flung myself into the final details before the president and the vice-president arrived on the scene.

Managing a large political gathering in which the prime exhibit is the president of the United States is an exercise in doubt and torment. There are barriers and obstructions, mostly man-made, as well as the prevalence of nagging fears that something will go wrong, images of chores untended, instructions overlooked, and a barrel-full of egos of local politicos to be warmed. The list is endless.

I knew we would have our crowd. I felt that. But I also hedged my bet. I had considered the debacle of being short of customers, a fate worse than being fired at the stake with slow-burning faggots. I had told the press we would have 3,500 in attendance. Unbeknownst to anyone but my aides, I had instructed tables and chairs for 3,000 to be mounted. In reserve, ready to roll, were additional tables and chairs to seat an extra 500. We deliberately kept a wide aisle in the rear of the hall, for quick access to make serving dinner easier (so I had casually mentioned to the press). But my floor managers were triggered to set up the extra tables in that spacious aisle space on a moment's notice. Thus, it would be dutifully reported "an overflow crowd exceeding already generous estimates." So it goes.

To the rear of the speakers' platform, shielded from the backstage area by a flowing, heavy curtain, we had constructed an enclosure made suitably private by thick red velvet fabric totally encircling it. Inside the enclosure was a carpeted floor, laid this very day, as well as comfortable chairs, tables, and a small refreshment bar.

Here we would house, before the ceremonies began, the president, vice-president, and their wives. Our head-table guests, some fifty of them, were being corralled in a private room off the main hall, leaving the backstage enclosure strictly for our stars. A short set of stairs had been built from the backstage area to the head-table platform so the president and his party would have to move no more than fifty feet to be visible to the audience.

The hall began to fill early. Almost ten minutes before my prearranged estimate, I gave the signal to start bringing in the extra tables. (One of my operatives passed the word to the press that we were beseiged with an overflow crowd.) It was now clear that while we might have other problems, a shortage of guests was not going to be one of them.

Soon I had the message. The president and his party were arriving at the side entrance of the coliseum. They would be escorted to the rear enclosure. I walked quickly around the dinner area to the backstage area. A somber-faced man stopped me.

"Sorry," he said, "this is off-limits."

"But," I protested, hopefully authoritatively, "I'm in charge of these arrangements. For God's sake, let me in."

"Sorry," he repeated, massively unimpressed, "no further, and no exceptions."

I was slowly beginning to boil. It was plain that this unsmiling Secret Service agent knew his duty and was damn certain to do it. At that precise moment when I considered a number of alternatives none of which, on reflection, would have succeeded, another agent sauntered over. "He's okay," he said. "He's running the show, he's one of Albert Thomas's men."

I have always accepted the fact that the agent who certified me, whose face has been blurred by corrosive memory, was due special awards. Had I been able to identify him later, I would have surely importuned the president to canonize him, by whatever special rites the Secret Service carries out pre-beatification.

I reached the private enclosure, stopped, hesitated, poked my head inside, and eased on in. The vice-president caught my eye, beckoned me to his side. He held me around the shoulder and brought me to the president. "Mr. President, this is Jack Valenti," he said, "I told you about him earlier."

The president smiled, a wide, friendly smile, and greeted me warmly. "Lyndon tells me I have you to thank for this terrific crowd in Houston." His smile grew wider and more hospitable. "I ought to carry you with me to handle other visits, particularly when I am not sure what kind of reception I will get." He grinned at the vice-president and they both savored their not-so-private joke.

Close up the president was more handsome than his pictures, more muscular, the body tight-knit, though there was an aging taking place. I could see it in the face, the furrows laying their line from mouth to cheek. But he exuded a litheness, an alertness as if he were ready to move quickly if he had to. Suddenly I thought a bizarre, unconnected thought. He reminded me of a Plantagenet captain, a wise, brave, splendid knight, stronger than he seemed and older than he looked, perhaps Richard I or Simon de Montfort, perhaps the Black Prince.

The president was obviously in a favorable mood and well he might be. The response of Houston citizens was an astounding thing for in truth this was the largest outpouring of people than any previous political visit had been able to muster. It had been a friendly crowd, with hostile faces and signs so rare as to be nonexistent. Even dour Ken O'Donnell expecting much less, relieved to discover much more, had commented earlier the reception had passed the most optimistic expectations.

The president took my arm, and four steps away he introduced me to his wife, who was seated in a large green wing chair commandeered for this occasion. She murmured, "How do you do," smiled, and I was, as were most Houstonians that day, enchanted with her beauty and with her. I turned to embrace Mrs. Johnson, who was seated next to Mrs. Kennedy, and returned to the side of a very relaxed and jubilant vice-president.

JFK and LBJ talked easily of politics, Johnson taller by half a head, leaning forward to emphasize a point.

I quietly withdrew, for there was still work to be done before they climbed the newly constructed pinewood stairs that would take them to the long head-table where all the ranking guests were now being seated.

It would strike me later, strike me with the impact of an axe handle that it was my lot to meet John Kennedy for the first time on the last night he lived.

The dinner was a huge success. Albert Thomas, surfeited and glowing with honors, gifts, the loving embrace of his constituency, the luxuriant words of the president and the vice-president, hugged me and thanked me profusely.

My own thoughts, however, had fled the Sam Houston Coliseum. The Houston job was done, over, and I had quickly unfastened my connection with it. Now, I ruminated about Austin, and its fund-raiser climax to the presidential tour.

When I later got aboard the vice-president's plane it was my first encounter with one of the presidential Boeing 707s. I learned later it was not a precise duplicate of 26000, Air Force One, but at that moment, it was pretty exciting to me, duplicate or no.

We landed in Fort Worth at midnight. I ran down the steps, and located the vice-president's car, a late-model Lincoln Continental. I stood quietly beside it while the lengthy welcoming ceremonies went forward. After concluding the greeting, Vice-President and Mrs. Johnson appeared, ready to get in and begin the motorcade to the Texas Hotel where we would spend the night.

To my total amazement, Senator Yarborough was fetched up by an aide, who whispered to me, "The senator will ride with the vice-president." If I looked as if I had seen an apparition, I could not disguise it. It became readily clear that JFK or someone close to the president had had a long talk with Yarborough for he was surely not the irritated man who balked in Houston. There was no sign of reluctance nor pique now, only a beaming Yarborough who greeted LBJ and Mrs. Johnson.

I sat in the front seat, Mrs. Johnson in the middle in the rear, the vice-president to her right and Senator Yarborough to her left. The conversation could not be described as spirited but it was nonetheless conversation, aided by a broadly tolerant vice-president who generated laughter when the talking became desultory. I was aware of the many sides of LBJ, and I admired the ease with which he handled Yarborough. He was full of humor and he accepted Yarborough's presence, uninfected by the bitter memory of a few hours before.

At the Hotel Texas, I joined Liz Carpenter and Cliff Carter in a huge four-bedroom suite which we would share with LBJ and his wife. Once we were settled in, the vice-president became even more expansive, relaxed, at peace with himself. We sat, the five of us, reminiscing on the unbroken success of the trip thus far. Mrs. Johnson said, "Didn't Mrs. Kennedy look pretty and didn't she handle herself with such charm and dignity?"

I could have described Mrs. Johnson in those same

phrases. It was typical of Mrs. Johnson to be generous to others, particularly those for whom she had admiration and respect. In all my years of close contact with this remarkable, incredibly warm and loving lady, I never once caught any sign of brittle humor or caged indictments, not once. Invariably she conducted herself with unfeigned, open honesty, with an inbred grace and unerring good taste, never on stage, never dissembling, always herself. She is a rare, unduplicatable human being, an impossible target for enemies, and was a sure, inexhaustibly steady pillar of strength to her husband.

Her political judgments were sound. She never spoke hurriedly about issues or problems. She thought seriously when asked about her views. She had definite opinions and she expressed them lucidly, and in vivid phrase, with that edge of softness that dulls a critical response when what she said was at variance with what was on the table. From every encounter she retrieved all the thorns. I would have to judge that in a crunch, the president valued her considered opinion more than any of his counselors because he knew that, alone among his entourage, she delivered her views without any self-interest or leashed ego that may have been hidden in the breasts of all the rest of us. She had lived with him and by him for over thirty years of rough political campaigning and though she was always a lady, she was also a sturdy political pro.

One has to be careful when describing Mrs. Johnson. There is the temptation to go overboard in heaping laurels on her. Yet the record is plain and untarnished. How she managed to combine several lives, wife, mother, adviser, activist, ceremonial White House partner, and retain her composure and her good humor is still not clear to me. She always did her job, uncomplainingly.

Years later I remarked to an audience that if anything had happened to Mrs. Johnson in LBJ's political career, he would have been severely crippled. I believed it then. I believe it now.

The morning hours came quickly and with the morning's light was brought the last day of the presidential journey. November 22, 1963 began as the previous day had ended, auspiciously, full of high possibilities, a hospitable day which all of us were ready to leap into, readying ourselves for the big dinner that evening in Austin.

We landed in Dallas and disembarked in the dazzle of a bright sun. The motorcade formed quickly and we were on our way. I rode with Liz Carpenter, Pamela Turnure (Mrs. Kennedy's aide), and Evelyn Lincoln (the president's secretary).

The crowds were as large as those in Houston. The atmosphere was barren of hostility, totally unlike the unfriendly ad that had appeared that morning in the *Dallas Morning News*. There was only this four-to-five-deep throng of thousands of cheering people, laughing, waving, screaming their delight, the epitome of what every happy political reception ought to be like.

Then it began.

Swiftly, without the rage of warning, the car in front of us accelerated to a dizzying speed. I saw a policeman, gun bared, awkwardly scaling a grassy embankment. We sped beneath an underpass. I craned my neck. Buildings began to blur. I saw a sign TEXAS SCHOOLBOOK DEPOSITORY on a building both undistinguished and dingy. Now we had lost the car in front of us. People were scurrying across our path as we swerved to avoid hitting them.

The whole spectacle turned grisly, grotesque, oddly tilting toward some unnamed possible terror. This was no sensible motorcade. It was an absurd raceway, flinging itself, skittering, wildly improbable. What happened? What is wrong? The mind is a peculiar machine. It has an automatic safety plate that shields the senses from ugly thoughts. The terrorizing, mind-boggling query becomes mute, shunted aside, not allowed entry for the brain to assay and test. The unthinkable is accorded no hospitality and the mind is spared the cutting edge that lances and peels and pains.

What thoughts crowded the others I do not know, but my automatic shield was furiously at work, disavowing any interest in mad surmise. So the quiver of the ultimate question that lay feathered against me was brushed away, as one would recoil from the unwanted cling of a spider's webbing. I did not want to ask "What happened? What is wrong? Is the president alright?" because I desperately feared the answer.

We caromed through the streets and wound up at the Trade Mart, the big cluster of roofs and doors where the president was to speak. We wandered to the back entrance to make inquiries. Surely someone could confirm what we so eagerly wanted to hear, that the president would make his speech though a bit delayed.

Now there was the clatter of feet, running feet. A distraught looking man, coat and tie flying, raced to a pay phone down the hall from us. We looked out to the parking lot. A man walked in our view holding up a transistor radio. The crackle of an announcer's voice, the static tarnishing the vowels: ". . . have been shot . . . Parkland Hospital . . ." I yelled at a man beside a dusty Chevrolet. He looked up, startled. I grabbed him by the arm and said: "I have President Kennedy's secretary with me. Can you take us to Parkland Hospital, right now?"

He was a deputy sheriff and he would take us. We emptied his rear seat of some tools and sprawled litter, then we climbed in, crowding front and back seats. We raced to Parkland, siren screaming.

When we arrived at the hospital, it was teeming with

cars parked helter-skelter in front and a swarm of uni-
formed police and plainclothesmen. We were admitted
through the front entrance, and each of us knew then that
the unthinkable, the unaskable, had burst through the
outer barriers of our silent mental redoubts. Our defenses
were down. We knew.

I gently escorted Mrs. Lincoln to the administrator's office where I left her in the care of an understanding hospital staff assistant. I ran down the hall, down the steps to
the basement where I had been told the vice-president
could be found.

The basement area was a mass of people. The faces of
all were a collage of grief, stunned, vast, penetrating grief.
There was aroma hanging in that basement, the dismaying
scent of hysteria and disbelief. There was much shuffling
of feet, men going and coming. I saw Congressmen Gon-
zalez of San Antonio, Thomas of Houston, Brooks of
Beaumont, Thornberry of Austin. Someone pointed to a
door, "That's the emergency operating room. The president is in there."

He was in there, stretched out, the flood of life drained
from him, the helpless form of the thirty-fifth president,
only a few feet away. This mad, incongruous, insupport-
able act. How could it have happened? Tears and fears
were now uncaged. Incredulity reigned on that basement
floor fetching up a blank and melancholy contagion.

Homer Thornberry was going to visit Mrs. Connally
and I fell in step beside him. She sat inconsolably in a
small room, her eyes reddened, her hands in her lap, her
cheeks wet with the moistness of her anxiety. Mrs. Johnson sat beside her.

"How is John?" I asked.

She looked up, the tears swimming again, "We don't
know, we just don't know." Mrs. Johnson embraced her.

I confusedly retreated, and wandered out into the hall again. I thought of Mrs. Lincoln. I must go to her to see how she is faring. I entered the stairwell to walk upstairs. I must have stumbled against the handrail and I halted and began to weep. I could not stop myself. I saw President Kennedy, I saw him clearly, and I could not stop myself. Finally I started my climb again. An arm flung itself at me. It was attached to Cliff Carter.

"The vice-president wants you and wants you now. I've been looking for you." He pulled at my arm and he stopped and said, "Now, Jack, pull yourself together. You have to." He hesitated. Then he said, softly, almost soundlessly, "The president is dead, you know."

The tears rushed through me again. I summoned all my discipline and still I could not baffle my weeping. Cliff stood silently for some few seconds, and then very gently he said, "We must go now, Jack, the vice-president is waiting for us." I murmured something or other, wiped my eyes and together we set off to find the vice-president.

We quickened our steps and found ourselves in front of a small room on the basement floor where Cliff said the vice-president would be waiting. The room was empty. There was a Secret Service man standing by the door. He was Lem Johns, later to become an important, trusted leader in the White House Secret Service detail. Johns spoke to us, "I'm to take both of you to Love Field. The vice-president wants you aboard the plane now."

The car was wedged in between other police cars and the officer behind the wheel said plaintively to Johns that he couldn't move. "Get this car moving," shouted Johns, pointing to an open space beyond a grassy area and curb. The officer gulped, nodded, and roared out of the parking space, leaping over the street curb, across the small grass spot, hurtling onto the street beyond. We caromed off another curb heading at an ungodly speed toward Love Field. When we approached the gate to Love Field, two burly guards plus two plainsclothesmen accosted us.

Lem Johns poked his head out of the window and displayed his Secret Service credentials. "These two men are aides to Vice-President Johnson. He is waiting for them on Air Force One," he said. The men gazed for an interminable length at the credentials, surveyed Johns vigilantly, opened the door and conducted a silent scrutiny of Carter and me. They asked our names and secured our identifications. They pondered each credit card I handed them, while Lem Johns fidgeted impatiently. Finally, they waved us through.

When we arrived at the steps leading up to Air Force One, another cordon of guards duplicated the surveying operation, this time with even more no-nonsense testing. We were passed through and I ran up the steps, and made my way through the aisle of Air Force One to the center cabin where the president's office space was located. It was crowded. Congressmen Thornberry and Thomas and Brooks were huddled around the small table in the cabin. I nodded to them and sat down, to wait.

I waited with some apprehension and more than a little doubt. I really didn't know why I was aboard this special plane. I was moving in areas where I had no exploratory knowledge, no hint of what was expected of me nor how I should respond. The weight of the measureless tragedy, only a few hours old, was still draining me of thought and energy. Why was I here? It was obvious that I was on board to travel with the new president to Washington. Cliff had made that clear to me on the ride out. I was not sure I even wanted to go now that the moment was here, nor how long I would be gone. I was leaving a life that was congenial to me and a business that was mine. I was proud of it and pleased with what it gave me in both challenges to surmount and material things to enjoy. I was reluctant and uneasy.

Suddenly the talk abruptly halted in the midship cabin. In the narrow aisleway that led aft from this cabin to the private bedroom of the president stood Lyndon Johnson. He was grave, solemn. Automatically, we all rose to our feet. Albert Thomas spoke first: "Mr. President, we are ready to carry out any orders you have." Johnson smiled briefly, waved us to our seats and sat down in the president's chair, on the port side of the airplane, a large beige chair with a small portable table in front of it.

It was the first time I had heard LBJ addressed as "Mr. President." The man to whom it was proffered was in a strange way another man, not the same man I had known. I believe with others who have an intimate notion of what the presidency is all about that something inexplicable and possibly mystical takes place when a man is transported across an infinite flight of time and duty, from where he is businessman, academician, politician, whatever, to that place called the presidency. It is a transmutation, an alchemy of human form and human burden and natural glory, where there is no settled formula to guide a man's steps, nor any covenant that determines his precise response. It is both dimly marked and garishly illuminated and each man who stands there by whatever habits he has known or by whatever instincts that inform him makes his own way as best he sees that way. The presidency transforms the man who holds the office. The obligation (and it is that) which fixes his attention, and the power (and it is also that) which now is girdled round him are both splendid and terrifying. Now, in an abrupt transition he assumes the role of arbiter and the inspirer of millions of people who look to him, and hopefully follow him.

LBJ sat in his chair, his face masking whatever he felt and thought. I sensed that this friend of mine was now deploying all his volatile passions and intellect into a tightly circumscribed web of disciplined emotion.

What lay before him no one could accurately predict. No one could ascertain whether some devious and incomprehensible conspiracy was now unraveling. One had to stretch back a hundred years to the Lincoln murder plot to draw adequate comparisons.

Unknown to me LBJ had just placed a call to Robert Kennedy, the attorney general, both to express his deeply felt condolences and to officially ask for advice. Both Johnson and the attorney general had determined that the oath of office should be given on the plane before Air Force One departed for Washington. Johnson had also made his first command decision, on his own, to wait for the body of the dead president to be brought aboard before he gave an order to be airborne. This was an instinctive decision and a good one.

Months later Johnson had mused to his associates about his feelings at that moment. He knew that the entire world, as well as the nation, was in shock. A gallant, proud, captivating leader had been slain in sunlight and the nation and the world strained to glimpse and take stock of this oddly alien figure who now was at the controls. LBJ had to demonstrate beyond any doubt that the helm was in strong hands. He had to prove, swiftly, that while the light in the White House may flicker, the light in the White House can never go out. The world must know that the constitutional apparatus binding this country together could withstand the cruelest kind of disjointing and stay intact. It was essential that no hesitant hand be shown, no doubts be visible, no slippage in continuity be detected.

I sat within two feet of LBJ and I ached to blurt out my own innermost feelings of affection and loyalty. But I kept silent. He beckoned to me. I put my ear close to him and he murmured, "See that Marie Fehmer gets the precise wording of the presidential oath."

I left the cabin and went to Marie's side. She sat in front of a typewriter a few feet beyond. Deputy Attorney General Katzenbach had, on instructions, phoned the wording to Marie.

Marie had typed the oath and she handed it to me. I got on the phone. My first official act was to talk to Nick Katzenbach in his Washington office and have him read the oath again while I checked it with the typescript. It was correct.

Within minutes, Judge Sarah Hughes, an old friend of Johnson's and newly appointed to the federal bench by President Kennedy, came aboard. She would administer the oath of office. Judge Hughes came to the center cabin. Now it was packed tight with as many as could be squeezed in: press, aides, congressmen.

Mrs. Kennedy came from the aft portion of the plane where she had been sitting with Kennedy aides. She stood beside the Johnsons, at the left side of LBJ. Her pink suit was caked with the blood of the slain president. She seemed vaguely frightened, her eyes wide and steadfast in their gaze though she looked at no one in particular. Her hands were trembling slightly.

Judge Hughes began reciting the oath, her voice cracking and ragged. Johnson answered her in clear tones, decisive, firm. At 2:40 CST, Lyndon Johnson became the thirty-sixth president of the United States.

He kissed his wife, embraced Mrs. Kennedy and Judge Hughes, who was plainly pleased to have it over with. As the judge was being escorted off the plane, the new president said, "Let's get airborne." Within eight minutes, the wheels of Air Force One were drawn into its body and through scudding clouds the president's plane flew northward and eastward to the nation's capital.

During the historic swearing-in, Malcolm Kilduff, the assistant press secretary to President Kennedy, had held up a tape recorder to the speaker. Kilduff gave the dictating belt to Cecil Stoughton, the White House photographer who had imprisoned the moment on film, and ordered him to get it transcribed and distributed.

Stoughton's picture remains of that scene. To the right is the stolid visage of Congressman Jack Brooks, visible over the left shoulder of Mrs. Kennedy. Mrs. Kennedy, her hands in an uncharacteristic awkward posture in front of her, her hair flowing over her upper left cheek, the gaze fixed, opaque, and unseeing. The new president, his hand clasping the bible being clutched by Judge Hughes, his right hand raised, the palm and fingers at the height of his ear, a pinch of white handkerchief peeking out of his breast pocket. Mrs. Johnson to the president's right, somber, sad. Barely visible above the president's upheld right hand was the head of the Dallas police force, Chief Fritz. Looming up at Fritz's right, lips pursed, a straight line of solitude, was Congressman Albert Thomas. At Thomas's shoulder, hair awry, eyes looking up, dark in the background is my own picture. At the lower left hand corner of the frame is a distraught Kilduff, holding up his tape recorder.

Mrs. Kennedy quietly moved back, and to the aft of the plane where she resumed her vigil over the casket containing her husband's body.

The president called Congressmen Thomas, Thornberry, and Brooks, Bill Moyers, Liz Carpenter, and myself to sit with him in the presidential cabin. There he sat and watched the television set to hear the news reports coming in. The president sat calmly as if he were assessing the news that was now crowding the TV set. He leaned over to his wife, "I think we should call the president's mother," he said. Within minutes they were talking to Mrs. Rose Kennedy.

"I wish to God there was something I could do for you, Mrs. Kennedy," the president said. He handed the phone to Lady Bird Johnson. "Oh, Mrs. Kennedy," she said, "the heart has been torn out of us today. Our love and our prayers are with you." The president then called Nellie Connally and talked to her, as did Mrs. Johnson.

Later, the president asked me to find Bill Moyers who had slipped out of the cabin. I walked to the rear of the plane without knowing who was back there. Sitting, talking to General Godfrey McHugh was Mrs. Kennedy. She smiled hesitantly, her hand floated to her cheek, paused there, puzzled, surprised for a bare second. She dropped her eyes and turned to General McHugh. I murmured my apologies, stumbled backward. She smiled again, this time more positively as if she understood my awkwardness and I turned and quickly retraced my steps. As I withdrew I saw the dark coffin resting in the rear of the plane. Inside was the body of John Kennedy. I fought back strange, unsettling thoughts.

The president was busily engaged in conversation with the congressmen when I returned to the center cabin after locating Moyers up front. I pondered what the president was thinking at this time. I knew to my certain knowledge that Johnson never expected to be president. He had offered vague and imprecise suggestions some months before that he would live out his political life as vice-president, and return home to Texas when Kennedy's second term had expired. He had said on numerous occasions that a southerner (though he considered himself a southwesterner, a fine turn of geographical precision) would never be nominated for president on the Democratic ticket in his lifetime. It was his notion that had the Democratic party sought the weight of brilliance and wisdom, Richard Russell of Georgia would have been the nominee (though, of course, LBJ recognized that Russell's civil rights position was the unwrenchable bar to any presidential bid). He also felt, with those unerring instincts that guided him in matters of politics, that no matter how many offerings he made to the altar, the left wing of the Democratic party had veto power over the nomination and they would never spring to his banner. In some curious way, the left wing of the party placed greater store by crusades mounted than by results achieved. It was an act of pious and irremeable faith, anchored in shrouded, contorted guilt complexes, that steered this wing of the party toward holy doctrine rather than specific advance. Johnson knew this. So, like other men of strong and galvanic pride, while he fretted he nourished no quixotic aims. He accepted what he had to accept and in this vice-presidential post—which John Nance Garner described in terms of power as not "being worth a bucket of warm spit"—he believed himself to be forever shorn of holding further direction of authority.

Now he sat in the presidential plane, catapulted by "a senseless act of mindless malice" (as Theodore Sorensen once wrote) from the most frustrating job in the world to the most valuable. He never expected it. But it had happened.

The plane sped on its straight-line journey to Washington. We would be landing at Andrews Air Force Base some two hours and eighteen minutes after our departure.

The president motioned to me, Liz Carpenter, and Bill Moyers: "I want to speak briefly when I arrive. I want to make it clear that the presidency will go on and I want to speak of my terrible sorrow which everyone else in this country feels. Put something down for me to look at. Remember, I want it to be brief and to the point." He turned away to scribble something on a notepad.

Liz and Bill and I chatted for an hour or so and we enscribed a paragraph for the president to review. Actually, each of us wrote our own version and then we tried to mingle them. It may be taken as uneditable gospel that speechwriters cannot mingle their words. While one speechwriter may examine something others have written, and while he may muse and nod and even murmur "well done" on a phrase or two, the refractory nature of writing for presidents (and candidates) interposes itself and it may be taken as a solemn maxim that a speechwriter is congenitally unable to substitute prose of someone else for that which has sprung so eloquently from his own pen. And so we labored, Moyers, Carpenter, and I. I must be honest and confess that at this moment I forget whose draft was finally brought to LBJ. He took the typewritten page, double-spaced and began to scrawl, in that full-flowing handwriting I came to know so well, his own editing. The draft had ended with the line, "I will do my best. I ask for God's help." LBJ held his pencil over this line for a brief moment and then quickly scratched out the last sentence and wrote: "I ask for your help—and God's." It was not the flourish that any of the three of us might have finally gone with, but it was simple, to the point and LBJ liked it. That settled it. We quickly retyped the brief paragraph on an index card and he stuck it in his jacket pocket.

Consider now in the mid-journey of Air Force One the state of mind that existed aboard. The bleakness of the murder hung like miasmic mist over everyone. The new president, seemingly the calmest man aboard, was fastened to his own thoughts beating inside him with God only knows what ferocity. The Kennedy aides, now huddled together in the rear of the plane, were still in shock. The enormity of the blow was only now beginning to be felt, the pain now beginning to slice through skin and thought, the numbness wearing off and now the pain, cruel, incessant, and without known antidote. I read much later in William Manchester's book about the hostility that supposedly was rampant. If it was I was not aware of it. Then, as I remember all that happened, it is possible that

I am reconciling what I *believed* to be so only because the names and the faces of the Kennedy people aboard were largely unknown to me. Could I have mistook what I thought was an immense sadness and dispirit for open hostility? No, I think not. I can understand now what I could not really perceive then. To sit in the White House, inside the magic inner circle where only the anointed of the president could freely move, to be there amid power and celebration of power, to be the confidant and trusted emissary of the president, and now, by a freakish, ghoulish act of assassination to be isolated, alone, adrift, with the captain missing and a new helmsman in charge, this abrupt transition could not be managed by mere mortals.

O'Donnell, O'Brien, military men Clifton and McHugh, press man Kilduff, and all the rest would have had my understanding even if I had glimpsed the hostility which the writers later told us was invested in every moment of that ride back. But I didn't see hostility. All I saw was grief—bitter, dry-teared grief.

The president called McGeorge Bundy and Walter Jenkins in Washington. There were meetings to be held. It was a blow to the president when he was reminded that much of the cabinet, Secretary of State Dean Rusk and five other cabinet members, were aboard an Air Force plane on their way to Japan. Get them back, said the president. Reschedule the cabinet meeting for Saturday. Get the legislative leaders alerted and prepared to meet as soon as we land. Kilduff had already, at the president's order, been in contact with Andy Hatcher, assistant press secretary, to have full press coverage at Andrews. Inform the press about the meetings with McNamara, Bundy, and the legislative leaders. Keep the mechanism moving, don't let any lapse be visible or even happen.

Soon the word was brought to the president. We would be landing at Andrews in minutes. The big plane began its descent, and we could feel the big wheels detaching themselves from the Boeing's belly, dropping into place.

The president sat quietly, chatting with his wife. I was sitting a couple of feet from him. He asked for a glass of water and when the steward brought him the glass he reached out for it. His hand brushed near my face and I watched the large palm, the outstretched fingers. The hand and fingers were steady. Not a tremble. Strange, how that tiny fragment stuck in my mind. Perhaps the president's calm was so out of joint with the queasy embrace in which all of us found ourselves. I know that I was watching all that transpired as though I were in a movie house sunk in rapture over what the actors were saying and doing, a fantasy, a piece of dramatics that would end when the lights went up. Except we knew that this was not the ending, but only the beginning and many of us on that plane were anxious, even afraid. It is cabined in my memory that Lyndon Johnson alone among us was applying his will and resolution to the torment he had to face and he was prepared, quite prepared, to confront the hours and days ahead without fear.

Months later I came to understand some of the complexities that flowed so buoyantly within Johnson. Some, but not all. It has been written before and it will continue to be chonicled that LBJ was a massively complicated man. I concur. There is no one, save perhaps his wife, who began to plumb the mysterious and diverting depths of Johnson. But one aspect of his character I did come to vaguely understand. It was the stern discipline that persuaded him to be relaxed, cool, appraising, patient in moments of crisis. Recently I came across a description of Henry II, the first and the greatest of the Plantagenets, that square, bull-necked, intense man who created the civic environment from which sprung modern England.

Churchill once wrote about Henry II: "It was said that

he was always gentle and calm in times of urgent peril, but became bad-tempered and capricious when the pressure relaxed." The similarity is more than casually apt. Johnson did in truth comport himself with dignity, authority, accessibility to counsel, and an almost casual dismissal of fear when dismay and doubt were running down every corridor. The early hours of his presidency (when these values were on vibrant display) were to be repeated time and again; assistants, cabinet officers, and sometimes newspapermen would take note of the special command LBJ exerted over his own person when peril stood in the shadows. On the other hand, it was equally true that nit-picking little blunders by others, insignificant staff errors, trivial and almost unseen niggling would incite Johnson to towering wrath.

We were nearing the capital. General Clifton came to the president's cabin to tell him that we were minutes away from landing.

Even as the plane plunged ahead toward Washington the president had firmly slotted in his mind exactly what he wanted to do. First, the statement on landing. He wanted the full focus of the TV cameras on him, to let the country and the world see him and to demonstrate that the government was moving forward without any disruption. This was essential. Already Malcolm Kilduff was coordinating with the White House press office to set up the arrangements for the Andrews Air Base ceremony. It was a full press call. They would all be there.

Second, the president wanted to hit the ground running. The word came back from Washington that Walter Jenkins and McGeorge Bundy had a full program of meetings set up. He was quite prepared now to be president in act as well as name.

I could feel the cabin pressure slackening. We were almost down. Soon, the screech of wheel against runway.

We taxied to an open area where there must have been a thousand newsmen and cameras gathered. Every high official in Washington not on that Tokyo-bound plane now reversing course was anxiously waiting to see and talk to the new president.

Then, a curious event occurred that has always puzzled me. When we had parked, it was the president's belief, and mine, that a forklift would gently remove President Kennedy's coffin and the new president would disembark with Mrs. Kennedy. I was standing beside the president in the narrow passageway that led from the president's cabin to the aft portion of the ship where the disembarkation would take place. Mrs. Kennedy and the Kennedy aides were already pressed around the aft doorway waiting for the forklift to take off the coffin. It was our intention to have the president follow Mrs. Kennedy off the plane.

At that moment, Bobby Kennedy, the attorney general, who had obviously boarded the plane from the front came full speed down the aisleway into the passageway, moving past us. I cannot tell whether or not he spoke to the president. I have to believe there was some recognition, some gesture of greeting, but I heard no words pass between them though there might have been. Bobby was moving fast, murmuring "excuse me" as he forced his way through the crowded, people-jammed aisleway. There was much jostling and pushing. The president was pressed against the sidewall of the plane. It was literally impossible for him to move any further. Secret Service men were in front of him and the Kennedy entourage was in front of them. Bobby had managed to get through, and he disembarked with Mrs. Kennedy.

When the president finally got to the aft doorway, Mrs. Kennedy and Bobby and the others had already alighted, and had left the ramp by automobile. There was no evidence of frustration within the president. I counted this act of disembarkation ahead of the president a massive dis-courtesy, almost unbelievable, but it did happen and the president of the United States stood trapped in a passage-way like any harried commuter hurrying by subway to his job. But the president, if he felt any anger masked his feel-ing behind the solemn expression he had worn for the last hour. He was quiet. He did not fret. He stood motionless until a way had been cleared for him.

(I had regrets about my thoughts later. It struck me that Bobby's shock was still active. What he was thinking when he raced through that plane had to be dark dreams of a brother murdered in the street just a few hours ear-lier. No man can sustain that kind of blow and still be nor-mally acquainted with either protocol or courtesy.)

The air was chilled when we stood in the eerily illumi-nated darkness. Television lights stabbed the night making day out of a strange oblivion. President and Mrs. Johnson stood before a microphone. In a large semicircle was of-ficial Washington and every newsman with a press pass and transportation to Andrews Air Force Base.

At precisely 6:10 P.M. Eastern Standard Time, the thirty-sixth president of the United States began to speak:

> This is a sad time for all people. We have suffered a loss that cannot be weighed. For me, it is a deep personal tragedy. I know that the world shares the sorrow that Mrs. Kennedy and her family bear. I will do my best. That is all I can do. I ask for your help—and God's.

That was all. A fifty-seven–word message, forthrightly and simply delivered, the Texas accent for the first time being contrasted with the Boston-toned voice of John Ken-nedy.

> Now, I lay in bed, trying to sleep and unable to.
> The strange turn of fate had tilted a nation, set into ava-

lanche a train of events which no seer could have foretold.
Just a few feet away a new president was in his bed, getting ready for his first day as the nation's leader. This was
the beginning, and I was eager to join the morning as fast
as it could come.

PART II

The West Wing

The
White House Staff

Working on the White House staff is the ultimate seduction. Afterwards, everything else is a tasteless passion. From the days of Franklin D. Roosevelt, as the dimensions of the president's power have expanded, so has the arena of action for that band of men called White House assistants.

The White House staff is so peculiarly the instrument of the president that its make-up depends entirely on the needs and the demands of the individual president, as he prescribes them.

It is quite likely that all presidents select their staff from those persons they have known and tested through the years. The staff relationship is a family value, and like families, the blood of a tried and triumphant friendship is far thicker than acquaintances or referred talent. That is why most presidents have, and will continue, to pick their closest aides from the catalogue of old friends and associates or campaign-blooded allies. Nothing unusual or sinister about this, only human nature replenishing itself.

My sole suggestion to presidents is to include, if at all possible, several staffers who have held public office. More on this later, but there is no specific more valuable than the time spent scouring the precincts for voters and votes on one's own behalf, no body of work more instructive than the applause and obloquy of the crowd, and no training more informing than rubbing up against fragile public temperament. Humility is the most hard-learned and sourly-taught of human virtues and the most noticeable by its absence. The public man without it navagates a surly river in a leaky boat. A presidential staff without a goodly number of its personnel schooled in the pain of humility is apt to get a president into trouble. Big trouble.

My own view is that a staff can be too large, too cumbersome, which in turn develops curious ailments such as a tendency to insulate the presidency and isolate the president (more about this danger later on). This is not good. Also, a large staff, in geometric progression, increases the possibility of staff blunder, and staff arrogance.

Large White House staffs breed an inner bureaucracy that can get as crusted with official barnacles as a cabinet department or independent agency. Since the prime essential of a White House staff is its ability to inform the president swiftly and free him from tedium and minutiae, the sheer bulk of a fat and slovenly staff lacerates its very function.

The ideal White House operation is one with just enough bodies to do the work, and with a capacity to call on the executive departments and the OMB (Office of Management and Budget) for detailed research and information gatherings, as well as tapping those non–White House groups for imagination and ingenuity.

Crucial White House staff work can be broken down in the following categories:

1. *The schedule of the president.* This is heavy work, indispensable to a smoothly functioning White House for it is the shaper and mover and conserver of the most precious White House asset, the president's time.

Too much accessibility is as defeating as too little. There are no rule books or readily available guidelines for use by appointments secretaries. Between the president and his appointment staff there has to be built a delicate balance of usefulness and withdrawal, a fragile sorting that is so easily disturbed and misused, a design that allows the president to be open to his staff and to his constituency (the Congress, the press) and yet free, as far as is humanly possible, from counterfeit counselors and the frittering of time.

2. *Conduits from the White House to the president's action managers in the departments, as well as the Congress.* Unless White House aides are going to be line managers as well as staff assistants (a dual role riven with the possibilities of disaster) the president's assistants must provide, and keep open, information channels to the departments and the Congress. Legislation, executive action, ideas, strategy have to be conveyed from the White House to the departments and a counterflow of facts, intelligence, and suggestions back to the Oval Office. While the president must be available to his cabinet officers and to key members of the Congress, he quite obviously cannot personally attend to every problem, even every crisis. His staff, with precision, discretion, and sensitivity to the human ego must provide this extra presidential scrutiny. Domestic business, foreign affairs, and congressional matters have to be handled in the absence of the person of the president, so that the channels never get clogged or corroded.

Too much emphasis cannot be given to the care and feeding of key members of the Congress. The leadership must be consulted often, warmly, carefully. Then there are the chairmen of important committees (e.g., Appropriations in both houses, Finance in the Senate, and Ways and Means in the House) as well as those members who rule subcommittees whose writ runs larger and farther than the general public imagines. One surly, offended subcommittee chairman can give a president hives. LBJ used the phone to reach out to these "dukes of the Hill," to give them affection, respect, attention, and most of all the sure knowledge that they knew he cared about their opinions. LBJ used to say that five minutes on the phone was the equivalent of thirty minutes in his office. "If you use the phone right," he would say, "you can save a couple of hours everyday." He saved them.

3. *The eyes and the ears of the president.* A president has to know what is happening in the government and in the country. If he doesn't, he half-governs. The staff is his radar, picking up tremors and soundings and bringing these readings to the president, as factually and as unvarnished as information can possibly be. Sometimes what is heard and seen and felt may or may not be congenial to the president. He may be riled, infuriated, cross, or comforted, but an uninformed president is only breeding tardy reactors which in time can shatter him or surprise him or defeat him, none of which will find hospitality in a president's memory or state of mind.

4. *A sounding board for the president.* A president usually chooses his staff because he trusts them as human beings, which means he can rely on their loyalty as well as their competence. Loyalty for the record is not defined as blind, mute obedience but rather a refusal to betray either a presidential confidence or a presidential command. The alternative to either, if the staff member cannot in good conscience fasten his fidelity to the sticking place, is to resign. This is the honorable and practical way to inform one's conscience as well as be free to speak out, to oppose, or to disengage.

Therefore, assuming loyalty in this form, the effective staff can hear out the president as he ruminates about a decision which puzzles him, weighing presidential musings and suppositions and responding frankly with a viewpoint or a counter-suggestion or an appraisal. The so-called yes-man is a blight and every wise president knows this.

5. *An idea bin for the president.* Presidents are not, as may be commonly supposed, inexhaustible reservoirs of ideas, the meaty stuff of presidential achievements. Chief executives need to be constantly offered ideas with a possible fit to a specific problem, whether it be an appointive vacancy, a gristly crisis, a need to be filled, or a charting to be explored.

* * *

Access to the president is quite a valuable asset. The one or two or three members of the staff who have entree, day or night, to the president possess coin of such value that there is no known gauge to measure it. The sport in which all Washingtonians indulge with the installation of a new administration is picking up the spoor of those presidential aides who will be in the inner ring where only the anointed dwell, where presidential access is sure and where presidential faith is held.

I was bewildered at first by the growing number of phone calls I received the first week I was on the job. There had been a story in the *Washington Post* about how "close" I was to the president, and almost as if a dam had burst somewhere, the calls started coming into me. They came from congressmen who wanted to meet me, from newspapermen who suddenly found me "good copy," and from lobbyists who figured I was somebody they "ought to know."

It is hard for anyone, not used to this adulation to be unaffected by it. This is the curse of sudden accession to the White House. After a while a White House assistant begins to believe he is a fellow of considerable charm and intelligence. LBJ used to tell us the story of Sam Rayburn and Harry Truman on the day that Truman became president. "Now, Harry, a lot of people are going to tell you you are the smartest man in the country, but Harry, you and I know you ain't." A crude, cutting blow, but the cagy Speaker was only trying to do for President Truman what LBJ tried to do for his staff, armor them against the virus of self-importance which the White House breeds with graceless speed.

Of course, real power does not reside in any staff member. He has as much or as little, and no more than the president chooses to give him. It can be withdrawn as quickly as it is preferred.

The White House assistant learns quickly and readily, that the closer he is to the president, the nearer he is to the pot of power at the end of the political rainbow.

Power in Washington is measured by a stern gauge: The direct proportion of access to the president, for the asset of the realm is information that flows only from the president. If you were to fluoroscope the brain and conscience of any top official within the government, you would be able to chart the flight of agony caused by lost intimacy with the president, or denial of access to him. It's a peculiar ailment, but one doesn't need the Mayo Clinic to diagnose the cause. Conversely, when a man leaves the side of the president, he is hit hardest by his lack of information, that awful chasm that separates what he once knew from what he does not know any more.

The mesmerism of the White House assistant lies in the aide's use of three little words: "The president wants . . ." Every time he sits in a meeting, or picks up the phone to call a Cabinet officer, agency head, or important congressman, it is the voice of the staffer that one hears, but all who listen know it is the arm of the president that reaches through the line; therein lies both the mysticism and the magic. A mere stripling armed with these three little words can turn a lot of levers. But once he leaves the squat, white building west of the Mansion to work in the "other world" of business or the arts or the professions or education for all his life there is only the numbing truth that his magic is gone, and all he has left are intelligence and charm which, as the head waiter at "21" will tell him, can buy about two kopecks' worth of nothing on the power market. It may explain why old White House assistants never die; they pray for restoration.

Power to a White House aide is an enchantment. It is more than that. It is a mainline fix every morning, shoved into the bloodstream of the aide so that he shortly comes to believe that he really is someone extraordinary, possibly beyond the pale of ordinary restraints, reeking of the smell of command. It is difficult for an aide to consider that his power is linked to a fixed time schedule, that he will leave not one hour later than his chief leaves, and then it will all be over, a memory, brute-strong in its cling but still a memory.

From my own personal experience, however, it was more than just the sensual caress of power that made work in the White House so inviting. I woke up each morning eager to be about my duties, no matter how little sleep I had the night before, no matter how exhausted I was when I put my head to pillow, no matter how monastic the routine, the endless, bone-wearying routine. The reason why is quite simple, though to some it might appear quite corny. It is because the White House assistant (speaking for myself here) understands that if he has contributed one jot of aid to the president, he is, by this contribution, serving his country in ways that are not measurable in any bank account or spacious home or easy living. He is doing something that enlarges a better life for millions of people he will never see or know. The plain truth is that no ascent to high corporate levels, no coup in the market or fame in the world of art and culture or academia, can compare with the juice of this sensation.

I cannot help but believe that every man and woman who serves a president in the West Wing finds this same sense of excitement inhabiting his every waking moment.

There is really nothing quite like it.

Most White House aides, with obvious exceptions, have no previous connection with personal glory or publicized achievements of their own before they ascend to the right hand of the president.

When Sam Rayburn grumbled to Lyndon Johnson (in regard to the new and bright young aides of President Kennedy in the early days of JFK's administration), "I'd feel a lot better if some of them had run for sheriff just once," he was pointing out his concern at the vacancy that usually exists among most White House assistants: they lack the abusive and abrasive consorting with political life which is the most humbling of human experiences, and the most valuable in dealing with power; running for and winning public office.

*   *   *

President Johnson gathered around him a band of Johnson men and women whose individual merit put them on a level as high as or higher than any previous administration. It was surely no gathering of mediocrities. It was, even to my biased and tilted view, a talented and enormously gifted group, with varied interests and expertise, bound in loyalty to the president (though not as tightly as many have surmised or as the president definitely wanted), and not at all reluctant to make their own views known to their boss.

The president wanted to retain the services of the Kennedy White House cadre, but only two stayed on—McGeorge Bundy and Larry O'Brien.

Bundy and O'Brien stayed on for reasons peculiar to their own themes. Mac Bundy concluded his duties transcended presidents or party; therefore, the claims on his loyalty were larger than any one man. To O'Brien, working the corridors to the Congress in the interest of suitable legislation was of a higher cause than retirement simply because his own idol and leader had been murdered.

But to Theodore Sorensen, to Kenneth O'Donnell, the ties that bound them to JFK had now snapped forever, and could not be repaired to allow them to serve in the employ of another. They were ravaged by grief, disappointment, and disbelief. The fun and the grit had gone out of their jobs and they left as quickly as they could. Moreover, they knew (as I came to know later) they could never achieve the same kind of personal closeness with LBJ as they had with JFK and it was this intimacy, now fled, which was the glue that they could not live without.

No LBJ aide was allowed to "go public" on TV as a visible spokesman for the Johnson administration. This was left to the president himself, and cabinet officials. President Johnson grumbled, not without reason, that if a public blunder was to be made, he damn well would be the one to make it.

It is a fact that President Johnson was unusually accessible to all his staff, though some more than others. I counted it one of my larger responsibilities to keep the Oval Office gate swinging open on easy hinges so that LBJ's men could freely express themselves to the president.

The channel of communication most often used was the written memorandum, which I made sure would be put in front of the president's eyes. By this method, the staff could importune, enlighten, incite, inform, and often oppose. They would receive in response to their memo a presidential reply, either by phone or in the president's angular script, at the bottom of the memo, a "NO" or a "YES" or a "SEE ME." Sometimes there would also appear a paragraph or a sentence which left no doubts about the president's considered judgment as to the memo in question.

The president's men and women, the key aides he relied on (and raged at) deserve some special detailing.

Joe Califano came to the West Wing when Bill Moyers took over as press secretary. He became the steward of the White House domestic programs. He was serving as special assistant to Robert McNamara in the Defense Department when he came to the attention of both Moyers and myself. We both recommended him to the president. An honor graduate of Harvard Law School, Califano was a kinetic bundle of raw energy. He reacted intuitively to ideas and with great agility and ease seemed to leap from one intellectual crag to another. He gave the president one asset which LBJ counted of no insubstantial value—quick, quality implementation of presidential commands. He worked long hours, with no hint of weariness, moving confidently over a score of crisis points. He was a brilliant lawyer, and he thought like one, assembling facts, weighing them, everything compact, fitted together, bringing all the facts to muster in shining, logical, straight lines. He was an extremely valuable piece of manpower, as the president might have put it, and LBJ relied on him heavily.

Both Joe and I were the "house Italians" and the president used us in what they call in Hollywood "dress extra" tasks. I was always amused by this and so was Joe. We realized that whatever faults the president had, one could never accuse him of not being able to count ethnic votes.

* * *

Bill Moyers was perhaps the most celebrated of the Johnson aides. His "press" was invariably good. He knew with splendid instinct how to live and work and survive in the Washington political swamps. He came to work for LBJ a raw, untested youth just out of college. He came to the office of Majority Leader Johnson in the Senate a shiny-faced Baptist minister, fresh as a new-picked peach, with that horn-rimmed–glasses innocence which was to confound so many who thought him easy to ride over. One looked at Bill and could almost hear hardy Baptist hymns and the rustle of river water drenching the newly baptized.

But behind the ministerial facade and the smell of fire-and-brimstone sermons was a brass-knuckled street fighter who knew every side alley and fire exit. He was never run down or cornered. Early in the LBJ years he did what every durable bureaucrat and power-gatherer does—he installed friends and colleagues in damn near every nook and cranny of the government so that he was the most knowledgeable and best informed of all the aides in the West Wing.

Moyers had a soft and easy charm, ingratiating, supple, and oftentimes overpowering. He knew with whom and when to be deferential. Whenever he smiled that engaging grin stern enemies had second thoughts of guilt. His talent was highly visible and highly effective.

When George Reedy left the press secretary's office, the president called me into his office. He said, "I want to make you press secretary but I am afraid to. You are too close to me and the press lobby will set out methodically to murder you in order to hit at me. You would have a miserable time no matter how smart and skillful you were. I am going to name Bill Moyers. He can handle them. He's got a special license with those guys." The president, as usual, was right. Moyers was superb in his job.

Later on, in 1966, Moyers and the president drew apart. It was a dangling piece of business that never got put together before the president died.

* * *

Harry McPherson was special counsel to the president. The most literate and culturally civilized of the Johnson aides, Harry should have been a working poet, which he once aspired to be, though from the president's viewpoint it was a happy chain of events that led him to his side and not to the university cloisters.

McPherson is one of the few lawyers (Louis Nizer is another) who does not write as if he were riding bareback on a tractor. His memos to the president were models of lucid thoughts elegantly paragraphed, bound together with sweet rhythms. Harry was universally admired and liked by the staff because we never felt uneasy in his presence. He was always humane, eager to be compassionate about others' problems. He had an easy camaraderie with the Irish intellectuals (Pat Moynihan, John Roche), and was more at home in the university library than in the political pit.

The president had affection for Harry, sometimes ribbing him, and poking a conversational finger in his chest by suggesting Harry was "in bed with all those bomb-throwing, ass-kissing, fuzzy-headed Georgetown liberals." It always got a laugh, but in truth Harry did have a special rapport with the liberal intellectuals of the party, those who sat around grinding their teeth over the president. I considered this a grand asset for the president, but then as the president used to say, "it depends on whose ox is being gored." McPherson brought a touch of class to our circle.

* * *

Every president needs, as they say in Texas, a real, tough, "sumbitch." Someone who can say *no*, and make it stick. Marvin Watson was the president's sumbitch just as Sherman Adams was Eisenhower's, Ken O'Donnell was Kennedy's, and Bob Haldeman was Nixon's.

But Marvin in life and purpose and reality was not the man one would have thought would have been chosen for this snake pit of a job. He was gentle, always kind and thoughtful (he was the first man to send you a letter and a gift when you were sick, the first to ask if you needed help when you had just fallen on your butt as a result of an accident or a political avalanche). Washington never really understood Watson, and surely only a very few of the press got a glimpse of his stout and active mind, tuned to the finer specialities of a problem. He was viewed suspiciously by the liberal members of the Congress and received the total distrust of the loyal Kennedy people.

Between Marvin and the liberal democrats was an uneasy truce, tilted to the collapsing point at times when Bobby Kennedy and his band of followers suspected Marvin of poisoning their political wells. The truth is Marvin never regarded Bobby and his people with anything other than mistrust and they responded in kind.

In Texas, Marvin was a leader of the conservative Democrats, and only his love and loyalty to the president caused him to support legislative measures that in Texas he would have vowed to defeat. Marvin swallowed his contempt for a number of LBJ's legislative aims, and argued brilliantly for their passage when I knew in his heart he wasn't too sure of the rightness of the measure.

But the press was wrong about Marvin. They attached to him the neanderthal label, plainly viewing him a blinkered one-dimensional servant of the president. They were plainly wrong. He was one hell of a lot more. Few knew he was an assistant professor of economics at Baylor University, and few were witness to the flawless skills he brought to the job of administering the White House operation.

He had one unimpeachable asset that in the White House and Washington is coin of such worth it cannot be counted by weights and measures. He had the unlimited confidence of the president.

* * *

Horace Busby was the oldest Johnson aide in tenure, with the exception of Walter Jenkins. Introspective, sensitive, with a glittering mind, he flitted in and out of the Johnson staff group, moving to his own business research enterprise from time to time, and then returning on a full-time basis. LBJ had relied on Busby through the years as his first-ranking speechwriter. The famous civil rights speech that Johnson made at Gettysburg, when he was vice-president, was created by Busby. It contained those oft quoted lines: "Until justice is blind to color and education knows no race, then Emancipation is a Proclamation, but it is not fact." The Busby style and temper were eminently suited to Johnson. He admired Busby and throughout his career in moments of great crisis, he called on "Buzz." (Even in the "final" crisis—his decision not to seek renomination—he summoned Busby to the White House to help him plot and construct the fateful sentences.)

George Reedy was, next to Walter Jenkins and Horace Busby, the longest-tenured of the LBJ aides. This was the *bête noire* of his existence for it bore primogeniture rights which Reedy found, to his dismay and frustration, evaporating swiftly with the incursions made by new, and younger, men coming aboard the LBJ staff. When Johnson was so precipitously borne to the White House, Reedy had been his press secretary and spokesman. He had been such in LBJ's majority leader and vice-presidential days. Reedy thrived on the late-hour seminars he conducted for the press who were searching out the legerdemain of the majority leader, or probing the solitary fate of the vice-president. Reedy would sit by the hour engaging in endless talk, fastening his voice onto the various reporters who came to hear and to learn about the magic and the mysteries of the leader. He was never happier. When Johnson became president, Reedy found himself shoved to the rear of the bus. He didn't like it. He sulked.

Ponderous in movement and speech, a sworn enemy to neatly pressed clothes, with an enormous globe of white hair afroed, before it became fashionable, George found brevity a burden. He disengaged himself from that gift as much as he could, which was often. When a reporter asked George the question, "Is LBJ going to Europe?" George responded with a bottomless dissertation on the state of mind of western civilization beginning with the Venerable Bede. As one exhausted reporter put it: "I feel like the boy after school who told his mother 'today the teacher told me more about penguins than I wanted to know.'"

Reedy brooded when Pierre Salinger remained press secretary and when Pierre departed hastily to run for the Senate in California, George rejoiced in replacing him. But a confluence of bad luck, ill timing, and an opaque insensitivity to the delicate balance needed to be struck be-

tween the press and an increasingly beleagured LBJ suf-
focated Reedy's position. Credibility gap was born as both
a phrase and a calamity. The press grew waspish, restless,
and sorely irritated at the Reedy monologues and his di-
versionary, interminable homilies. Whatever threads connected the press to the press office snapped abruptly.
Reedy was in deep trouble and both he and the president
knew it.

I can still see George, sweating profusely, clumping
around the asphalt ellipse on the South Grounds, when
LBJ began one of those fabled "long march" press conferences. The press in a great wad collected around the president, trying to keep pace with his long strides, and George
would bump along in the rear, unable to stay abreast of
the locust-like swarm in front of him. Oftentimes, when
the president disappeared back into the Mansion, the press
would gather with George in the briefing room to inspect
their notes and to belabor Reedy for expositions on what
the president said. "How the hell would I know," grumbled Reedy. It is a fact that one cannot monitor a presidential press conference two furlongs behind on the turns.
I had much sympathy for Reedy in this matter, for it was
a torment and whatever George's assets, he was never
much of a half-miler.

The president was affectionate toward George but
worried about Reedy's progressively worsening stature
with his clients and decided to give him a gentle way out.
George was to have an operation on his feet (he suffered
from hammertoes). The president garlanded him with praise,
made certain he would have a well-paying job in private
industry after his hospital stay, guaranteed payment of his
hospital bills, and announced Bill Moyers as his successor.

Nothing to George could have run a fingernail across a
blackboard with more grating results than the designation

of Moyers as press secretary. Moyers's subsequent success in the job rumpled Reedy's every waking hour. He regarded Moyers with all the tender warmth one reserves for leper colonists.

The president never lost his loyalty for George. When Reedy's private job collapsed, LBJ retrieved him, and brought him back to the White House at the salary of his highest-paid assistants. Reedy spent most of his days, the last year of the LBJ presidency, writing memos on various subjects.

Perhaps all these dolorous events minted bitter memories for Reedy, and when LBJ departed the White House Reedy sat down to write a book about the presidency. It was highly praised by the critics, mainly, I thought, because its thesis fitted the aims and bias of many of those who reviewed the book. LBJ was, at that time, only vaguely perceived to have any hopeful qualities, and it appeared to be "on target" for a close, longtime assistant to Johnson to nail him hard to the pilings with accusations of "imperial court," "blind courtierism," and other less mild hectoring.

I speculate that nothing wounded the president more in his last days than Reedy's detailed savagery of description of an unnamed president resembling no one so much as a Blanco County Caligula, with no redeeming qualities.

It was a sad finish.

* * *

Liz Carpenter was the staff director and press secretary to Mrs. Johnson, but she should have been desking in the West Wing, with LBJ's top aides. She was witty, smarter than any of us, and I think President Johnson made a mistake in not making her his own press secretary (and I would wager she would have been one of the all-time greats in that job) but possibly he hesitated for it would have left his wife without Liz.

She was a merry warrior, never giving an opponent any quarter, but never gunning him down without a quip to ease the pain. The president had asked me to hold staff meetings in the morning with his key aides, to go over the daily schedule, to look at the future—in sort, to try to anticipate problems for him. These staff meetings petered out (as I expected they would) for we soon became so busy doing chores the president had assigned to us, and had no time to spend an hour or so in the morning with each other. Moreover, I found myself absent too many times, yanked out of the meeting by a presidential summons which would always begin by saying, "Sorry to take you out of that meeting, but . . ." I invited Liz to sit in and I was right to do so. She cleared the early morning shadows.

Bess Abell was the first lady's social secretary. But she was more than that. She was an emollient, softening every crisis with an elegant imperturbability which mystified and calmed me. The rafters could be shuddering and the entire White House falling down about our heads and Bess would stand there, undismayed, smiling easily, never a tinge of despair or panic. She never raised her voice. The words would come slowly, every edge of hysteria carefully smoothed away, with only sounds of softness patting one's ears.

She counted dullness as the original sin. If you were invited to an evening in the State Dining Room or East Room, then, by God, you weren't going to be starched with tedium. She worked at her job, although it was impossible to search out any signs of nervousness. She just simply went about her tasks with no minute wasted, pursuing every void until it was filled.

She and Liz Carpenter were about as finely matched a pair of pros as could be brought into action. The first lady depended on them, and they loved her and served with fidelity as well as perfection; and when you bring those two assets into balanced harness you are mingling with the varsity, which was the way both President Johnson and Mrs. Johnson wanted to operate.

* * *

No account of the Johnson White House Staff could be complete without including two women of disparate personality, but both so competent as to boggle the mind: Juanita Roberts and Marie Fehmer.

Juanita Roberts, an Army professional (Colonel Roberts we used to call her when some one of the LBJ aides was ready to wring her efficient neck), was another experienced Johnson hand. She had been with him in his Senate and vice-presidential days and she fought incessantly with the male aides to claim her place in the hierarchy. She saved everything, I mean *everything*, for the Johnson archives. In the days when LBJ was vice-president Bill Moyers once sent a package which when she opened it revealed some old chicken bones with a note from Moyers: "The vice-president just ate and I thought you might want these for the archives." Juanita was not amused. But with all her insistencies that many of us found damned disagreeable, she managed the secretarial office of the president with monumental skill.

Marie Fehmer summons up all the cliches one reads in Gothic novels. She *was* sweet beyond all possibility. She *was* soft and feminine and invariably gentle-tempered. When Mary Margaret Wiley departed the LBJ environs to be married, Marie took her place. Prying secrets out of Miss Fehmer? She would have given up her fingernails, pulled from her with wicked pliers and nary a peep of anything. I dearly loved her.

* * *

McGeorge Bundy, special assistant for national security affairs, was a special favorite of mine. In him are exhibited all the genetic codes that design the New England brahmin. He is supremely confident of his own responses, with neither fear nor doubt seeping into any confrontation he has with person, problem, or crisis. Winston Churchill wrote of Arthur James Balfour, Conservative prime minister of England from 1902 to 1905, and a nephew of another prime minister: "He had that composed, detached, uplifted mental and moral vision combined with the art of dexterous and practical management requisite for those who guide the course of permanent societies." It is a perfect fit for the public Bundy.

Mac Bundy, the *wunderkind* of the Harvard faculty, brought into high office by President Kennedy, was not confused by political labels or narrowed party loyalties. He was a Republican who idolized Henry Stimson, and in truth, may have modeled himself after that patrician Olympian who served, not presidents or parties, but country.

President Johnson was attracted to him mainly, I believe, because Bundy represented to him the embodiment of the New England artisan, Yale-educated, Harvard-trained, with a tough intellect and that casual, almost negligent confidence that seems to be part of the bloodline. Moreover, LBJ admired Bundy's thinking, always aiming at the essential, and uncomfortable with the trivial. Bundy quickly accustomed himself to the LBJ style, using wit and humor to accompany his views. It was that special Bundy kind of wit, couched in the civilized tongue spoken jauntily by what LBJ used to call the "eastern breed."

Never were there two more dissimilar men than LBJ and Mac Bundy. They were as different as two men can be, in background, humor, facade, style. And yet they were suited to each other. Their relationship was not an intimate one, but somehow one can imagine that Henry Stimson was not a jolly companion of FDR. The FDR guile would not have been congenial to the austere Stimson, and possibly vice versa.

There was something else in Bundy, again a legacy from his ancestry and interwoven in his Stimson connection. It was his sense of public duty. This commitment to service was bound up in Bundy, and from it flowed the assured rapid-fire assessments which according to one's lights are either brilliant or arrogant. It is unlikely that Mac Bundy would be elected to office, for I doubt that Bundy would obligate himself to the tedium—and the discomfort—of playing "jest plain Mac" to the constituency; it may be true that Bundy's principal defect was his aloofness from the rude knowledge of political campaigning. Or as Ramsay McDonald, the Labour prime minister, said of Balfour: "He saw much of life from afar."

Bundy and I got along quite well. He never patronized me, though others pointed accusatory fingers at him for doing just that. I liked him enormously for he was never dull or commonplace. Moreover, he never became casual about the business at hand. He had a cool bravery which never shirked a head-on collision with those who found his views not in accord with their own. And he persisted in giving the president the full flavor and exactness of his thoughts, always flintily expressed, unplumed, and dryboned. The fact that his thinking paralleled the president's in no way was due to flattery or the desire to please. They simply saw the world through the same prism.

I quarrelled with David Halberstam when his book *The Best And The Brightest* battered Bundy, among others, for his role in Vietnam. My concern was that Bundy, as well as Bob McNamara, and all of us, were being indicted for the wrong crimes. If Vietnam was wrong, then we are indictable for bad judgment. But to spear a man for bad judgment is quite apart from smearing him with bad motives. Mac Bundy, to my certain knowledge, fulfilled his commitment, which simply stated was to serve his country honorably with all the skills he could offer. That he did. He did it as he did most tasks, with much style and competence.

* * *

Larry O'Brien was the other Kennedy holdover who stayed with LBJ, and indeed, became the highest-ranked Kennedy holdover in the LBJ team when he was elevated to the cabinet as postmaster general.

Larry is a jovial extrovert, a public relations man in private life who was attracted to John Kennedy, and along with that band of Massachusetts men followed JFK along his ascent to ultimate political power. He gloried in the mechanics of politics, rummaging through the precincts in search of levers and fulcrums that would cause voters to go to the polls and choose the right candidates, which, by some natural selection, would be O'Brien-backed.

O'Brien got along splendidly with President Johnson. LBJ reckoned Larry to be honest in his dealings, trusting him to be loyal to LBJ after President Kennedy was murdered. Their relationship was professional, one in which they surveyed the political pastures, agreeing over which directions their journey should take.

I enjoyed Larry, he was accessible, easy to relax with, full of buoyant, fluid conversation, with no incongruities of temperament or stodgy arrogance. He was an energetic captain of the LBJ congressional praetorian guard, instantly knowledgeable, and after a time tuned in perfectly to the all-seeing, all-pervading LBJ eye for detail.

* * *

Douglass Cater became the president's specialist in education, and the extent of his skill and ingenuity in this area is amply verified in the roll call of educational legislation that is without compare in the history of the nation.

Doug is from Alabama and even the influences of eastern intellectuals and a career in the very den of sophistication have not blurred the southern accents of the Cater tongue.

He was the most published of the Johnson aides, having written four books on the Washington political scene, particularly as it touched and affected the journalist in the federal city. When I first met him he was the Washington correspondent for the *Reporter*, at that time one of the most influential of the small journals, read and studied by all the power brokers in Washington. The president had known him much earlier and was impressed by the mingling of southern understanding with a hard-beaked approach to what was real and practical.

One afternoon in 1965 the president invited Bill Moyers and me for a swim in the presidential pool. Doug Cater was our guest. Splashing around the pool, all of us nude as Adam, the president bobbing along in the water queried Doug about coming to work at the White House. To Cater's every parry the president thrust again. "You've been writing a long time about what was wrong with how the government was run, now I'm giving you a chance to put your theories to work. Come on in and help run the country instead of writing about it."

It was heady stuff and Cater was clearly weakening, a sign the president knew and without stint he kept up the drumfire of importunings. After what seemed like an English Channel swim, we finally climbed out of the pool, exhausted, but the president was grinning widely. He had nailed his man. Cater became a special assistant to the president.

With that unmistakable ambling gait, his large grin in place, Doug became a goad and a conscience in the White House. More and more the president gave him his head, so that Cater in time became an indispensable link to the educational community in the country.

He wrote a lucid English sentence, easily clear to the minds of a grand theorist or a hard-sense politician. His wife, Libby, was a brilliant woman, equally at home as Doug in the fierce political conversations that took place, and possibly Doug's special asset when he worked out answers to tough problems.

Doug was an amiable man, not given to erratic temperament. He was solid, always on track, both as an independent thinker and as an aide who worked well with his colleagues.

In the dozens of educational bills that LBJ rammed through the Congress, it was Doug Cater who rode point, clearing the way with stubborn congressmen and sometimes paranoid academicians and school professionals who saw darkly what the rest of us saw clearly. When the president declared himself in favor of public broadcasting, it was Cater who did the original architectural work on the design of the first federally-financed public broadcasting apparatus.

* * *

Richard Goodwin was an important staff member to LBJ. Goodwin was a prickly chap. At his worst, he was as lovable as a sullen porcupine; at his best, incandescent and possibly a near-genius in his field. For when Goodwin is collaborating with his muses, he is the most skilled living practitioner of an arcane and dying art form, the political speech.

Goodwin was the principal author of three of LBJ's most memorable speeches: the famous "Great Society" speech at the University of Michigan on May 22, 1964;* the celebrated "We Shall Overcome" speech to the joint session of the Congress on March 15, 1965; and LBJ's precedent-shattering address to the graduation exercises of Howard University in Washington, D.C., on June 4, 1965.

To say simply that working with Goodwin is not easy is to admit a deficiency in the English language. I learned quickly the Goodwin code: to hold onto the speech until the very last minute to prevent some lower form of animal life (me) from fooling around with his prose. To actually withhold the speech until the president mounted the ros-

---

* Goodwin, by felicitous chance, unearthed a phrase that was destined to be the canopy under which the Johnson legislation program flowed. The origin of phrase Great Society emerged from no search for a slogan or some label. As in the case of many a prize *objet d'art* it came in the night, unheralded and unsought.

The president was scheduled to make some remarks on the occasion of presenting the Eleanor Roosevelt Award, on March 4, 1964. The former first lady was a special favorite of the president and Richard Goodwin prepared a first draft in which he searched out some answers to how a nation could redress its grievances. Included in the draft was the phrase Great Society. I liked it because it seemed to encircle what the president was trying to do. Late that evening I discussed the speech with the president. He too liked the phrase and I suggested that we scrap this specific speech for this event because the draft had a more spacious theme.

Why not enlarge the theme, coupling the phrase with a new outline of what the president felt would be his philosophy, his précis of his move to the future, his aims and objectives for this country here at home. The president okayed the idea and the Great Society was formally exhibited at the University of Michigan.

trum was really Goodwin's objective. He was seeded number one in vanishing acts when he was working on a speech. He actually couldn't be found for days. He performed his act with steadily growing skill.

Once Goodwin came close to striking his banner, but only because the intruder was a Nobel Prize laureate.

The president found John Steinbeck a man of continuing appeal. He liked his rough and careless manner and his fidelity to excellence. He respected his achievements. He asked me to confer with Steinbeck, particularly to get the novelist to offer some ideas for the president's inaugural address in 1965.

Steinbeck was not a man who wrote in inspirational outbursts. He took his time, burnishing each vowel as if he were hoarding it. He wrote on long yellow foolscap with a pitch-black pencil. He kept a hundred or so of those black writing sticks in front of him on his desk, with an electric pencil sharpener at his elbow to keep the points freshly honed. The handwriting was gnarled, but precise, though hard to read without working at it.

About a month before the inaugural, Steinbeck sent me his material. I passed Steinbeck's prose to the president and to Richard Goodwin who was assigned the task of putting the speech together. Goodwin was noncommittal when he read Steinbeck's piece.

When the first draft of Goodwin's speech came to me, I quickly noted that nothing of the Steinbeck material was in it. I made no comment, but passed the draft to the president.

When I met with LBJ, he had encircled two paragraphs of Steinbeck's prose and said: "I want this in the speech. It is much too good to leave unsaid." He had encircled the following:

The Great Society is not the ordered, changeless, and sterile battalion of the ants.

It is the miracle of becoming—always becoming, trying, probing—falling, resting and trying again—but
always gaining a little—not perfect, but perfectible.

I made some minor changes in the Steinbeck prose, the
solitary time I ever mucked around with a Nobel
laureate's material. I changed "miracle" to "excitement"
and dropped out the last phrase—"not perfect, but perfectible." I returned the edited draft to Goodwin. I pointed to
the Steinbeck paragraphs and said, "A must, the president
wants."

Goodwin gave me that shuffling grin he wore when he
was really thinking that presidents ought not interfere
with professionals. The Steinbeck paragraphs were inserted and the president delivered the lines with delight.

* * *

To flesh out the speech-writing brigade, I brought in
two young men, of more than ample craftsmanship: Bob
Hardesty and Will Sparks. They were both extremely
hard workers, the clock was only a decorative piece in
their offices. Mostly they turned out what we laughingly
referred to as Rose Garden garbage—those triumphant
soundings which the president gave to Bible groups, women's civic clubs, veterans' associations, and other assorted gatherings, in the perennially lovely garden a few
yards east of the Oval Office. But the president demanded
that whatever he said to whomever and wherever bear the
imprint of at least a minor excellence and what Hardesty
and Sparks turned out more than met that specification.In
fact, they wrote with such dispatch—never missing dead-
lines—that I personally felt their creative work was of a
superior caliber, on or near the level of the cool cats Goodwin and Busby. (After his White House tenure, Will
Sparks wrote a humorous book called *Who Spoke to the Pres-*

ident Last which recounted some of the absurdities of life in the West Wing).

* * *

Some time after the 1964 campaign, Liz Carpenter called me. "I want you to meet a terrific young man. He worked as an advance man on the Lady Bird Special (the train ride through the South on which Mrs. Johnson served as surrogate for her husband). He's eager, bright and he wants to work for you."

I had Jim Jones come in to see me. He was an open-faced, absurdly young-looking man. Slightly built, with thinning brown hair and a friendly manner, he made it clear he wanted more than anything else to work in the White House. At first blush, there was nothing really striking about Jim, except this persistent amiability. But if one examined him closely, there was visible a hint of the hard edge of resolve that later characterized him. I judged him as a prime candidate for employment (and later I counted that swift judgment to be one of my better calls) but I had nothing available in my own area. I told Marvin Watson about Jones, and suggested to Marvin that if he had any kind of spot, he ought to hire Jim. He did. In the years that followed this mild, easy-going young man proved to be made of equal parts of stamina, juice, and sprung steel.

He became assistant appointments secretary and when Marvin Watson was elevated to the cabinet as postmaster general, Jim took over his chores with no noticeable slackening in the efficiency of the office. Always alert, keenly aware of the political landmines that dotted the White House landscape, he served the president with consistent high quality performance. In 1972, he was elected to the Congress from his home town of Tulsa, after losing his first time out in 1970. With typical Jones good humor and tenacity, he merely grinned at his first defeat and set about to win the next time out. He did.

*   *   *

Larry Levinson, a scholarly lawyer, unusually bright, ceaselessly in action, was the principal aide to Joe Califano, and managed the day-to-day flow of material and traffic that was part of the domestic affairs group. Levinson had a keen and exceptional sensitivity to the pitfalls and booby-traps that lay across the course of the domestic legislation. He was never caught napping.

*   *   *

Clifford Alexander, a tall, engagingly handsome black attorney, superbly educated, served in the counsel's office. Cliff was noticeably energetic in presenting his views and the president found him useful and imaginative.

*   *   *

Three of the first class of White House fellows were key assets in the West Wing: Charles Maguire, an ex-advertising executive, who was my assistant, and who stayed on to the end of the LBJ term as a talented and valuable staffer; Tom Johnson, mature beyond his years, was assistant to Bill Moyers, and who became in time the assistant press secretary and is now publisher of the *Dallas Times-Herald;* John de Luca, intelligent, quiet, introspective, worked in the Bundy office. (De Luca became the deputy mayor of San Francisco during the Alioto administration).

*   *   *

A group of original Kennedy assistants stayed on for varying lengths of time. Serving as chief counsel when LBJ took office was Mike Feldman, a tall, stooped lawyer of calculating and perceptive brilliance. When Feldman resigned to return to private practice, Lee White, short, balding, shrewd, an activist and innovator, became the counsel. White later was appointed chairman of the Federal Power Commission where he served with distinction.

* * *

In the congressional liaison office was a platoon of hardened, battle-tested professionals. Mike Manatos, of Greek ancestry, covered the Senate and he covered it with such intensity that he was never off guard. Henry Hall Wilson (later to become the president of the Chicago Board of Trade) a gangling, drawling North Carolinian was the House expert and he did his job with much precision. Claude Deshautels manned the liaison headquarters on the second floor of the West Wing.

* * *

But at bottom the core of the White House staff was the cadre of secretaries and staffers who were apolitical and who stayed at their desks and performed their jobs no matter who was president. My own secretary-assistant was one of those enduring pros who came to the White House when President Eisenhower was in office. Nell Yates was a quietly intelligent woman, even shy, always charming, who spoke seldom but who was a fountainhead of information, who knew where every piece of paper ought to go, and who ought to get it. She steered me and unobtrusively advised me in those early days so that I avoided error and boobytrap. The plain fact is, Nell made me look good when sometimes I really didn't know what the hell I was doing, allowing me to get the credit when she surely deserved it.

The White House is peopled largely by these nonpolitical types, who survive administrations to help guide the new power-clad assistants who come and go. The whole West Wing would come crumbling down in confusion and inefficiency if it weren't for these men and women, whose names the public never hears or knows, but without whom the complex machinery would grind to a halt.

And no report of the White House can be assembled without some mention of the most awesomely efficient human apparatus ever devised by anyone at any time. I am speaking of the White House switchboard operators. These cheery-voiced ladies perform such flying communications wonders that one assumes they are children of Mercury. Twenty-four hours each day they are on duty, alert and ready. A White House staffer has only to pick up the phone, ask for whomever, and know without a peradventure of doubt his quarry will be located and brought to heel at the ear of the staffer.

* * *

Any catalogue of LBJ aides would be horribly incomplete without Walter Jenkins. Though he was only on board in the White House for some eleven months, he had been with LBJ since Johnson's early days as a congressman. I still cannot understand the bizarre turn of events that caused Walter to depart the White House, but I do know one thing and I know it well: He was the kindest and saintliest of all the men I have ever known; always unfailingly helpful to rookies who shipped in to serve the president. He knew more, did more, said less, and complained not at all. He left a hole that was never filled.

Often I used to wish for him, his counsel, his large shoulder on which all of us assistants leaned for more times than we cared to remember. LBJ gave him complete and total trust and there was never anyone to really take his place.

* * *

The internecine scrambling of the White House staff was never put so clearly as in the case of the Sorensen office.

When Ted Sorensen resigned in early 1964, his spacious office became vacant. It was a corner room with one absolutely priceless and attractive asset: it had a john, the only staff office so equipped in the West Wing. Because whomever occupied this office would be vaulted by eminent domain to the top of the presidential aide list, and because LBJ instinctively realized this, he ordered the office remain vacant. But to Bill Moyers, capture of the Sorensen office became essential, and he stalked his prey with all the wily cunning of Henry V at Agincourt.

Moyers sat in a shared office with Ken O'Donnell, JFK's chief political agent, next door to the Oval Office. This large room was the lair of the appointments secretary, a chore I was assuming more and more, though at that particular time I sat in a smallish office next to the appointments secretary room.

One day, when Moyers and I were closeted with LBJ, Moyers asked, innocently, casually, almost a throwaway line, if he could sit in the Sorensen office for a few days while he completed work on a presidential speech. It's quiet in there, Moyers said matter-of-factly, as if the Sorensen office was of no real consequence, only a refuge from the tempo and bustle of the West Wing. Nice place to do this important presidential speech. It's only temporary, shrugged Moyers. The president nodded absently.

The speech was duly completed, and then Moyers, again with a query offered so negligently, solicited the president's permission to sit in the Sorensen office to lay out some crucial domestic legislative programs. More room to spread papers, was Moyers's reasoning. The president frowned, and possibly was about to haul Moyers down, but Bill then suggested he wanted to call several meetings of key cabinet people and other experts. No place to put them, except in the Sorensen office, said Moyers, but, of course, we could hold the meeting in the White House Mess, knowing full well the mess would be too open, too easily a site for leaks. The president nodded hesitantly.

A day later, Moyers's secretary, Carole Welch, moved in, typewriter, bag, and baggage. A day after that, Hayes Redmond, Moyers's assistant arrived to take up residence. For several weeks, nothing more was heard. No one was called to Moyers's domain so that the conquest was not flaunted to others on the staff who had understood the takeover was merely temporary.

But day by day, the Moyers colonization continued, until, like the Saxons, the staff woke up one day and found the Normans had moved into the palace. Late one evening, some weeks after the Moyers conquest, LBJ raged to me that Moyers had "disobeyed orders and took over the Sorensen office." (Ted Sorensen would have been pleased to learn he was memorialized in the Johnson White House much as explorers get an obscure peak named after them in the Arctic wastes.) I tried to soothe it over with the president. He grumbled, but subsided after a bit.

Moyers stayed. I always felt a mite serene over the entire affair. Here we were involved in cosmic issues of state, fighting to, as we were wont to say, "lift the quality of life in the nation" and Moyers had, in the midst of all this, staked his claim to the largest office in the West

Wing. It was splendidly trivial, and of the stuff gathered in casebook material for *How to Steal a March on Your White House Colleagues and Gain Fame and Power without Getting Your Ass Torn Off by the President.*

On the other hand there are those times when the back-fire of well-meaning plans damn near blows you off the cliff. It happened to me and I never really knew what hit me. It had one lasting effect: I think I created for myself an entry in *Bartlett's Quotations,* but like Lincoln's character who was about to be run out of town on a rail, "if it wasn't for the honor I'd just as soon walk."

Like a good many events that have larger meaning, this one started quite innocently. Since I had been in the advertising agency business I was invited to speak to the annual convention of the Advertising Federation of America, in Boston, on June 28, 1965.

Since I had been in the White House I had never accepted any speaking engagements. But this one intrigued me. I talked to the president, who told me to go ahead, though he did, with presumption of what later happened, remind me of Sam Rayburn's admonition to young congressmen—"When you're talking, you ain't learning." I decided to go ahead and make the appearance.

I delivered my speech with some fervor and, if I am perfectly honest, with some skill. It was well received. The theme of the speech was the presidency, what it was about, how Johnson handled it. Perhaps I was a bit gaudy in my appraisal and approval of the president, but as I told one of my critics, "Do you expect a president's assistant to get up and denounce his boss?" I never once read or heard any newsman in print or on the air make a public denunciation of his editor or publisher or network president. At any rate, I returned to Washington ready to carry on my duties and promptly forgot all about my Boston speech-making.

I got a call from George Reedy, the press secretary. "What the hell did you say in that Boston speech. My staff tells me we have run out of copies. Every bureau in town is nagging us for a copy. What did you say that was so interesting?" I told George I didn't know. I reread the speech and scratched my head. No secrets revealed, no promulgation of new policy. I just didn't know what was intriguing the press.

Then, the mortars began to land, and it was guerrilla war in the West Wing, with the press kicking the hell out of one lone special assistant, and they did a job.

It seemed that in my address to the ad convention I used a line "I sleep each night a little better, a little more confidently because Lyndon Johnson is President." This got shortened to "I sleep better at night." It all climaxed with Herblock's cartoon. (Herb Block is the resident genius of the *Washington Post*, and the nearest thing to a Hall of Fame cartoonist in the nation. No one compares with him in the precise brevity of his comments, apt, devastating, ingenious, dipped in *curare*. Herb Block is also one of the most self-effacing, companionable men in Washington.) He drew a cartoon, with a top caption "Happy Days on the Old Plantation," depicting a master with whip scourging hapless slaves, with the nearest slave obviously a cringing Jack Valenti. The lines beneath the cartoon read: "A sensitive man . . . a warm-hearted man . . . I sleep each night a little better, a little more confidently because Lyndon Johnson is my President." This turned up the volume a little higher at the Washington cocktail parties and dinner fests.

The press excoriated me because my speech had been, to use one of the descriptions bandied about, sycophantic. Too lavish in praise, just too much syrup, said the press. Some friend sent me a speech by Sorensen which he made while President Kennedy was alive in which he likened JFK to Roland, Charlemagne, St. Francis, Apollo, and

Thor, and possibly the Mormon Tabernacle Choir. And then later, several years later, I read Daniel Patrick Moynihan's praise of Richard Nixon which, I thought, made my own speech seem a denial of Lyndon Johnson. No one had taken the time to see what I really had constructed in that final paragraph which contained the "sleep better at night" phrase.

This is what I wrote in the last two paragraphs of my Boston speech:

Once during the deadly days of the Nazi terror, when France had been overrun and the heel of the Nazi was on the neck of the French, Winston Churchill spoke to the French people: "Français, c'est moi Churchill." He told them not to lose heart, that in due time, the free world would stir itself and relieve the French of their long night. "So," he said, "sleep well, my Frenchmen, sleep well to gather strength for the morning, for the morning shall come."

I sleep each night a little better, a little more confidently because Lyndon Johnson is my President. For I know he lives and thinks and works to make sure that for all Americans, and indeed, the growing body of the free world, the morning shall always come.

But, no matter what I did and said, my phrase had been enclosed, wrapped, and mailed to *Bartlett's Quotations;* I have been assailed and assaulted by it on dinner rostrums and in auditoriums whenever I appear to speak. It follows me like a shadow, it is glued to me and I have finally given up and said, alright, damn you, follow me and be damned.

I am comforted by one thought. Once I was lightly complaining to the president about this "sleeping better" attachment to me and I told the president that it seemed as if I were destined never to be rid of it. The president looked amused. "Why are you fretting?" he said. "Do you know how few presidential aides ever utter a memorable phrase?" Then he laughed. "Come to think of it, not too many memorable phrases are ever uttered by presidents anymore."

The president enjoyed his staff people. Unlike other presidents, there was with LBJ no dichotomy of working and social friends. He gathered his staff about him because he enjoyed being with them, much as a father would be with his family. He relaxed with them, he was comfortable and at ease with them. He was capable of being very tough on his staff and, to be quite honest, was brutal with them at times. Because I felt so secure in my relationship with the president, while these moments embarrassed me, and sometimes pushed me into a kind of blue despair, it never unhinged my enduring respect for him, or caused me to believe I was flung out into the cold. I knew where I stood. I knew he cared about me and trusted me and needed me and so I, possibly, didn't reel under these LBJ blows as did some of the other members of the staff. Many times, I would try to be the conciliator and meet privately with the president to take the side of Bill Moyers or Doug Cater or Joe Califano or Harry McPherson or someone who, at that moment, was in the presidential doghouse. We all inhabited it for varying lengths of time. My duties demanded my nearness to the president and so when he had "flogged" me I acted as if nothing had happened, went about my chores and soon the president's arm would be about me, a grin on his face, and a squeeze of my shoulders as if to say "I'm sorry. Forgive me."

The president knew when he had been excessively tough with those around him. While he never really apologized in words, he surely did in deeds. One day we had a

problem, its origins escape me now, and the president accused me of fouling up some well-laid plans. Possibly I
did. At any rate, he lit in to me with a fury that seemed to
have no human limits. I said nothing, merely listened, and
when he had finished, I excused myself, went back to my
office and continued my work.

Late that evening, my buzzer rang loudly. (Each of the
chief assistants had a red button on his phone console. It
was wired directly to the president's office console. When
he wanted a particular assistant, he rang that assistant's
buzzer and by depressing the red button, we were on a
direct line with him. The red button had a sound that
every assistant knew as if it were wired to his nerve center. When it rang, we jumped, pushed, and answered.)
The president's voice was soft and gentle. "Why don't you
call Mary Margaret and see if she can come down to the
White House. We can all have supper together. Would
you like that?"

It was the president's way of saying "I'm sorry. I love
you. Be with me. Let's forget what I said." "Fine, Mr.
President," I would answer, "I'll call her now."

My wife would be picked up by White House car, and
at 10:00 P.M. or later, she would appear. The president
would greet her warmly. We would sit in his office, the
three of us, and then Mrs. Johnson would join us, while
he and I did some work together. He would take Mary
Margaret by the arm and we would walk into the night,
under the covered walkway to the Mansion. The president
now would be full of good humor. He would joke, josh,
tell stories, and the early day's outpouring of discontent
would have vanished, never to be recalled.

He did this with all his assistants. He wanted his staff
around him, with their wives and husbands. He knew better than anyone the long, tedious, exhausting hours we
worked and he used these late-evening suppers as his way

of giving affection and individual interest to wearied aides.

For years to come, historians and social scientists and Ph.D. candidates will inspect the grand design of the LBJ personality. They will survey the flaws and the authority, the warts and the competency, the fissures and the capacities. The searchers will find none of these are separable. It is quite possible that LBJ was precisely what Oliver Goldsmith was describing in his *The Good-Natur'd Man:* "We must touch his weaknesses with a delicate hand. There are some faults so nearly allied to excellence that we can scarce weed out the fault without eradicating the virtue."

Once, my father, then in his late seventies, came to the White House to visit me. His eyes were as big as saucers for he had never been so close to the seat of ultimate political power. He was trembling with excitement. I took him into the Cabinet Room where the president was involved in a public ceremony with several cabinet officers present, and the press crowding that historic room. When the president's eyes fell on my father, he grinned widely, and said, "I want you all to meet a great man from Houston, Texas, Joe Valenti, who is the father of my assistant." My father gulped, the color fled his face, and then he pressed forward to be hugged and greeted by the president. His eyes became moist. Never had anything so splendid ever happened to him. To be embraced by the president of the United States, in front of all these people! He never forgot it. The president joshed with him, introduced him to all the cabinet officers, and later took him back into the Oval Office to give him some presidential souvenirs. My father was so overcome with joy he could hardly speak.

Later that day the president said to me, "Your father is a good man, Jack. You are lucky to have him with you." I understood. The president was telling me that he was glad he could give my father the gift of recognition and public affection. He knew what that meant to my dad, a simple, decent man to whom the presidency was some shining holy place and the president a man of saving, divine power. It was a generous and thoughtful gesture and I told the president, "Thank you, sir, for this morning, it meant so much to my father."

He did the same with all his aides. He never had to be asked. He knew instinctively what was right and wonderful and he did it with good humor, warmth, and unaffected grace.

The fabled screen actor Kirk Douglas recounts with relish a story about the president. Kirk had come to Washington in 1965 to visit with a high U.S. government official. He waited on the official for over an hour and was told he was too busy, could Mr. Douglas come back tomorrow. Kirk, vexed, called me and asked if he could come to see me. Of course, I said. Within minutes Kirk and his wife were in my office. We chatted, and then I suggested they see the president. See the president? "My God," said Kirk, "how could I see the president when I wait an hour to see some functionary?"

I buzzed the president and told him the Douglases were in my office. "Have them come in," was his response, and instantly they were in the president's office. He greeted them affectionately, and made them feel comfortable and at ease. He told Kirk how much he enjoyed his movies (he had just seen a film called *In Harm's Way* in which Kirk and John Wayne had starred).

As Kirk and Anne Douglas left, they marveled at the whimsy of Washington. The easiest guy in town to see is the president!

Before the president's grandchildren were born, my then two-and-a-half-year-old daughter, Courtenay Lynda, was his special favorite. No matter how important the meeting Courtenay was always welcome. He reveled in her and made her a "star," so often did her picture appear in the newspapers and on television, consorting with her boyfriend, the president.

Once I was sitting with the president in a somber National Security Council meeting about 6:00 P.M. A note was passed to me. My wife and daughter were outside, could I excuse myself for a moment? The only time I ever got to visit with my child was in the late afternoon. My wife would bring her down so I could see her and kiss her. I left the house in early morning and got home very late at night, so my little daughter was growing up not knowing precisely who her father was.

I whispered to the president: "Mary Margaret and Courtenay are outside. I'd like to see them for a few minutes." He nodded, "Bring Courtenay in. I want to see her too."

I told my wife when I reached my office that the president wanted Courtenay to say "hello." I picked her up in my arms and went back to the Cabinet Room. I opened the door noiselessly and peered inside. Secretary of State Rusk was speaking, going over a complex diplomatic idea on which he was discoursing steadily. As I opened the door wider, Courtenay caught a glimpse of the president, and in a loud girlish voice she shouted, "Prez!"

The entire room-full of serious-minded men turned as one to face me, with the secretary of state looking wracked and astonished. The president held out his arms. I put Courtenay down on her feet and off like a shot she raced toward the president. She leaped onto his lap, giving him a moist kiss, and the president cradled her in his arms, smiled hugely at her, and then nodding to Rusk, said, "Go ahead, Dean, continue your report."

Dean Rusk is not a man to discomfort easily. He has

amazing powers of resilience. But this time he had some difficulty in gathering together his senses in what may have been one of his few awkward moments. It challenges a man to discuss matters of critical policy with a two-and-a-half-year-old girl staring at you as she perches on the lap of the most powerful public man in all the world.

But Courtenay was plainly used to being present when the great and the near-great gathered in the White House. There exists a marvelous photograph of the president sitting in his rocking chair in the Oval Office surrounded by Senator Russell, Senator Mansfield, and other chieftains of the Senate. By his side, with her back to the assembly, and the president's phone in her hand and ear, is Courtenay. It is a study in democracy, and the ascendancy of the young. I often remind my eleven-year-old daughter today that she is the youngest political has-been I know. Many of us fall from political power, but at age five?

*　*　*

As American newspaper readers and television viewers know, the chief executive who took John Kennedy's place in the White House had a tough act to follow when it came to grace and wit before an audience. Still, LBJ was essentially a man of humor. He could no more resist spinning a yarn to illustrate a point than he could curtail his breathing. It would not be accurate to describe LBJ's stories as "wit" in the Kennedy sense. They were not. It was simply that Johnson and Kennedy were two different kinds of men. JFK used wit, irony, and sardonic thrusts as one uses a rapier to prick the skin, to give spice to otherwise dull recitals. LBJ used mimicry and folksy tales of Texas to score and underpin a crucial issue or to make known a point of view.

He was a funny man in the sense that he was skilled as a

mimic. Most of his stories emerged from his central Texas hill country home, a land where the living was plain and difficult. He built up a family of characters from his boyhood and early political days that would be cast in the various stories he told. LBJ would sit by the hour to tell his stories and though I heard most of them several times, I have to admit they were full of fun and comic images. Maybe it was the way he told them.

I used to try to persuade the president, for example, that he ought not read so much of the news and editorials when they gave him hell. "Mr. President," I would commence, "who the devil reads all that stuff you read? Sure, some people in Washington, but very few of the citizens out there know what is being printed. You take too much of this to heart. Forget it." The president would peer at me, with that opaque gaze, and grunt without answering. And he would continue to read.

One morning I reached his bedroom early with a stack of documents to discuss with him. He was propped up in bed with papers sprawled over the blanket. This morning, he was frowning as he perused some story in the *Washington Post*. Without determining just what it was he was reading, I began: "I can tell the news is bad, Mr. President, and my suggestion is to toss all those papers in the wastebasket and just forget what they are saying."

He put the paper down, half-grinned at me, and asked, "Oh, you would, would you?"

"Yes sir, that is exactly what I would do."

"Well," said the president, "you may be right. You see, this story is about you."

I stood upright and while I cannot describe my expression it must have been a bit strange, because the president now widened his grin, tossed me the paper and I read, to my consternation, an interpretative story in the *Post* which said, among other things, that Jack Valenti was a bit of a dolt. "That lying son of a bitch" was my first reaction, the words leaping out of me with enough force to scrape paint off the wall.

Now, the president swung his legs over the bed and onto the floor, whopping merrily, "Sort of depends whose ox is being gored, doesn't it?"

Yeah, I muttered, it sure as hell does.

Oftentimes, leaks occurred in the White House. The president would fume and try to locate the source of the leak.

One story about leaks went like this: When the president was a boy of fifteen, he helped his father, Sam Johnson, on a road contract. The elder Johnson was building a small turn in one of the country roads and the work was going slowly. Sam Johnson was unhappy about the delays, and he prayed that the district engineer who lived in Austin, some eighty miles from the work site, didn't get any knowledge that the work was way behind schedule. One day Sam Johnson sent young Lyndon into Austin to buy a piece of equipment for the tractor which had stalled on the job. Lyndon bought the missing piece and was headed out of town when he spied the district engineer coming out of a building. Young Lyndon loped over to the district engineer, greeted him, and the engineer said: "Howdy, Lyndon, how's the work going with your father?"

"Oh," said Lyndon, "we are not having such a good time of it. We're way behind schedule"; he proceeded to unload on the engineer all the troubles that had plagued them. The engineer frowned, said goodbye. The next day, he showed up on the site to Sam Johnson's intense regret and after delivering some choice words of reprimand, the engineer departed. Sam Johnson thought a while, and then he said to his son, "Now, Lyndon, how do you suppose the district engineer found out about this?" Lyndon shuffled uneasily and confessed to his father what he said.

Sam Johnson fixed a fierce gaze on his son, and then he said very softly, "Lyndon, now remember this very carefully. You just ain't smart enough yet to talk to a district engineer."

I heard this story a number of times, as did others on the staff. Then, whenever a press report appeared that bore the mark of some staff member's leaking something that had happened in the White House, the president would hold up the press report to the staff member and say softly, "I see you've been talking to the district engineer again."

Invariably, I always enjoyed hearing the president tell one of my favorites, a story about a very famous congressman of the thirties who had a higher opinion of himself than others had of him. Once the congressman recounted to his colleagues how he stormed into President Roosevelt's White House office, and told the president this and such and by God and by damn, oh how he told the president. To which Speaker Rayburn is alleged to have replied: "I am not interested in what you told Roosevelt, but I am damn sure interested in what Roosevelt told you!" Whenever a staff member or some government official recounted to the president the essence of a conversation with someone of prestige and influence and spoke too long about his own point of view, the president would break in with a smile and say, "Now, that's all very good, but I sure am interested in what Roosevelt told you."

There was another story LBJ told often: Once when he was driving through East Texas during the Office of Price Administration days when coupons were needed to purchase items, LBJ stopped at a rural country store deep in the East Texas thicket. The grizzled old man who owned the store tended to LBJ's gasoline purchase, and when it was done, the president asked, "How many coupons?"

The old man looked puzzled. "Coupons?" he said.

"Sure," said LBJ, "you know, the OPA?"

"Oh," exclaimed the old man, "you mean the O, P, and A. Well, we didn't put that in down here."

The president had a thing about assistants forgetting crucial parts of a task, or even noncrucial parts. He got mad as hell whenever anything was forgotten. Once his anger subsided he was apt to look up at the offending aide, and quizzically say, "I suppose you didn't put that in down here." We knew.

I suppose the story he told most often to a hundred different groups was one of my favorites also. He constantly tried to implant in the minds of his White House staff the terribly urgent necessity of reining in your emotions when dealing with senators or congressmen. Over and over again, he forced on us the imperative of being respectful of congressmen and senators, and never losing one's cool when talking to someone from Capitol Hill.

When he was a young congressman, his guide and mentor was a sage and clever lawyer, Alvin Wirtz from Austin. Because Wirtz had once been a state senator in Texas, he wore the prefix senator. Thus, Senator Wirtz, brimming over with wise patience and a philosophic understanding of the frailty of the human spirit, tutored the rookie congressman in the wily turns of life. There occurred a dispute between the Texas private power companies and the public-power-minded Congressman Johnson. Senator Wirtz finally arranged a meeting between LBJ and the power titans of the state in Austin. After an hour or so of fruitless wrangling, LBJ exploded, rose to his feet and poking his long forefinger in the face of the senior power executive present, said, "Goddammit, you can just go to hell!" Then he turned on his heel and left the meeting.

The next morning, Senator Wirtz asked LBJ to come by his office to chat. When he arrived, the old senator sat him down. "Now, Lyndon, it took me six months just to arrange that meeting," he said. "And in one minute you blew all my plans sky high and also your chances for a settlement. Now, I am going to give you a piece of advice and some truth. It is this. It's one thing to tell a man to go to hell, but Lyndon, it's something else to make him go!"

LBJ relished this story. He stuffed it in the ears of all his aides time and time again. Stop, look, and listen, he said, because while you can tell a man to go to hell, you can't make him go.

The
Johnson Caution

The fracturing of a president's administration is a possibility he always lives with. It can come with suddenness over an issue badly searched; over a decision too impetuously made; because of follies and disasters no prescience could have divined; or the indiscretions of aides unaware and insensitive to the pitfalls and landmines that invest the Washington environment. Almost from the first day of his accession to the presidency, President Johnson began to build those fences of professional integrity which he vowed no aide of his would ever vault.

He was very fussy about campaign contributions and particularly who handled them. He told me, not once, but dozens of times, I was never to handle a campaign contribution. "Never, never get involved in contributions," he said. "If anyone comes to you and wants to make a contribution, don't ask him how much or what for or anything. Just send him to the National Committee finance chairman and let it go at that. Do you understand? And do you also understand that it is a federal crime to accept a contribution in a federal building? Do you? You'll be clean if you don't touch money, don't look at money, don't ask about money. Let the finance chairman handle all that. Do I make myself plain?"

Yes, he made it plain.

He knew that for some years now the press and others had been on his trail trying, vainly, to link him with the so-called Bobby Baker affair. I knew very little about what it was that Bobby Baker had engaged in. But when LBJ became vice-president, disengaged from the vast power he exerted as Senate leader, the sniffing around his door became intense. I think that President Johnson's distaste for wiretapping had its origins during his vice-presidential days. He told me on several occasions, he was absolutely certain his own phones were being tapped in the abortive hope that his conversations would reveal some link to Baker. To say the investigation was total and unceasing is to understate. But nothing came of it, for the simple reason that nothing was there. LBJ regarded politicians on the take as stupid.

There were always rumblings about the "Johnson fortune"; that by some devious and possibly illegal act the Johnson family had acquired their TV station in Austin. Also, there were always hints that the Johnsons had large land holdings near some federal establishment. That no one could ever find even the slightest sliver of proof didn't quash the gossip.

In truth, the Johnson television station came about in a perfectly routine fashion, which any inspection of the records will show. In 1952, applications were open for one VHF station in Austin, Texas. Because of the nearness of neighboring cities like Waco, San Antonio, Houston, Dallas, and Bryan, only one VHF was allotted to Austin. For some months, no one applied for the Austin outlet. In 1952, television was not the darling of investors. It had yet to display any long-range profitability; people with money to invest shied away from this unstable and as yet unsupported-by-facts venture.

After months of no person or company filing for the single VHF station, Mrs. Johnson, operating in the name of the Texas Broadcasting Corporation, filed for Channel 7, the lone VHF station, on March 11, 1952. The FCC put out further notice to entice other applicants. None came forward. On July 14, 1952, four months after Mrs. Johnson's filing, with no competitive applicants on file, the FCC granted a license to Texas Broadcasting Company for KTBC-TV, channel 7. On the same day, the FCC also issued a license to C. H. Coffield, operating under the name of Capital City Television Company for a UHF station, channel 18. In that time, no one really knew where the future lay, in VHF or UHF.

What happened to the value of KTBC, channel 7, was the same as happened to any other station in any other similar American city. As the city grew, as more people came to live in Austin, as more homes installed TV, so the value of the station rose. At the president's death, the station was sold to the *Los Angeles Times* for nine million dollars, some twenty years after it first went on the air. Most financial experts would attest to the value-rise as being reasonable, and duplicated in almost any other growing city in America where similar stations went on the air at approximately the same time. (In the same year, 1952, the *Houston Post* purchased channel 2 in Houston for some $700,000. Today that station is worth many millions.)

LBJ was extremely careful before and during his presidency to stay far away from any involvement in the FCC.

In all the years of the Johnson family ownership of KTBC-TV, no one, not even his political enemies, filed any charges with the FCC. Every three years the station's license came up for renewal. The FCC would ask for any critical comments, but none ever came. And so the license was renewed, without controversy, and routinely.

To the charge that no other VHF station was ever officially allowed by the FCC (Austin has two UHF stations today), the facts respond. With the first FCC engineering map of the U.S., Austin was accorded only one VHF. It was never intended, by engineering and scientific fiat, that Austin would ever obtain another VHF because another VHF in Austin would interfere with a similarly-channeled VHF in another nearby city.

And so LBJ, on attaining the presidency, never even wanted to connect himself to appointments to the FCC. His first move as president, was to name a Republican already on the FCC, Rosel Hyde, as chairman of the commission. He wanted no criticism that he had chosen a "crony" to head the commission.

He told me, as he told all of those whom he brought to power: "I want you to remember the fate of Matt Connelly, a fine and decent man. He was Truman's appointments secretary and he went to jail because he committed one indiscretion. He got an appointment in one of the departments for a man who had contracts to talk about and they convicted him. I am going to say this once and never again and you better listen hard. If anyone on my staff even so much as makes a phone call for an appointment for someone to see any official in this government about contracts in any government department, or about lawsuits in the Department of Justice, he automatically has his resignation on my desk. I don't care who asks you, or how much money he contributed to the party or how important he is in this country, there are no exceptions to the rule. Understand?"

I understood. So did every other staff member.

How then to explain that rule to a large contributor when he called and asked for me to make an appointment for him?

I can't recall how many times my phone rang with an "important person" at the other end of the line. "Can you make an appointment for me to see the assistant attorney general or the assistant secretary of defense?" When I responded that I simply couldn't do that, incredulity and oftentimes anger exploded in my ear. "I don't want you to do anything except get me the appointment. Is that asking too much for . . ." and here my caller would specify either his service to the party or his contribution to the campaign or his closeness to the president.

My answer was always the same and usually settled down my frustrated caller. "The president has given me orders that I cannot make any appointments for anybody at Justice or Defense, in particular. Now if you insist, I will try to connect you with the president and he can take this up directly with you." End of conversation.

I fouled up one time. And I never forgot the dereliction.

An important senator wrote me a letter expatiating at length on his exasperation with the Defense Department for being slope-headed about one of his constituents who operated a manufacturing plant. The Defense Department, it seemed, had neglected to give this man a contract.

I was busy the day the letter arrived. My frustrations at that moment clouded my good sense. I brushed the letter to my assistant and told him to buck it to the department for a draft answer I would sign.

Within a day or two the draft was on my desk, I read it quickly and signed it. What it said, in essence, was that the senator's constituent had too high a price on his product, and besides the quality wasn't much either. Not a particularly helpful letter as I recall, indeed a bit hard-nosed. I promptly forgot about it.

In two or three days, I was summoned to the president's office. He was scowling, the deep lines in his cheeks and chin set with that intensity I knew so well. The danger signals were hoisted and I braced myself for the storm, whose source was not clear to me and about whose direction I was completely in the dark.

The president waved a piece of paper in front of me. "Read this letter," he said quietly. I read it. It was from McGeorge Bundy to the same senator who had written me. The letter went as follows:

Dear Senator:
I do not handle contracts. I do not respond to any requests about contracts. I suggest you take this up directly with the Department of Defense.
                                        Sincerely yours,
                                        McGeorge Bundy

I felt the goose bumps. God, I had indeed forgotten. How stupid of me.

Now the president stepped from behind his desk to approach me. He stood close to me, and handed me another letter. "Now, read this one," he said. I didn't have to. I knew instantly it was the letter I had signed to the same senator. How the hell he found it was beyond me.

"I want you to take a copy of this letter from Mac Bundy. Keep it on your desk at all times. Memorize it. This is precisely the way I want you to answer every letter you get from anyone about contracts or selling anything to this government. And I want you to remember Matt Connelly." Whereupon the president turned, returned to his chair behind his desk, sat down and began to read some documents. I had been dismissed.

As I turned to leave, he said, "Wait a minute." I faced him. He beckoned me to sit down in the chair next to his desk. "I know you think I am mighty tough on you. But dammit, this is a poker game with the highest stakes. You just have to understand that the tiniest, the very slightest misstep and you can bring down the whole presidency on my head. That stuff about Caesar's wife was sound advice. What's one little letter to a senator going to do to anyone? Plenty. I don't know what could happen, but if that senator's friend got himself mixed up in some stupid scheme that was crooked, that letter of yours would surface and you would be testifying before some congressional committee trying to explain it. And you couldn't, even though you are innocent. The best way to stay out of trouble is not to get near it. Not only for your sake, but mine. They would bleed you because they know the trail of blood would lead to me. You understand?"

I understood, though it was a hairy lesson to learn.

But the president wasn't through. He stood up, beckoned to me, and led me to my office. Then, half-smiling, and all-serious, he spoke: "I want you to put this letter of Mac Bundy on your desk and every time you get a hair up your ass to write some damn-fool letter or call someone about anything that has to do with Pentagon or Justice business, read Mac's letter again." With that, he lifted up the glass top on my desk and inserted under it the Bundy letter. He let the glass down gently, and turned to me: "That is now the eleventh commandment and from your standpoint and mine, maybe it is the most important one."

He clapped me on the shoulder, turned, and left.

I never told Mac Bundy that he had been canonized. I didn't want Mac trying to walk across the Potomac in order to verify himself. After a week, I removed the letter.

The president never mentioned that he missed it though every time he came to my office to chat, I always suspected he would browse my desk to see if it were still in place. Perhaps the fact that I never again violated his rule was sufficient to his wants.

Yet even as I left the Oval Office, I knew the president was right. Though my letter was not by any stretch of the mind favorable to the senator's constituent, (it was exactly the opposite) the fact I had responded at all to this request was the nub of the failure and I knew it. The president's harsh reception of my omission was his way of letting me know how serious, how deadly serious, was the error. This precaution was suitably made, though. Many times the only way to assault a president is to wound an aide. If one brings down the assistant, perhaps the blood will spill on the president. The only possible way to prevent this happening was to close every fissure and make sure the White House was a seamless web of integrity.

How to judge the president's results? One may fault LBJ for many things, and one may with impunity criticize those around him for mistakes or misjudgments, but at this writing there is no evidence that someone near the president in the West Wing committed the kind of indiscretion that tarnishes the leader. It is significant to note that in all of the Johnson years in the presidency there was no hint or smell of scandal of any kind in appraising the conduct of the public's business.

In the early days, LBJ would, with a merciless persistency that both puzzled and angered me, strip his staff of pretension. "You're only an extension of this office and don't you forget it. Don't push anyone around because all that you have and are is temporary, damn temporary. Remember that."

He pressed the thought, endlessly, that we were custodians of a trust. If nagging, badgering, even brutalizing his staff was the necessary means to achieve his end, then the staff would have to understand. It went with the job.

We were bruised, but we got the message.

LBJ deliberately kept his staff very small. And he ordered that the staff of his staff be limited in the same way.

When I ran the appointments secretary office, one of the most important of staff responsibilities, I had one assistant and two secretaries. That was it. Total. I was also responsible for all written presidential material. For that assignment I had a staff of two, count them, two speechwriters. Total.

Joe Califano ran the domestic affairs office with a total of four assistants. Bill Moyers handled the press office with two assistants. Larry O'Brien ran the congressional liaison office with three aides. Harry McPherson conducted the affairs of the counsel's office with one assistant. Douglass Cater was in charge of educational matters with one assistant.

Indeed, the *entire team* of presidential staff resided in the West Wing of the White House, with the exception of three domestic affairs assistants and the two speechwriters. If the White House staff has proliferated in size, it surely has no ancestral ties to the Johnson concept of a streamlined White House staff. The more bodies you had in the White House, according to the LBJ political theory, the more your chances for blunders, problems, and mismanagement grew—in geometric proportion. Ergo, keep the staff small, keep down the number of assistants, and assistants to assistants, and you reduce the probability of bloopers and stupidities.

When the president travelled to his ranch, he took only one or two assistants. I suspect one of the reasons why the travelling troupe was kept so small was because there was simply no working space for any of us at the ranch. The thought of transporting a large staff to the LBJ Ranch was abhorrent to the president. Our working facilities consisted, in its entirety, of one room in the ranchhouse, the president's study. In that small room the president shared his office space with two secretaries and no more than two assistants. If two assistants were there, we both used the same telephone, unless we leaned over the secretary's desk to use hers. Our "desk" consisted of one small table where we juggled elbows and knees. Everything any of us said, including the president, was heard by everyone else. We worked, it may be said, in surroundings something less than opulent and spacious.

Whether the country was run properly is a matter of personal opinion. But beyond any doubts, it was mighty inexpensive to taxpayers.

* * *

The Johnson caution did not extend to his own personal safety when, in his judgment, larger matters were at stake.

In 1966 the president was invited to visit Mexico by the then president of that republic, Gustavo Díaz Ordaz. This visit was to take place only shortly after the Dominican Republic involvement in which several thousand American troops were hastened to that Caribbean nation; first in order to evacuate Americans stranded there when the civil war broke out, and then to intervene in the civil fracas to bring about a ceasefire and peace, of a sort.

LBJ called me and said: "I want this trip to go well. I want you and Bill Moyers to fly there and handle the advance. Bill will take care of the press arrangements and you handle the rest."

Within hours Moyers and I were aboard an Air Force Jetstar heading toward Mexico City where, upon landing, we set up headquarters in the American Embassy.

Without warning, one of those small but indispensable details came up behind me and pasted me a blow I will never forget.

Arrangements had gone swimmingly—from the inspection of the presidential guest bedroom at the Mexican president's palace, Los Pinos, to the motorcade route. The bedroom was spacious, the bathroom large and pleasant (LBJ had a thing about bathrooms—they had to be just right, particularly the showerhead. While the Constitution would not have unraveled if the bathroom were not exactly right, it is also possible to state, weighing the LBJ reaction, that perhaps it would be better if it were the Constitution at fault and not the bathroom).

The presidential motorcade course, from the airport some fourteen kilometers to the presidential palace, was traversed, in company with the Secret Service. We all agreed that it was a long line of presidential travel, but we acquiesced.

In short, all of the difficult and numerous little details were beginning to fall into place. Late one afternoon, two days before the arrival of President Johnson, I sat with U.S. Ambassador Tony Freeman and a number of Mexican officials. Almost casually, I inquired of the ambassador if the president's limousine (armor-plated, bulletproof glass, bomb-proof underside) had arrived by cargo plane. The ambassador quickly responded that it was due that afternoon. I nodded and prepared to go on down the check list I had assembled, when the ambassador interposed with a question: "Why does the president need his limousine here?" A rather silly question I thought.

Laughing, I answered him. "Well, the president has to ride in his limo on public occasions like this. The Secret

Service would go into total hysteria if he did otherwise." The Secret Service man present nodded.

The ambassador looked at me worriedly and obviously puzzled. "Jack, I think you better talk to the foreign minister. We have a problem if you insist on the president riding in his own limo."

"Problem?" I said. "No problem, he has to ride in his car, no other way for him to get from that airport to the palace. We'll pass a million people."

The ambassador, a highly intelligent total professional, and immensely understanding of the Mexican character, pride, and temperament, made it clear to me that if I insisted on the president riding in his own limousine, we would have a *contretemps* of the first rank on our hands.

"You have three alternatives," said Ambassador Freeman. "One, the president and Mrs. Johnson ride in his limo and the president of Mexico and his wife in the Mexican open car; two, the two presidents ride in the open car; or three, we cancel the visit."

I chewed on this a bit. It was quite obvious, more than quite obvious, that the president could not ride with Lady Bird, *without* the president of Mexico with him. That was out. Cancellation was definitely out. That left what I chose to regard as the unsalable alternative.

Freeman again was softly inquiring. "Perhaps I should talk to the foreign minister (Antonio Carillo-Flores, a former ambassador to the U.S. and an intimate friend of President Johnson) and see if it is at all possible for this problem to be settled as you would like."

Within an hour, Tony Freeman had returned. "No chance," he said. "The foreign minister has talked to President Díaz Ordaz. The Mexican president must ride in an open car."

Freeman reiterated to me this ancient and unbreakable rule of Mexican politics: the Mexican president must never appear in public with anything barring him from his people. A closed car is a barrier and therefore unacceptable.

I quickly adjourned the meeting to ponder this cheerless turn of events. We had, as the Secret Service put it, a crisis. I retired to a private office and without hesitation, I called the LBJ Ranch, where LBJ was staying prior to his taking off for the Mexican trip. I got the president on the phone.

"Sir, we have a problem, and it is this . . ." but before I could go further, the voice of LBJ came flying into my ear, strong and unmistakably out of sorts.

"For godsakes, Jack, that's why I sent you to Mexico City. You handle the problems there, I've got enough of them right here without your adding to them. Whatever the problem is, you solve it."

"But, Mr. President, you don't understand. Only you can solve this one," and before the interruption came, I quickly unfolded my story, laying it right on the line so that there could be no misunderstanding.

When I finished, the president spoke again, this time, quieter and slower. "Jack, I don't care what kind of car I ride in. I will even ride a burro if that is the only way to get into the city. You are there to handle such matters. Whatever you and Ambassador Freeman decide is the right course for me to follow, I will do it. Now, let me get back to *my* problems."

Click.

One final source of authority remained. I called J. Edgar Hoover in Washington. When the director of the FBI came on the phone, I told him of the predicament I was in and of the president's own cavalier brush-off of his personal safety. I told Mr. Hoover I sure as hell didn't want to be responsible for something happening to the president, and yet the dilemma was here in front of me, a gigantic piece of a dilemma.

Mr. Hoover was calm. "If I were you, Jack, I would not worry one bit. Just put yourself in the hands of the Mexican Secret Police and the local constabulary. They will take care of everything. Indeed, I would think the president would be safer driving down the boulevards of Mexico City than he would be in New York City."

Mr. Hoover did promise to dispatch to my aid a dozen crack FBI agents from nearby cities in the southern part of the U.S. They would be in Mexico City within hours. But "don't worry" was Mr. Hoover's parting shot.

I did worry. But I did as he bade. I met with the head of the Mexican equivalent of our Secret Service, a gracious, charming, and totally menacing man whose whole bearing indicated he knew what efficiency meant in Spanish *and* English. He assured me that all was under control. His confidence began to infect me, and within an hour after talking with him, my pessimism lessened. Moyers, Ambassador Freeman, and I conferred at length; with the ambassador's firm recommendation to go ahead with the open car motorcade, with President Johnson pitching the decision to us, we agreed. The president would ride in the open car.

On April 14, the president flew by chopper from his ranch in Texas to Randolph Field in San Antonio. There he boarded Air Force One and landed in Mexico City at 5:30 P.M. He and President Díaz Ordaz greeted each other warmly with a comradely *abrazo*. They mounted the open limousine for the fourteen-kilometer drive from the airport to Los Pinos.

It was in the waning hours of daylight. Some three hours later—in the midst of almost three million spectators, the gathering cheers leaping to higher crescendos, signs and placards of affectionate greetings hoisted in every block, throngs pressing in a weaving, never-immobile mass—the two presidents finally wound their way to the palace. It was a jubilant hospitable welcome for LBJ, one of the largest and the most friendly crowds he would meet in all his presidential career, matched perhaps only by the hysterically loving Australians and Koreans on LBJ's Asian tour a year later.

And not one thing went wrong.* Our worst fears were never confirmed. Mr. Hoover's remark about the president's safety was totally verified.

---

* After the president had departed for Washington the Mexican authorities showed Ambassador Freeman a three-volume set of plans and operational orders that were carried out to insure LBJ's safe conduct in Mexico City. Thousands of dissidents and potential intruders were rounded up. Every single window in every building on the route had been inspected. The Mexican police knew the name of every occupant of every room with a window in every building. Armed soldiers were on every floor of every structure the two presidents passed. Thousands of soldiers and police were stationed at strategic placements along the route, so that every window was in view every second of the motorcade's procession. Seventeen first-aid stations were set up along the route, each manned by an English-speaking doctor and English-speaking nurse. Blood plasma of the type of the president and Mrs. Johnson were provisioned in each of the locations. Each driver in the motorcade had special instructions and a map, easily readable, that would take him to the nearest first-aid station along the route. It was a total immersion plan, exhaustive, finite, specific, in more fine detail than one could have imagined. It was a stunning example of the Mexican organizing genius, and the splendor of its meticulous scrutiny was in the result: success, without a hitch.

The
Bobby Kennedy
Matter

There are few subjects guaranteed to pique public interest and stir public debate more than the relationship between President Johnson and Robert Kennedy.

It was perhaps inevitable that between these two resolute and complex men there would develop a mutual antagonism seemingly unfixable by any friend, baffling both allies and observers, an unlinkable void separating each from the other. And I daresay no single person could have accurately divined what truly went on in the minds of either of these men when they thought about each other.

Every meeting they had furnished new speculation, ladled on by anyone who claimed to have any connection with either man. Had they ever been congenial to paving over past wounds, and real or imagined slights, and if from this congeniality there had been built an alliance between the two—an alliance to last with no reproofs or breaches of faith—it is likely that these two men, linch-pinned together, could have constructed a political combination unbeatable by any known political force.

My first meeting with Bob Kennedy was as unlikely a first meeting as a man is to have. In the early part of 1964, before Bobby had resigned as attorney general, though it was speculated in the press he was determined to make some move, he came to the White House to attend a cabinet meeting. I had just stepped into the corridor outside the president's office, and Kennedy and Mike Feldman, were striding briskly down the same corridor. I was on my way to the Cabinet Room, as was Kennedy, for the meeting with the president.

Bobby stopped in front of me. I looked at him, smiled, delighted to see him; before I could speak, he spoke to me: "I don't appreciate the leaks coming from the White House and from you. I suggest you cut it out." There was no expression on his face, only flint and gray smoke in his eyes and a straight, hard line across his mouth.

To say I was stunned is to utter one of the great understatements of the decade. My surprise was amplified by the fact that I had just learned what a leak was, so green was I to the Washington jungle. I stammered something, I can't remember exactly what. I probably tried to blurt out both my astonishment and my denial, all mingling together in some garbled sound that came from my throat, but not recognizable as my voice. Bobby turned, and with Feldman a few steps back of him, strode off.

I gathered my senses, all of them in disarray, and followed Bobby to the Cabinet Room. Feldman had already doubled-back to his office and I took my seat behind the president's chair. Bobby sat in the attorney general's chair, two chairs from the president, and not more than three feet from me. He never looked at me, nor I at him.

I brooded about this all the next day. It was clear to me

that Bobby had singled me out as the source of stories published in the press about him and his relationship to the president, and the probabilities about Bobby being the vice-presidential nominee. Stories about LBJ and Bobby were ballooning all over Washington, and I could not for the life of me pinpoint any specific story Bobby was referring to. Enough to say that he had determined I was his enemy in the White House and I could not imagine why. First, whatever else I might have been, I was not leaking anything to the press; indeed, I was chary of saying much to any reporter that even suggested substance. Second, my only feeling about Bobby Kennedy was one of admiration. I was drawn to him as a person; I found him a man of considerable magnetism though I knew him not at all. Like so many Americans in 1960, I was mesmerized by John Kennedy and the so-called Kennedy charisma had not left me untouched. Thus, I suppose one could say that the residue of my own innermost affection for President Kennedy had now, by political osmosis, been transferred to Bobby. I found it not at all troublesome or peculiar to be totally loyal to President Johnson, to give him fidelity and even my life and at the same time have a spiritual rapport for the second Kennedy around whose shoulders the entire Kennedy legend was now mantled.

In those days, it never occurred to me that one would have to choose between Kennedy and Johnson. I would not have hesitated to make my own personal choice, but then I would have found the matter of choice disturbing and unneeded, and later on when I discovered that a good many people in Washington believed that one must take sides I found the entire enterprise quite repugnant.

I made it plain to all I knew that I was an "LBJ-man" not to be turned or torn from him and what he chose to do. Once a wise old politician in Washington told me when we were discussing a former aide of President Johnson who was now a voice of dissent against the president: "If so-and-so will desert the president to go with someone else because he thinks it politic to do so, then one day he will defect from whomever he supports now to go with another when the mood strikes him."

I recall what advice I was given once when I was very young. My friend was exploring the definition of a "friend." "A friend," he said, "is somebody who stays with you even when you are wrong!"

To this hour I have retained a respect for the late former Secretary of State Dean Acheson. When at the height of the Alger Hiss affair, before Hiss was convicted, it was Acheson, that intransigent, aloof, imperious man, who said, "I will not turn my back on Alger Hiss." In my home state of Texas where I lived then, many of my own friends were furious with Acheson for his binding loyalty to a man they considered a spy, but as yet untried by his peers. But I began then my mounting admiration for Secretary Acheson and the courage it took for him to state publicly his friendship for Hiss. To a politician, in or out of office, the grandest, most valuable asset he can have is the loyalty of friends, unshakable, defect-proof, enduring in triumph *and* defeat.

When one sits at the summit of power, or on its slopes, friends abound, they are everywhere and vocal in their admiration and fervent in their nearness. It is when you are hauled down either by elective disaster or executive fiat or collision with a higher authority that a man gets to truly count his friends.

Indeed, I believe that the one man who understood this, and held to its tenets with fierce devotion was Bobby Kennedy. I think he had a clear notion of what I felt about President Johnson, and while I have not the slightest inkling of his own feelings, I want to believe, and do, that

Bobby expected that kind of loyalty from his friends and was prepared to give in kind.

Through the intercession of friends like Governor Averell Harriman and Charles Bartlett, the nationally known syndicated columnist, relations between Bobby and myself warmed and possibly might have developed into something deeper and more enduring. On Governor Harriman's seventy-fifth birthday, in 1965, Bobby hosted a laughing, merry group at his home at Hickory Hill. My wife and I were among the guests and when we arrived, Bobby greeted Mary Margaret and me with unfeigned warmth, and immediately summoned Ethel to tell her we were present. The warmth of Ethel Kennedy has a force all its own. She embraces you without hesitancy, no ceremony or stuffy protocol. She is pre-eminently a woman of open grace, with a brisk and beguiling energy. Bobby and I chatted for a moment. There was no tension, and I felt as if he were saying in a quiet and gracious way that he was glad to see me, as I was to see him. In a funny way, I felt very close to him. I wanted to tell him how much I admired him, but it would have sounded silly, I thought. Now I regret I didn't. I wanted to be his friend, and to let him know I cared about him.

On March 6, 1968, the Senate Commerce Committee met to hold confirmation hearings on the newly appointed fifteen members of the Corporation for Public Broadcasting, created by President Johnson to fund a national public broadcasting system. I was one of those nominees. It was at these hearings that I again saw Bobby Kennedy, in a happy and congenial setting. He had come to the committee hearings to speak affirmatively about the New York residents nominated to the board.

Bobby nodded to me, came to my chair and greeted me

warmly, with that furiously engaging smile on his face. He noticed that no Texas senators were present (though he did not know that my commission of appointment had specified District of Columbia, thus the absence of a senator from my home state). After he had spoken on behalf of John D. Rockefeller III, another appointee, Bobby paused, and then joshingly said, "Mr. Chairman, I am bound to point out that Mr. Valenti has no senator to speak for him, and I would be pleased to say a word in Jack Valenti's behalf, as if he were truly a New York resident." There was appreciative laughter from those in the room, Bobby bowing to me and grinning wider. That was the last time I saw him alive.

I had felt that President Johnson might have been a bit brutal in kicking Bobby over the side, and taking all the cabinet with him, in that celebrated announcement in 1964 that no one in the cabinet or who met with the cabinet would be considered as vice-presidential material. But I think Bobby was not dismayed by this. It was the kind of ruthlessness that both these proud men understood, the sort of alley-fighting that a public man must be willing to engage in if that course is the only way to get from one side of the street to the other, and if the course of action is necessary to a larger issue.

The issue of the vice-presidency was bound to be drawn. It was seeping into every cranny of the White House and we all knew it, most of all the president. The pulling and tugging of the Kennedy partisans, the tiptoeing around the subject that was the staff ballet in the West Wing, the grim, unsettling political climate it was creating, all these pushed and shoved against the daily schedule. Something was sure to give. I personally favored Hubert Humphrey for the post, as did most of the White House aides. And I was convinced in my own heart he was the choice the president was going to take. Yet, there often were signs and signals which unfastened my fixed opinions, imperceptible, shadowed, yet full of soft sounds and veiled movement.

On June 4, 1964, the president and Bobby Kennedy met in the Oval Office. The subject was the Olympic Games and problems that had arisen about them. Bobby had great interest in this enterprise and was urging the president to take an intimate involvement. General James Gavin, of World War II airborne fighting fame, had been the prime mover here and had been importuning me to get him (Gavin) in for a visit with the president. I had demurred, politely, until we had more facts than we possessed at the time. Bobby intervened through Kenny O'Donnell and the presidential meeting between RFK and the president was set up.

They talked together for one hour and twenty minutes. The correspondents in the West Lobby were in various stages of hysteria, breeding and hurdling all sorts of rumors which filled that lobby with tangible contagions. What were the president and Bobby talking about? Olympic Games? Bullshit. Give it to us straight, it's the vice-presidency, isn't it? And so it went.

O'Donnell, chatting with me nervously while our two principals closeted themselves, said that the New York papers were going to carry in tomorrow's editions a story that Bobby was preparing to resign from the cabinet and run for the Senate in New York. O'Donnell didn't elaborate or confirm this and I didn't press the point, merely shrugging my shoulders and listening to him. O'Donnell was not what one would call a long-distance–running talker. I always felt that O'Donnell gave up spoken words with all the grudging reluctance of Hetty Green spending two dollars. Dave Powers came in, his merry Irish face in torment. A large group of photographers and reporters had clustered around the attorney general's limousine outside the West Basement and Powers had ordered it removed to the South Grounds which was off limits to the press.

Finally Bobby emerged from the Oval Office. He nodded perfunctorily to me, his mood appeared pleasant enough, surely not the demeanor of a man who had run a bludgeon gantlet. O'Donnell and Powers accompanied him through the rear of the West Wing to where his car was waiting.

During the rest of the day, though I was in and out of the president's office, and though we were together for much of that time, he offered neither assessment nor recounting of the talk. I said nothing, asked nothing.

The next morning early, in the president's bedroom as I ate breakfast with him, he threw out his first words about Bobby's visit. "I was very impressed with Bobby yesterday," he said. "He was right up to snuff on his facts, knew them cold, and made a very able presentation. Damn able."

"Did you discuss anything else?" I asked.

"Yes, we did," said the president. "I asked him about the civil rights program and told him I was going to move it forward if I did nothing else. He was very informative and generous in his conversation. All in all, it was a good meeting."

The next day, O'Donnell again raised the subject of LBJ-RFK. He said that if Bobby and the president were able to spend more time together privately their relationship would grow closer. Bobby, he said, was continually more impressed with the president and his steadfast resolution in the face of opposition, particularly on civil rights. O'Donnell was vehement, even scornful, about the intervention of second-level, low caliber, so-called aides of RFK. He came down hard on Paul Corbin (who was an assistant of some kind to RFK, and who had been active in a clandestine manner—or so it appeared to LBJ aides—in New Hampshire, stirring the countryside in favor of Bobby for vice-president). This did raise, as one might suspect, some rigid hackles among the Johnson men in the West Wing. O'Donnell poured out his distaste for Corbin to me and reiterated the need for LBJ and Kennedy to spend time together.

I offered no dissent. What passed through my mind was the intent of O'Donnell in parading his contempt for Corbin. Was this a false scent across the trail, or was Corbin truly acting on his own without orders or approval from the attorney general? I said little, nodding and suggesting that O'Donnell continue. It was a bit unusual, as I had thought before, for Ken to be so outspoken about those whom one would consider a part of his own band of brothers.

The day's schedule bore down on the president. He met with the National Coal policy people, with John L. Lewis and his mine union executives as well as the mine owners in a forty-five–minute session. Then he called in O.A. Knight, and his oil, atomic, and chemical workers union executives to meet the coal group, as the Lewis group left. LBJ enjoyed the mingling of union and business executives. It was part of his life-long conclusion that getting people of disparate views in a room together was bound to produce something better than stalemate. It was all very fraternal, this odd mix, and LBJ found it splendidly attractive.

Nearing 7:00 P.M. on June 5, 1964, after these union conferences had finally concluded, I accompanied the president to the Situation Room in the basement of the White House.

The Situation Room, centerpiece of information-inflow

and strategy-planning for the White House is located in the basement of the West Wing, amid a coil of communications apparatus and a rabbit warren of small offices and cubicles that comprise the province of the national security enclave of the president. It is austere and antiseptic, a room beyond the pale of any decorator's touch, unless he was a specialist in metallic blandness. Its furnishings could be best described as "early sterile," designed for functional pedestrian activity.

It is about fifteen feet by twenty feet. A rectangular metal table sat in the center of the room, flanked by a number of straight-backed, metal-bottomed chairs, calculated to make meetings short. On one wall was a large world map on which was displayed by pins and colored markers the disposition of U.S. naval forces at that particular moment. On the other wall was a long curtain, floor to ceiling, behind which communications experts could tend to their electronic devices without disturbing meetings going on. Along another wall was a battery of phones, including a direct wire to Number 10 Downing Street, as well as direct, instant pick-ups to the War Room in the Pentagon. Of course, there was a direct line to the president.

Just outside the Situation Room was the main area of White House communications, machines and teletypes constantly clacking and whirring with incoming messages. Several teletypes on twenty-four–hour vigil ceaselessly transmitted cables to our embassies all over the world, cables coming into the State Department and the Pentagon and sped through to the Situation Room for transmission to national security assistant's staff and to the president. The famous "hot line," a teletype residing in the Pentagon, when activated, spewed its incoming messages to its counterpart in the Situation Room communications center. With only a few seconds delay after its reception in the Pentagon, the Russian language message would be click-clacking in the basement of the White House. Several minutes later an unofficial translation would clatter through.

There were two entrances to the Situation Room. One was through the main communications center and the other would be approached directly from within the office area of the national security adviser.

On this June 5 evening, Secretaries Rusk and McNamara together with McGeorge Bundy awaited us. We examined top secret documents and intelligence reports on the situation in Laos and South Vietnam. The president, as usual, bypassed all the military jargon and military assessments. He questioned the lack of diplomatic intervention. "We need more diplomatic ingenuity, not more hardware," he said.

Bundy was pessimistic that diplomacy could entice any other nations to give us a hand. The president said we simply had to try to with all the fervor we could muster. He looked with great care at the reports in front of him.

"Why can't we bring in," he said, "more civilian governors and administrative advisors to help improve the civil problems. Why not get AID, Agriculture, and Peace Corps people in there to help their farming." He turned to McNamara: "There's nothing that will give a farmer greater hope for the future than to see larger yields from his planting."

The president stood up, and as he was wont to do, roved the floor, jingling keys and coins with one hand in his pocket, gesturing fiercely with the other.

"Dammit, we need to exhibit more compassion for these Vietnamese plain people. When their own armies move across the countryside and destroy crops and livestock, the poor farmers get no recompense. When I last talked with the South Vietnamese foreign minister this was one of the problems he outlined. Can we move in this civil and agriculture side? Can't we push the South Vietnamese to get their compassion out in the open where the people feel it and see it? Exhaust every possibility, check out every idea, look at every possible move. We've got to see that the South Vietnamese government wins the battle, not so much of arms, but of crops and heart and caring, so their people can have hope and belief in the word and deed of their government."

He sat down next to Rusk, and with a smile, said: "You know when I was a schoolboy in Johnson City, we had a teacher that none of the kids really liked. He was a kind of bully and not a very good teacher either. A bunch of us talked about giving the teacher a good lesson by punching him around a bit. Sure enough, one day about seven of us boys ran into the teacher as he was crossing a small footbridge. Somebody said let's get him and I took the lead, trotting toward the teacher. When I got right on him I realized he was a pretty big fellow, and he was ready to take us on. So when I turned around to get support from my friends, to my surprise and to my horror, they had turned tail and run. I was with the teacher alone. I got out of there fast. What I am saying is if I have to turn back I want to make sure I am not in too deep to do so."

The meaning was plain. The president wanted to do all he should do short of invoking reprisals from the Chinese and the Russians, when we were too deeply involved with men and material to withdraw prudently. "No one," said the president, "would be a winner."

As we left the Situation Room, the president grabbed Bundy by the arm and asked him to talk to Bobby Kennedy about Vietnam, and particularly how Kennedy viewed Lodge's work in Saigon.

On June 6, after a National Security Council meeting on Laos in which it was determined to overfly Laos with frequent reconnaissance, we boarded helicopters for New York.

The president was scheduled to unveil a bust of David Dubinsky at the health center of the International Ladies Garment Workers Union in New York City. Hubert Humphrey accompanied the president. I had talked to Senator Humphrey earlier and suggested he ought to go on his own. I feared newspaper speculation about HHH and the vice-presidency and I fretted lest press surmise damage Humphrey's chances to receive the vice-presidential nomination. Humphrey agreed to take my advice. Within an hour after this conversation the president buzzed me. "Call Hubert and see if he and Muriel would like to go with us," he said. I was about to suggest this was unwise, but I knew the president hadn't made this decision idly. He had calculated the impact and had decided to take Humphrey with us. Not knowing precisely what the president had in mind, but knowing he had something, I felt I would not try to persuade him to reverse gears.

I eagerly looked forward to seeing John Steinbeck again. This gruff, bearded genius was a favorite of the president. Steinbeck and his wife Elaine would be along on this trip. The president felt comfortable with John Steinbeck, which was as high a recommendation as a man got with LBJ. He would not consort with anyone, living legend or not, if he felt ill at ease.

The garment district scene was a wild one. Thousands of New Yorkers surged to greet the president when he arrived. Dubinsky, spry, elfin, shrewd, was jubilant. The president embraced him, laughing uproariously, with Dubinsky glorying in every minute.

After the unveiling was a small luncheon gathering including Mayor Robert Wagner, Congressmen Emanuel Celler, the late Congressman Bill Ryan, then Congressman Leonard Farbstein, Senator Humphrey, and others. It was fortuitous that Wagner was there for I had business to transact with him. The luncheon was in a small room and full of talk, and I had no chance to approach Wagner. After lunch, we both made our way to the men's room, and standing there side by side, I determined that the mayor had no choice but to listen to me. I urged him not to get involved in a blood feud with Adam Clayton Powell. The president had asked me to ride shotgun for Powell, who as chairman of the House Education and Labor Committee was crucially commanding the House legislative battle for our education measures, and in particular the War on Poverty bills.

The mayor and the chairman were locked in furious combat and rattling sabers over who was to be in charge of the poverty enterprise in Harlem. The mayor's man was Dr. Kenneth Clark. Powell had put his banner in the hands of one of his key lieutenants. The New York City newspapers ran red with the blood of the fight.

"We need Adam free to concentrate on his committee work, Mr. Mayor," were my opening words. Fetching up logic, instruction, and presidential admonitions as quickly as I could, I pushed on, encouraging the mayor to understand the president's plight and his needs. I was also aware that I needed to complete my missionary work before Wagner buttoned up and was able to disappear into the hail of conversation upstairs, to be lost among admirers and courtiers. I knew that a Higher Being would forgive even my thoughts which visited upon the mayor a whole sea of kidney and bladder problems—anything to delay his departure. Wagner seemed convinced, and still importuning him, I effectively blockaded his escape via the only exit door. Finally, he agreed to be amenable. He would call a cease-fire, but only for the time being. Fine, Mr. Mayor, wonderful. I reported all this to the president, without going into detail as to the locale of Wagner's conversion.

The president, with Dubinsky by his side, walked through the streets, amid a jostling mob of thousands of cheering, cheerful people, with us all the two blocks from the health center to the ILGWU auditorium, packed solid with every one of the 1,600 seats filled.

The president, jovial and in visible good spirits, remarked to Dubinsky, "I'm going to do much better in New York than a lot of people think." Dubinsky bobbed his head in total agreement. There was no question in the old labor leader's mind about the majority in New York, and absolutely none about which way his union members were going to vote.

On Sunday, June 7, Michael Forrestal called the president at 3:00 A.M. to inform him that one of our planes had been shot down over the Plain of Jars in Vietnam. Forrestal, the son of the late first secretary of defense, is a remarkably composed and intelligent man, then an aide to Mac Bundy. His emotional ties were to Bobby Kennedy, but he carried out his duties with steady fidelity to the president. I was deeply regretful when he chose to leave the White House basement group.

At 10:00 A.M. the same day, Forrestal phoned me to ask me to call the president for permission to set up a National Security Council meeting. The president agreed. The meeting was held at 12:30 P.M.

At this meeting, the decision was made to continue reconnaissance but the president pressed for more specific recommendations and plans. "Where are we going?" he asked with some vehemence. All those around the table, with the exception of General Curtis LeMay, were in agreement about the plan of action, but LeMay wanted to get tougher, much tougher now. The president though not displaying irritation, told me as we left the meeting that he worried about LeMay and his truculent visions. "I get anxious and look for the fire exits when a general wants to get tough. LeMay scares the hell out of me."

The president was steady and disciplined in these meetings. His questions were searching, and his dismay at what he considered lack of forward planning held in check so that his questions were given softly, quietly. Forrestal agreed with this estimate of the president. He told me privately that he thought "the president is putting his finger on the deficiency in our total planning now."

I became aware, the more I participated in these national security and cabinet meetings, of how few times Bobby Kennedy spoke up. He was silent, withdrawn, keeping his own counsel. This was in contrast, Forrestal told me, to the meetings over which President Kennedy presided. There Bob Kennedy was outspoken, quick, and ready to advance his opinion.

It was on June 13, 1964, that Bobby revealed his willingness, his desire, to go to Saigon as our ambassador.

The president had called me into his office on that day. We talked of some pressing issues that were embracing his attenton and he turned to me abruptly and said, "Have a talk with McGeorge Bundy. The two of you come back to me with suggestions about who should go to Saigon to replace Lodge."

Ambassador Lodge had written the president with a veiled suggestion that he (Lodge) thought it was time for him to depart Saigon. At this juncture in the Johnson-Lodge relationship, the president was uncertain about the former Republican vice-presidential candidate. LBJ assessed Lodge's public image as of increasing value, but in the president's judgment, expressed to me, he felt Lodge was leading with slackened reins. The president was troubled by what he called "poor administration" which is not the stuff of which good leadership is constructed. Lodge was having problems (though one could not with accuracy pinpoint the source) with his staff stemming mainly, as I read in the memoranda from State, from his insistence on making every decision himself. The president thus found himself content with Lodge's willingness to be relieved.

Later that day I called Mac Bundy and we chatted. Bundy told me, as I already knew, that Bobby Kennedy had written the president that if LBJ desired, the attorney general would be willing to go to Vietnam as our ambassador. Bundy with some delight informed me that the attorney general felt his relationship with the president was improving. Bundy reported that Bobby told him of his conversations with the president, and Bobby believed that their tattered, imprecise, and soured past experiences were being overcome, or at least being forgotten.

The president had asked Dean Rusk, Bob McNamara, Mac Bundy, and Bobby Kennedy to give him three names, those names of the men they thought best qualified to be sent to Saigon. Interestingly, all four men put their own names at the top of the list. Bundy, in that spare, bleached way of his, suggested this was to show the president that each of his top advisers was willing to make whatever sacrifice the president chose them to make.

At this juncture, Mac and I talked about the possible use of a congressional resolution to give the president visible and legislatively sanctioned support of our efforts in Vietnam. I told Bundy I didn't think the time was propitious for the introduction of the resolution. We both knew, of course, that the president fretted because there had been no open congressional debate and passage of congressional approval of what we were doing in Indochina. All the past mistakes of other presidents neglecting this key and crucial embrace by the Congress paraded before the Johnson memory. He expressed to me many times that at some point, he wasn't sure precisely when, he must go before the Congress to gain their sanction and support. He would be willing to endure all the tumid and endless oratory that must precede congressional action, but the Congress's support was essential. Bundy had been laboring over a series of working papers outlining the use of a congressional resolution. Would I look them over and then take them to the president, he asked. I said I would, and as I paused before leaving, Mac asked, "Did you know that Bobby has suggested the name of Terry Sanford as a possible candidate for Saigon, also?" I knew Sanford only casually. He was the governor of North Carolina and a man of considerable abilities. "What do you think about Sanford?" I asked.

Bundy replied and unshadowed some interesting aspects of high official thinking. Bobby had seemingly mentioned Sanford to McNamara and the secretary of defense was not congenial to the idea; not because of any lack of faith in Sanford's obvious talents, but because McNamara assessed the most valuable asset of our Saigon ambassador to be his ability to report factually and accurately. He wasn't sure of Sanford's ability to do that. Mac Bundy, on the other hand, put small worth in the reporting on the premise that a good administrator could make use of reporting facilities available to him in Saigon. But, said Bundy, what we need is to know the man in Saigon so well that his voice and thoughts can be analyzed with precision ten thousand miles away in Washington. Thus, Bundy's logic fled the Sanford suggestion because as Bundy put it, "Nobody here really knows Sanford and no one would therefore be able to pluck out of his reporting the kind of analysis that goes into whether you take a man's recommendations or not."

Bundy's choice was George Ball, not Bobby Kennedy. I offered my doubts to Bundy about Ball for this job. I regarded George Ball as too valuable a man to position so far away. I felt Ball was a wise counselor of the president, and he ought to stay where that counsel could be heard and heeded. Little did I know that a year later George Ball would prove to be the most prescient man in the room when the great decisions on the war were being taken.

Early the next morning I was in the president's bedroom at his request to breakfast with him. I reported my visit with Bundy. The president, propped up in his bed with a tray in his lap, chewed listlessly on a piece of bacon. He sipped his hot tea, stirring with the tea bag as he listened to my report. "Are you going to name Bobby Kennedy?" I asked him.

He was thoughtful for a second, then said, "No, I am not. I would be accusing myself for the rest of my life if something happened to him out there. He could do the job. He could do it damn well, but I can't trust the security there and someone or some group might want to do him in. I couldn't live with that." He paused and asked, "Who would be your choice between Maxwell Taylor, George Ball, or Roswell Gilpatric?"

I was prepared for the question. Without hesitation I answered, "My choice would be Roswell Gilpatric."

The president surveyed me. "Why?" he asked.

"First," I said, "I think Ball is more suitable to your own needs here, where he can be in constant touch with you. Talking to you by cable ten thousand miles away is not the same. I count Ball too important a voice at your council table to risk him having him in Saigon.

"Second, I think Gilpatric is one of the ablest men I know. He would be a first-rate administrator, a no-nonsense captain and he would turn in accurate reports. I think he would be tough enough when he had to be. You could trust his judgment.

"Third, but I am bound to say that from the standpoint of whom the country would feel more confident in, would have more faith in, the man who would give the people a sense that their ambassador in Saigon is someone they can feel comfortable with, Max Taylor is your man. But I would send Gilpatric because I think he would do the job you want done."

The president nodded, and we talked at length about this matter. Finally I gathered up all the papers that we had gone over after we had finished our Saigon ambassador issue and prepared to go to my office to wait the president's arrival in the West Wing.

He clambered out of bed and put on his robe. He seemed to be engrossed in his own thoughts, then he looked up, and waved as I left the room. "Have lunch with Clark Clifford and me today. We will be discussing what we talked about this morning."

That noon, I sat with the president and Clark Clifford in the family dining room on the second floor of the Mansion. We began talking as we sat down. The president questioned Clifford about his choice for ambassador. But before Clifford could answer, the president began, as he often did, to ruminate and unharness his own views as if he wanted to expose them to the pressures of thrust and heat and counter-thrust. And to my surprise, he floated the names of Taylor, Ball, and Gilpatric and, with language more pungent and incisive than my own, he used the thoughts I had offered him that morning, with emphasis on Taylor and the national confidence he inspired. Clifford agreed. The president mentioned that Bobby had volunteered his services, but Clifford gave no response to that.

And so General Maxwell Taylor, confidant to President Kennedy, close friend and trusted counselor of Bobby Kennedy, a ramrod-straight soldier with numbing qualities of tenacity combined with a scholar's mind and inclination was the president's chosen instrument in Vietnam. In a way, Max Taylor was coming full circle since he, with Walt Rostow in 1961, had authored for President Kennedy's sanction the blueprint for America's intrusion into South Vietnam in numbers and commitment larger than anyone could have conceived then.

I have often wondered what would have happened if President Johnson had thrown aside his fears for Bobby's safety and named him to the Saigon post.

On June 17, 1964, at 6:30 P.M. the president, Larry O'Brien, and I met with Congressman George Mahon, chairman of the powerful House Appropriations Committee, Carl Albert, majority leader of the House, and Congressman John Rooney, an influential representative from New York. The president wanted to plot strategy to pass the foreign-aid bill without Otto Passman, an energetic Louisiana congressman and persistent foe of foreign aid, as the president said, "butchering it up."

"Either Otto Passman is going to run the foreign policy of this country, or I am," said the president firmly. He pointed out with some salty language the troubles that burdened the world, the meetings he was going to have the next day with ambassadors from Latin America, how freedom was besieged everywhere in the world, and how could he face the ambassadors and his own conscience if foreign aid, which he deemed essential as a prime instrument for peace, were blunted. What he was asking, said the president, was one-half of one percent of the gross national product for foreign assistance. "I'm sending up a bill one billion dollars less than the last bill President Kennedy wanted and exactly what Congress appropriated last year. This is a bare-bones bill," said the president, "with no fat on it."

He leaned forward, looking full in the face of those congressional leaders and said: "Look, I have resisted all attempts to fatten it up so Otto Passman can chip away at it, and then give me what I really wanted in the first place. But that's not right. I want an honest bill and that is what I am sending up."

The congressmen agreed with the president and they would try to remonstrate with Congressman Passman, as well as round up the votes needed to pass the measure. It was an impressive LBJ performance. He was indignant and firm; he recited fact after fact without referring to notes. I felt he had made headway with these powerful House leaders.

Afterwards, we sat together, the president and I, and he said, "I keep hitting hard because I know this honeymoon won't last. Every day I lose a little more political capital. That's why we have to keep at it, never letting up. One day soon, I don't know when, the critics and the snipers will move in and we will be at stalemate. We have to get all we can, now, before the roof comes down."

On June 21, four days later, the president had a bleak day. Congressman Bill Ryan of New York called me. He wanted to bring in the parents of two of the three young people who were missing in Mississippi, and feared dead as a result of racial hatreds there. Later in the day, before LBJ saw the parents, J. Edgar Hoover called to report that the car of the young people had been found. It was burned to a crisp and the FBI agents were unable to get inside.

The president looked stunned. "Oh, my God," he said. Shortly after, the parents arrived with Lee White, the president's legal counsel. When they entered, Hoover was again on the phone with the president. As I came into the room to announce the parents, the president was saying, "You are sure that you found the right car, the same color, the same markings." Hoover was obviously confirming this, the president listening, his face a dull mask of sorrow. "Where did you find it, how far from Philadelphia, Mississippi?" More Hoover responses, and then the president said softly, "Show them in."

I left the room. It was a conversation that I had no taste for, a mean, loathsome chore for the president.

On July 24, a most unusual event took place. The president had an appointment with Senator Barry Goldwater, the newly nominated Republican candidate for president. I had given instructions to Mike Manatos, an assistant to Larry O'Brien in the congressional liaison office to bring the senator in through the Southwest Gate to shield him from reporters. I told Manatos to station the senator in the Cabinet Room and I would bring him in at the appointed time to see the president. The president was meeting at that moment with some 400 labor laders and I suspected he might be a few minutes late.

At approximately 5:15 P.M., some fifteen minutes ahead of schedule, Senator Goldwater arrived at the Southwest Gate. He was ushered into the Cabinet Room and I greeted him by introducing myself.

"Oh yes, Jack, I know you. It's good to see you."

The senator, well-tanned, was dressed in a grey single-breasted suit, with white shirt and blue tie. He was a handsome man, suitable for one of those Marlboro cigarette ads, full of the outdoors, masculine, the planes of his face sharply drawn, as if Remington had cast him in bronze. But he seemed ill at ease, not quite confident of the moment ahead. When I had entered the Cabinet Room he was seated alone, reading. He got up when I came in and we chatted aimlessly for a brief moment. "Excuse me, senator, let me see if the president has finished his meeting. I know he is anxious to see you."

The senator smiled slightly, nodded, and I left to find my way to the president's office. Meanwhile I called Larry O'Brien and Mike Manatos and suggested they keep the senator company until the president was ready.

The president arrived in the Oval Office at 5:22 P.M. and I went to see him. He looked over two memos on his desk from staff aides about the Goldwater visit, "talking papers," we called them. The president was calm, even a bit bemused. He read for several minutes, and then stretching himself to his full height, beckoned to me. "Ask him to come in."

When I returned to the Cabinet Room the senator was talking with O'Brien and Manatos.

"The president is glad you are here, senator. He is ready to see you."

We walked into the Oval Office. The president was standing with his right hand outstretched. "Hello, Barry, it's mighty good to see you."

"Good to see you, Mr. President. You look wonderful," Goldwater replied.

The president grabbed the senator by the shoulder in an affectionate manner and guided him to the couch where they sat down. I shut the door and left them alone.

Even when the campaign was at its height, I never regarded Goldwater as an enemy. Somehow I never lost my sense of affection for him. While I thought he was wrong on many of the issues, he always came across to me as an honest, determined, forthright, open man, never devious. It was a matter with me of feeling comfortable with Goldwater, as a man, the sort of man one would enjoy spending time with on a hunting trip or the golf course, or as a friend who would stay with you if you were his friend, though your cause was lost. I liked him.

And the president never considered Goldwater a deadly enemy either. In fact, the president thought of Goldwater as a fellow ranchman, someone who, like him, cared greatly about the land and its resources. Of course, the president determined to win as hugely as he could, and in a political fight, particularly for the presidency, you go for the jugular. Senator Goldwater happened to be the Republican candidate for president. But that is as far as it went.

The time for deciding about Bobby Kennedy was close. And so, five days later, the president was to have a conversation with Bobby that drove a spike through the political heart of the Kennedy partisans.

On July 29, 1964, at 1:00 P.M., the president met with Bobby in the Oval Office where on many occasions the attorney general had conferred with his older brother, in those days when Bobby Kennedy was the second most powerful man in the country and no one doubted the reach of his power. On this day, Bobby came as another man, as gifted as once he was, but no longer carrying any weapons except those which his new leader would choose to give him.

They met and talked alone, these two disparate yet similar men. They talked for almost two hours. (After the meeting Bobby went to Mac Bundy's office where the two of them met and talked.) President Johnson minced no words, sought no refuge in dissembling or patching over what had been torn. He told Bobby that he would not take him as vice-president. The fight, the president said, was going to be waged in the border states and the southern states, as well as the Midwest, and that he, Bobby, was unacceptable in those areas. The president (as he later described the meeting to me *) took on Bobby face to face, hiding no fact or feeling, telling it to Bobby "with the bark off." The president, as was his wont, didn't hesitate to lay it out as tough as he had to be when the issue and time demanded it. He did not want Bobby to be told of his decision by anyone else. It was a stern political appraisal and I have no personal doubts that Bobby understood the unadorned political assessment given to him. He may have taken issue with the unreinforced view that he was "unacceptable" in those areas, but the brute strength of the logic, I suspect, had weight with him. According to Mac Bundy, the initial reaction by Kennedy was seemingly good. Bobby was calm when he emerged from the president's office (as was the president when I visited him minutes after Bobby had departed).

Shortly thereafter, Bobby announced for U.S. senator from New York, began carving out his new career, for the first time a public man jousting in the public arena for votes.

One never knows, but I have a feeling that the two men respected and admired each other. They were, to a surprising extent, much alike. They were both men of spectacular toughness, against whom lesser men bend and break. They were both determined to make their causes triumphant because each believed that what he espoused was right for the nation they both served.

I know that men around both of them helped poison those fragments of rapport that might have taken root. And because of the substance of half-truth, all that was said by aides of each became believable.

President Johnson had a deep affection and respect for

---

* Contrary to some reports of that meeting, the conversation was not bugged. The president was quick to dictate to his secretary his memory of what was said during the meeting with Bobby. He had a sheet of notes in front of him during the meeting with the essentials of what he wanted to tell Kennedy.

President Kennedy. He never once was disloyal to the president and JFK knew it. This respect was spacious enough to rise above the petty little humiliations LBJ suffered at the hands of JFK staff members, and possibly, inadvertently, Robert Kennedy also. This reservoir of admiration for a martyred president who at all times gave understanding and respect to his vice-president could have, I am convinced, been a large enough pool to wash away any recriminatory backlash that lived inside President Johnson.

Later on, a frail, seemingly inconsequential event occurred which, if handled differently, "might have been" the trigger to reconciliation. During the 1964 campaign, President Johnson went beyond what could have accounted as "enough help" to the then aspiring senatorial candidate in New York. President Johnson roamed all over the Empire State giving his voice and his person to the cause of Bobby Kennedy. When the votes were counted, the president had carried the state by over two million votes and Bobby Kennedy won by some 600,000. To the political pros, the coattails of the president had been long enough and strong enough to carry Bobby to victory over Senator Keating. Yet, somehow, somebody near Bobby must have cautioned him against giving any credit to the president. I sat with President Johnson in the Driskill Hotel in Austin on election night and we watched the returns. The camera picked up the newly triumphant Robert Kennedy in his New York City headquarters, with his wife, staff, and friends, beaming joyously at a noisy, wound-up crowd of supporters.

As Bobby started speaking, he began to thank all those who made the victory possible. He cited his wife, and by name lauded each one of his staff, and called out the names of several prominent Americans who had also aided him. At no time during this recounting of gratitude did he once mention the president. President Johnson made no outward sign that the omission struck him. His expression never changed throughout the speech by the senator-elect. But I felt the vacancy. I yearned for Bobby to say one word, just one, as a token of his appreciation for the hard stumping the president had done on his behalf, but no word came and suddenly the scene shifted and the moment fled. The president's demeanor masked whatever anger or disappointment he may have felt. But I was sick at heart. I knew the president well enough to be personally unhappy. I often speculated what would have happened if Bobby had spoken aloud to that television audience his gratitude for LBJ's assistance.

Robert McNamara, Charlie Bartlett, and I plotted how we might bring these two extraordinary men together and thereby strengthen the Democratic party as well as the country.

But once Senator Kennedy took a position on Vietnam that was in opposition to his own position on the same issue when he was attorney general, and when he began to move to the left, riding on the Vietnam conflict, the chasm widened.

The sad irony of it all was the inextricable entwining of viewpoint and commitment to human causes that bound LBJ and RFK. In every arena where the poor, the black, and the uneducated suffered indignity and neglect, President Johnson and Bobby Kennedy thought alike, and if their style of fighting to right wrongs was dissimilar, their ultimate aims and convictions were not.

Not very often on the American political turf at the same time do there appear two such large, unyielding, massively skillful political titans as Lyndon Johnson and Bobby Kennedy. Perhaps, when one examines it more closely, it was the eccentricity of their similarity which was the strange barrier that separated them.

The
Johnson Method

Cicero has said, "It is a difficult art to rule a republic," but he knew that if an effort to rule by other than republican means was abandoned, then the god-emperors took charge. LBJ did not have to read Roman history to fully appreciate Cicero's maxim. He knew.

On the first night of his presidency he sat propped up in his vast bed in his home and in low-voiced rumination sketched out his plans. President for less than fifteen hours, he was already pulsating with the specifics of tomorrow. He had no doubts about the course he ought to follow.

On that first night he talked about the economy and how, above all else, he had to give it whatever sustenance the government could provide. LBJ knew the family pocketbook was the root-and-branch crucial connection to all his plans and hopes for the nation. With a robust economy, everything was possible. Without it, nothing was do-able. He talked about civil rights. He had disagreed with the Kennedy approach and had so advised JFK by memorandum. He believed, as he wrote JFK, that the president should take civil rights to the people, over the heads of the Congress, and take it to the country as a moral crusade flattening all opposition with the sharp edge of principle and moral rightness. He had prophesied the civil rights legislation would bog down, led into quicksand by the crafty parliamentary-wise southern Senate patriarchs, unless special and visibly muscular effort were put forth. Now he was in the captain's chair and he spoke almost eagerly about his commitment to get civil rights off its backside in the Congress and give it legs. He would not cavil, he said, he would not compromise, for this was going to be a fight to the finish and he had no qualms about the outcome. He made it clear that night that medicare and aid to education would be at the top of the agenda. He mentioned that these two hopes always foundered on the bludgeoning of special interests.

He talked little of Vietnam that first night. I suspect he felt that Vietnam would yield to reason and informed judgment. LBJ really believed that if he applied his total intellect and concentration to a problem and if there was any alternative possible, he would find a way to an agreement. In all his career this reliance on reason and face-to-face challenge had never failed. He had no doubts it would succeed in Vietnam.

What he made clear that first night as president was his resolve to radically change the social environment of the nation in order to reset the out-of-balance scale of the chance for a quality life in America. He had thought much about this in those frustrating years as vice-president, though he never allowed the illusion of surmise to overtake the reality of his powerlessness. But now he was in command and his course of action was firmly fixed in his mind.

Now that he was in command he was committed, he told me, to the shattering of the political and social structure, for it would take no less than that to reintroduce the poor, the aged, the blacks, those denied an education, to a new opportunity which, as LBJ saw it, was absolutely essential to an equitable America.

No other president had attempted such a broad assault on social and economic rigidity. He now was prepared to do just that.

President Johnson's first half-year in office was hard on him. He had suffered from hurtful charges in the press and didn't feel he was getting his job done.

I recall very well the morning of June 12, 1964, shortly before 8:00 A.M.; I sat with the president and he talked, not so much, I suspect, to gain my counsel as to use me as a sounding board for his own thoughts.

Lying in bed, a small stack of papers in disarray by his side, he mused that he had made a decision the night before and felt better for it. He said he had just dictated a statement as to why he would not be a candidate for election this year. He had first determined to resign, but on reflection decided it was unfair to do so without a vice-president to step into his office. Then, he continued, he would be free to carry on with the program already started that year without being charged with "politics." He rubbed his chin reflectively, and murmured that he was disappointed in the Republican leadership who had that week accused him of playing election-year politics with Southeast Asia.

He was sick at heart, he said, that the Congress had no sense of urgency, lethargically doing its business from Tuesday through Thursday only. The apathy, the reluctance to grip hard the issues and the programs before them sorely vexed and frustrated him.

As he talked, he seemed to be even more absorbed in airing his own thoughts to himself, as if he was auditing freshly-minted opinion to assess its value. He said that he found it curious that some of those who observed him in office accounted him hungry for inordinate power. He knew this was not so and yet he seemed to be unable to rid himself of this public view, which clung to his every action and every word. Moreover, he was pessimistic over recruiting the highest-caliber people for the government. "There aren't enough Bob McNamaras and Dean Rusks," he said, "and their like is hard to find."

And finally he said to me that there was such a general disregard, even distaste, for him that no matter what achievements were made, no matter how far toward a more decent and abundant life he could bring the disadvantaged and the dispossessed of this nation, no matter how great the effort expended or how many of the obstacles removed, there would remain this exposure to the raw breath of relentless critics. For him there was no insulation, no higher ground where he could repair to work.

Needless to say, I remonstrated with the president saying, in effect, that this was not a valid view, and that the country needed him and what he could construct in this land. As I recall, he listened with a vague disquiet, and then the abrasions of the day began to intrude and our conversation ended. I never spoke to the president about this again, nor he to me. LBJ examined himself in the bleaker moments, and then went on to do what he had to do, what his duty (as he saw it) insisted be done.

On another occasion, I recorded a rather strange conversation that took place in the family dining room of the White House on Sunday, September 4, 1966. At the table during that noontime lunch were the president, Mrs. Johnson, my wife, and I. I had resigned from the White House earlier in the year to become president of the Motion Picture Association of America, but the president frequently had me alone and my wife and me together with him. In less than thirty days I would be accompanying the president to the Manila conference of Asian leaders.

The president was in a gloomy mood this Sunday. The phone rang. It was for Mrs. Johnson. She smiled graciously and departed to take the call in her bedroom. While she was gone, I said something about the election in 1968. To my astonishment, the president looked up bleakly and said, "I won't be around then. If I could figure some way to get out of this job I would do it now. They would say I was playing politics if I resigned and gave the job to Humphrey. But it is impossible to do the right job under these circumstances. My own party has turned against me, and the Republicans have chimed in. To be a good president and to handle all the problems that face a president, the very least that is needed is some kind of support from some group. If this is the kind of loss of support I can expect, then I should turn this over to someone else and let them start fresh. We have too many difficult problems and we need leadership that won't be attacked at every turn. We probably need a fresh face."

I truly believed at that moment he had committed himself to not running again. His voice was heavy, weary, flat. He seemed very tired, one of the few times I had seen him so. Naturally, I opposed the idea.

"Humphrey," said the president, "could start with a clean slate, he would be fresh. As it is now I have even lost the Congress."

Nothing seemed to torture the president more than the breakdown of support from the one arena where he always felt himself to be understood, the Congress. To be denied support from the Congress, from its leaders particularly, was a jolt to him.

At some moment, perhaps when he was elected to Congress, LBJ realized that the education he had received at San Marcos was not on a par with eastern universities, and he came to admire and to enlist within the ranks of those who followed him the finest brains from the finest schools. To have a Phi Beta Kappa key, to be a Rhodes scholar, to have graduated from a university in the higher reaches of your class was to the president an unerasable mark of achievement. It became quite difficult to bring anyone to the White House staff who lacked ingredients of superior scholarship. It is amusing, and a little sad, that the intellectual community which attacked LBJ so stingingly was the very breed of men for whom he had such sincere respect. The president gloried in brains. He was hospitable to anyone whose mental equipment was above average, and he never sought out anyone for heavy responsibility who could not be certified as "excellent in his studies." Every now and then we managed to slip by him someone the staff considered exceptional but who could not and did not produce a university record that might be described as very, very good.

I remember one day I was preparing a dossier on a young man whom I was recommending for a post at the assistant secretary level in one of the departments, assuming that the secretary of that department would approve. I talked it over with Marvin Watson who read it and with a smile said, "You would do better with that fellow if he had a Phi Beta Kappa key."

I frowned. But Marvin was right. So I took the dossier back into my office, had the man's educational attainments retyped and inserted under his college degree, "Elected to Phi Beta Kappa."

Later, the president flipped through the dossier, speed-reading it. To my amazement—and guilt—he paused for a moment, looked up, grinned, and said, "Sounds like he is a brainy fellow. Phi Beta Kappa, I see."

I slunk from the Oval Office with an unspoken suggestion to a Higher Being that He would understand. The fact that my newly manufactured Phi Bete acquitted himself splendidly in his job later persuaded me I had dissembled in a noble cause.

Once at a small dinner at Blair House, honoring the Rhodes scholar prime minister of Canada, Lester Pearson, the president lifted his glass in a toast to the assembly (which included McGeorge Bundy, Dean Rusk, Carl Albert, Nicholas Katzenbach, Bob McNamara, and a select few, all of whom had undergone the honing and beveling that only Ivy League and Oxford carpentry seemingly—to LBJ—afforded.)

"It is gratifying to see at this table tonight," said the president, "the most superbly educated men in the world, for in this room there are three Rhodes scholars, four graduates of Harvard, three of Yale, and one from Southwest State Teachers College."

Everyone roared with laughter, including the president, who was shaking with mirth, but I doubt that anyone around that small dining table truly understood the pride of the president in this assemblage of what he accounted to be the finest minds in Washington.

But LBJ had little reason to doubt his own spacious talents. John Gardner once remarked that, "Lyndon Johnson was one of the most intelligent men I have ever known."

No one who confronted LBJ in discussion, debate, or colloquy ever doubted that an active and divining mind was in fluid motion. He read quickly, and seemingly retained everything he ever read (or heard). He absorbed briefings and facts with a flawless mental digestion. I remember in January, 1965, when he called in the press to brief them personally on the new budget he had constructed.

Before a blackboard, in the manner of a teacher instructing hesitant pupils, he took the press step by step through the bloated arithmetic, material as dull as anything ever conceived by the hand and brain of man. Through the half-lit caverns of departmental allocations, he walked the press up and down and around the numbers of the federal accounting ledgers with a slide show exposition on the philosophy of why the money was appropriated, as well as a few lessons in the concept of the programs outlined. He did it without a note or referral to any aides. It was a bravura intellectual performance which slightly awe-struck members of the press generally conceded to be a *tour de force*.

He had almost total recall, fishing up from distant conversations full-fleshed pieces of what someone said, and precisely how it was said. Fragments of numbers leaped back to life under the LBJ memory prodding and, worst of all, a numbing recall of what he asked an aide to do some weeks past, and in the void of its performance, a terse reminder of the assignment and its neglect. This could be hair-raising on occasion.

LBJ had a contempt for noisy, reforming half-thought ideas, and he smarted under the pious arrogance of fashionable liberals, who rose to denounce and specify without really knowing what the hell they were talking about.

"He can talk, but he can't count," was LBJ's dismissal of a senator or a congressman who spoke in favor of measures that took a licking on the floor after the votes were counted.

The president had a special contempt for otherwise liberal allies who persisted in flinging rhetoric when they should have been doing a nosecount. "Always talking when he should have been listening," was the way LBJ described one famous liberal senator who won only a few floor fights, though he was always good for a few lines of type in the morning newspaper.

President Johnson set about quickly to organize his daily activities. Those of us who were his close assistants came to lament his work habits for we saw pretty swiftly that the president knew nothing about forty-hour work weeks.

That the LBJ work schedule was unending, a ceaseless collaboration of energy and a sense of duty, was beyond any question. But the president also insisted that no word leak at his ranch that he might have taken some time off to inspect his cattle or ride through his pastures to admire the sunset or the burble of the Pedernales as it flowed over his dam. His press secretary would always be careful to omit any of these excursions of the soul to note that "the president spent the day working on papers, discussing the monetary situation with his financial advisors in Washington, etc."

In truth this is a genetic aberration among presidents. Kennedy and Nixon were no different in this matter of publicly detailing their compulsion to do their job. In truth there is something about the office which seems to make men feel they ought to work longer and harder, and force everyone around them to do the same.

While it is difficult to contribute much affection to Louis XVI, though one may regard the loss of a royal head with some sympathy, he did have one unusual trait. He was not unruffled with letting it be known he was about things other than kingship duties. Once at Fontainebleau, the daily court bulletin laconically chronicled the king's day with these words, which you may be certain will never be uttered or published at any White House briefing: "Today, His Majesty is doing nothing."

The day began early for the president. He woke between 6:00 and 6:30 each morning. He slept in an ancient four-poster bed, in a medium-sized room overlooking the South Grounds, with the slim arrow of the Washington

Monument fixed squarely in the center of his south window. Next to him was a small table and his telephone console, a battery of buttons and lights giving him access to all officialdom in Washington and elsewhere. A fireplace, which I never saw lit, was opposite the bed, with a couch and two easy chairs near it. A large dresser stood between the southern windows and a smaller bureau nestled against the wall between these windows and the bed. A door, used infrequently, connected the president's bedroom with the handsomest room in the Mansion, the Yellow Oval Room. Elegantly contoured, gracefully designed, it was decorated with Cézannes, Renoirs, and a letter in Jefferson's handwriting was on an end table. A door from the room opened onto the Truman balcony which was used very often and with much pleasure by the Johnsons. At dusk, with the Washington Monument canopied by a blue sky and the dome of the Jefferson Memorial clearly in view, the Johnsons and their guests would sit on the balcony; this gave the president those precious few moments when he unwound, and found himself free from problems or torment.

In the southwest corner of the president's bedoom, just off the door leading into the second bedroom of the presidential quarters, used exclusively by Mrs. Johnson, were three television sets wired to a remote-control unit.

To the right of the bedroom was the president's bathroom, rectangular with a tub, shower, and a mirror and basin that ran almost from one wall to the other.

Opposite the president's bathroom was his clothes closet, and next to the bathroom was a smaller closet which stored the presidential mementos which LBJ was so fond of handing out to his friends.

In truth, the presidential sleeping quarters would not even by biased partisans be described as opulent. It was the bedroom of any well-to-do but not wealthy American executive or professional or academic. Except for the multiple TV sets and communication facilities, it was, in many ways, plain, utilitarian, but it was the way the president liked it.

When he stirred from his sleep, his first attention was to the mountain of papers that lay on the side table next to his phone console. This was his "night reading" which had already occupied several of his hours before he dropped off to sleep. He would sit upright in the bed, beside a sleeping Mrs. Johnson, and start his work. Shortly, Mrs. Johnson would wake, embrace her husband, and slip off to her bedroom leaving the president free to greet his aides, who were now outside the door.

Usually Bill Moyers and I, or Marvin Watson and I, would be on deck about 7:00 or 7:15; after knocking, we would enter the bedroom. The day had begun.

The kitchen personnel would by now have brought the president his morning tea and some toast, and the word would have passed to the Secret Service, and to the West Wing that the president was awake. Be alert.

The president invariably began the day with joshing. He would seize on my having been to a dinner party the night before and the ribbing would begin. First, he would want to know who had been present and what they said, not only to me but to each other. "You and Bill Fulbright settle the war last night, Jack?" would be an opening gambit.

"Well, I did talk to the chairman."

"And no doubt, you are full of plans and ideas which will give me heart all day long, is that about right?"—this was said with a big grin. "You and Bill Fulbright can surely fix things right, that I know." Moyers and Watson would try to suppress huge smiles. But I waited, for their turn would come.

Usually we would have coffee with the president and if

I suggested bacon and eggs, this would give rise to another LBJ rib. "Are we keeping ledger accounts on Mr. Valenti?"

In fact, I did consume a good deal of White House food. But then, a man doesn't wake his wife at 6:00 in the morning while waiting for a White House car. Either I ate breakfast with the president or I went without.

We could tell instantly what kind of mood the president was in. If there was no joking, only a grim "hello," we began to scramble to battle stations for it was going to be a bleak day.

On his bed, usually in the disarray that comes from use, were the ever-present newspapers: the *Washington Post*, the *Baltimore Sun*, the *New York Times*, and the *Wall Street Journal*. (In the evening, these would be exchanged for the *Washington Star*, the Chicago papers, sometimes the *Tribune*, sometimes the *Sun-Times*, as well as the *Christian Science Monitor*. From time to time, we would deposit the *Los Angeles Times*, the *Herald-Examiner*, the *St. Louis Post-Dispatch*, the *Philadelphia Bulletin*, the Texas dailies, as well as clippings from other newspapers around the country).

We dived into the night reading. The president would have scrawled comments, decisions or viewpoints on each piece of paper. We discussed those items which he had not yet read or on which he had not yet decided.

The day's appointment schedule would be gone over. Sometimes the president would have ordered other appointments to be put on, mostly off the record.

He would be on the phone during these early morning hours, always to Rusk and McNamara. "Bob McNamara is the only man in town who is at his desk when I call him at 7:00 in the morning," the president would say proudly.

Being on the job, alert, and ready to do business was a matter of high moment to LBJ. He didn't take too kindly to officials who were out of reach, nowhere to be found when he was doing his own chores.

Within an hour or so he would sweep the West Wing clean, calling each of his top aides with an opening line "What do you know?" which meant he wanted to dredge them for information.

The president thirsted for the full facts and total knowledge of everything. He wanted to know what you said to "Scotty" Reston and what he said to you and how you answered and what were his exact words. And if I spoke with George Meany, what did Mr. Meany say, exactly what did he say, and how did he sound and what were his comments on what I said to him. And so on.

It was obsessive, this need for information. It was unending and unceasing and the more information the president had, the more he wanted. He was never satisfied. I never saw him approach any problem where he was not in possession of a trunk-full of information, far more than any other man in the room, and oftentimes on subjects in which the official to whom he was talking was supposed to be expert. He was simply and clearly a fanatic about facts. He could never get enough; his appetite never waned for, or was sated with, information.

By 9:00 A.M. we had taken care of the unfinished business and the day's schedule was set; we had our individual instructions about special projects the president wanted completed. I went to my office, next door to the Oval Office.

Throughout the day we were on call. I usually attended meetings in the Oval Office with the president, particularly those with congressional leaders, and all meetings on Vietnam or the Dominican Republic or Panama or whatever the crisis was at that moment. Special sessions with larger groups were held in the Cabinet Room around the huge octagonal table given to President Roosevelt by his secretary of commerce, Jesse H. Jones. Here labor delegations, civil rights groups, businessmen, educators, special interest public groups, and assorted other assemblies were greeted and visited by the president.

At least a dozen or more times during the day I was on the phone to the president, answering a question, speeding to his side for some instant meeting, listening to him give an assignment which he wanted concluded within the hour.

Lunchtime would arrive. The president either ate at his desk or more often would have a working lunch with either newsmen or key government officials or opinionmakers in the nation, or his staff. And sometimes before lunch I would get a call from the president.

"You busy for lunch?"

"No sir."

"How about a swim first, and then we can eat afterwards?"

"Yes, sir."

These were good moments. Sometimes the president would invite guests to join us. I remember the day of December 21, 1963, just a month after LBJ had become president, he invited to lunch the top editors of the *New York Daily News:* F. M. Flynn, the president and publisher; R. G. Shand, the managing editor; and Ted Lewis, the *News* political columnist. Now at that time these key officials were, shall we say, past fifty in age. They had never really known President Johnson; moreover they had taken editorial pleasure in lambasting him without surcease for every conceivable breach of conduct they could rummage to find. In particular, Ted Lewis, Washington-based, a grumpy-faced old curmudgeon, with the temperament of a wounded rhino, found LBJ of a piece with a plague carrier, and he made that known every morning in his column.

The president was all honey. He greeted them warmly, guiding them through his office and the Rose Garden and thence to the swimming pool. There he invited them to swim. They looked a bit blank, muttering they had no swimsuits, which the president nonchalantly waved away as inconsequential. Then, the president of the United States emerged from the dressing room naked as the morning sun and dived into the pool where he began to swim with head bobbing above the water, still chatting. Ted Lewis's jaw dropped, he had the amazed look of a sinner come to judgment; his colleagues' eyes glazed over in sheer consternation. Bill Moyers and I damn near drowned in laughter. We both headed underwater before our whoops reverberated throughout the pool area.

Holding my stomach I surfaced; the *News* delegation, numbed by shock, was still in their catatonic trance. The president, innocently oblivious to his guests' exquisite discomfort, kept tossing conversational gambits at them, receiving garbled responses.

Finally the president climbed confidently out of the pool, headed for the dressing room and emerged fully clothed, glowing with health, and with an arm under the elbows of Messrs. Flynn and Shand. With Lewis alongside, he walked them to the private elevator and thence to the family dining room, where he continued the conversation. The *News* editorial chieftains were still in shock over this experience, an unerasable event in their mind.

For what it is worth, for all LBJ's nuzzling and caressing nothing changed. The *News* still painted LBJ in their editorials as some werewolf preying on the young. I still wonder though what these redoubtable *News* editors would have looked like, skinny-dipping in the presidential pool. Moyers and I considered that omission as one of the great regrets of our lives.

I recall another memorable luncheon involving another newspaper titan. On Friday, March 13, 1964, through the request of the late Edwin L. Weisl, Sr.—a Wall Street lawyer and one of the president's closest and most trusted counselors—a lunch had been scheduled by the president with Sam Newhouse, the tiny, intelligent, and highly successful publisher of some of the most important news journals in the nation.

Upon their arrival I drew Weisl aside: "Ed," I said, "the president is about to depart on Air Force One for inspection of the flood damage in the Ohio Valley. He would be pleased if you and Mr. Newhouse would accompany him and lunch with him on the plane."

Ed's eyes widened a bit at this astonishing news. He consulted with Mr. Newhouse and they agreed it would be a great experience. I accompanied them to the South Grounds, where we waited for the president to emerge from the Diplomatic Reception Room exit. He was there immediately. He hugged Ed Weisl, shook hands with Mr. Newhouse, and without delay we boarded a waiting helicopter and within minutes we were at Andrews Air Force Base, embarking on Air Force One, at 1:23 P.M. Aboard the president's plane were a number of congressmen and senators, as well as the secretary of agriculture, Orville Freeman.

For the next six hours we roamed the skies of the Midwest. We landed first at Pittsburgh where the president, with Sam Newhouse at his elbow, talked with Mayor Joseph Barr. At Pittsburgh we had a number of high state officials board the plane, among whom were Governor William Barron of West Virginia, Governor James Rhodes of Ohio, Governor Edward Breathitt of Kentucky, Gover-

nor Matthew Welsh of Indiana, and Governor Otto
Kerner of Illinois. From Pittsburgh we flew over the
flooded areas to get a look at the havoc wreaked by the
flooding of millions of acres of fertile land. At Cincinnati,
the president disembarked and briefly addressed a crowd
at the airport. Governor John M. Dalton of Missouri
joined us at Cincinnati while the rest of the governors left
the plane there. From Cincinnati, on the last lap of our
journey, we flew to Washington.

All during the trip, the president kept Sam Newhouse
perched next to him. Every now and then the president
would nudge Mr. Newhouse and say, "Look down there,
Sam. See where the flood ravaged that land?" Mr Newhouse would lean over, peer down through the thready,
tissued clouds, which partly obscured the view, and nod
his head.

The president would continue talking, holding Mr. Newhouse near him. A little after 7:00 P.M. we alighted again
on the South Grounds of the White House. By this time,
Mr. Newhouse's brief luncheon engagement had spanned
the day, he had flown several thousand miles, he had been
the recipient of presidential implorings and urgings and
declarations. He had been literally at the president's elbow
all the time. It was, in fact, one helluva lunch.

Inside the White House, the president was still not
through. "Why don't you call your wife, Sam, and tell her
you are going to spend the night here with me at the
White House."

Mr. Newhouse was brought to a phone and left to chat
privately with his wife. Suffice to say, he must have spent
a few minutes convincing his puzzled wife that he wasn't
kidding, that he had indeed just landed from a trip to the
Midwest and indeed, the president wanted him to spend
the night, and yes, he did have lunch.

Mr. Newhouse returned to inform the president that he

ought to get in his car and head home. It had been a special though demanding day. Again, the president cajoled and again Mr. Newhouse, though plainly weakening, demurred.

Finally they left, Ed Weisl and Sam Newhouse, with Ed saying to me under his breath, "Who the hell is going to believe this day?"

The president used the luncheon hour as his persuasion time. If there was an issue he wanted ventilated in the press, he would summon newsmen to share his luncheon table in the family dining room in the living quarters of the president. If the economy needed prodding, he would invite bankers and businessmen to lunch with him. If some civil rights venture was encountering stormy objection in the Congress, he would welcome the top black leaders to the second floor of the Mansion to lunch and talk. Then there was his staff, several of whom were lunching with the president (as I did) several times a week.

He found it intolerable to waste time; to him wasting time was not seeking and getting information from anyone in whom he thought reposed anything he wanted to know. He used the luncheon table to instruct, cajole, extract, inspire with logic or hope, or whatever he deemed adequate to his objective. The luncheon table and luncheon time were weapons to be used, and used effectively.

The president's midday hours were, at best, flexible. One might lunch with him at 1:00 or 2:00 or 3:00 P.M. He simply didn't accept the notion, put forward so vigorously by Mrs. Johnson, that one must regularize his eating habits.

Eating was not a major enterprise with LBJ. How to use the time one must otherwise allocate to having lunch was the prime concern with him.

About 4:00 P.M. each day, though even this varied, the

president would go to his bedroom, put on his pajamas, and climb into bed where he stayed for an hour. I cannot certify that he slept or even dozed. All I can verify is that he was in his bedroom, though even that environ wasn't sacred. I can recall any number of times when I was summoned to his side when he was supposed to be napping and find him propped up in bed pursuing some wisp of knowledge about the economy, or the war, or some congressional torment. It was both unexplainable and exasperating to his staff that a president wouldn't simply go to sleep for at least an hour and thereby give us (the staff) an unbroken sixty minutes without the intrusion of a presidential command.

Usually by 5:00 P.M., the second half of the president's day began. I would know when because my phone console would light up and start an insistent buzzing; the president would be calling. "Well, what do you know?" would be his first words, as though we had not spoken the hour before. He was doing business, inspecting the government after an hour's absence, to find out how the apparatus functioned while the leader was abed.

Now, the second half of the day would begin.

The president would be receiving in his office. There would be off-the-record appointments of congressional leaders or individual congressmen and senators, cabinet officials, and sprinkled among these would be on-the-record meetings with whomever the president chose to put on display.

The president worked out of the same office occupied by every president since Theodore Roosevelt. The Oval Office is aptly named, and its graceful contours are pleasing and comforting to the eye. The rug beneath the president's feet was pale green; the same rug that JFK used. In the center of the rug was the outline in blurred white of the presidential seal. The president's desk was one he had used in the Senate, a husky, rugged chestnut-brown desk, burnished and polished as the president liked it. To the left of the desk which was at the south end of the Oval Office were two teleprinters, clacking out the latest news. The president would step over to the teleprinters countless times during the day to find out what was happening, a faster scrutiny than anyone in Washington was privy to except for the newsrooms of newspapers, magazines, and television stations. On September 10, 1965, teleprinters flashed the news of the giant hurricane "Betsy" smashing the shores of Louisiana. Violence and catastrophe were combined in the news summaries. Still reading, the president grabbed his phone and ordered his pilot to ready Air Force One; in a second call, he alerted members of the Louisiana delegation who were still unaware of the tragedy unfolding in their home state.

To the far left of LBJ's desk, on the west side of the Oval Office were the ever-present television sets, three of them, mounted in a single unit, and connected to a remote-control apparatus which the president kept on his desk. The sets were so wired, that the picture was visible on all three sets at the same time, but the sound emanated from only one at a time. Thus, the president could see all three pictures and call up, via his control unit, any one of the stations to respond with sound. He watched TV selectively. In the morning, as he lay in bed, he would watch the "Today" show, particularly the news section, and any interviews with political personalities. His was a half-watch, half-read attentiveness, so that he could manage to go through his papers, and rivet his interest only when the screen demanded it. In the evenings, in his office, he would watch the network news shows, all three of them, carefully appraising what was said and by whom. In the late evening, at 11:00, he would occasionally turn on the local news shows to pick up any late-developing news.

LBJ detested news summaries. They were too sterile for him. He wanted to feed on the verisimilitude of the news personally. Voraciously he gobbled up the newspapers, and the TV screens and later I used to wonder why he tortured himself reading, watching, and listening to the badgering, the assaults, and the critical comments that flowed from newsprint and TV sets unendingly.

It is impossible for any man to give entrance to so much news and not know the country's mood; the antagonism of his opponents; the accusatory blight of critics; and the rising, fractious anti-war coalitions. He also watched the Sunday afternoon panel shows in which foes of the president would testify as to his obdurate and fiendish nature, his neglect of truth, and his malevolent torturing of democratic ideals. It was all there, and he saw it and heard it all, in living color, right from the lips of the righteous.

I make no claims that it was good for him. But I do establish the irrefutable truth that it did happen, that he was exposed to about as much news as any one man could take.

On the north side of the Oval Office was a round coffee table, marbled topped. The president's rocking chair (a duplicate of the one JFK used) sat in front of the table. To be near his treasured phone, the president had built into the coffee table an invisible drawer in which reposed a phone cradled into a console. He used it often.

On either side of the coffee table were two beige couches, each ample enough for three to sit comfortably. There were three other individual chairs in the room that oftentimes were brought to complete a circle when the population in a particular meeting grew too large for the couches.

Over the fireplace which was opposite the president's rocker was a large portrait of Franklin Roosevelt. On the east side of the office was a picture of George Washington and on the other side was one of Andrew Jackson.

Behind the TV sets, framing the door from the Oval Office to the hallway leading to my office, were bookcases filled with books about the presidency. In the hallway to the left going to my office (the appointments secretary office) was a smaller inner office. This was the intimate gathering place for the president. It comprised a desk, one large chair for the president, and a couch seating three. Here the president would repair for a quiet chat with an old friend (or, as I report below, to fashion an intimate lunch for two with a Senator Byrd) or sit by himself to read. When he ventured into this tiny office, it was a signal not to be disturbed except on urgent matters.

On the east side of the Oval Office were bay windows and a door leading onto the marble-topped veranda and the beautiful Rose Garden which was a riot of colors and marvelous smells, hedged in by lovely green shrubbery, and trees standing like sentinels, beyond whose branches and leaves could be seen the soft undulations of the Jefferson Mounds, as well as the Eisenhower-era putting green, unused by LBJ, but left there by him as a token of his esteem for the general.

The president's workplaces were his bedroom and his offices, though he was wont to sit in the West Hall living room of the Mansion to talk and have a drink with whomever was crucial to that day's plan.

As a senator and vice-president, LBJ drank Scotch, often in sizable amounts, though I never saw him drunk. He had a capacity for Scotch, as he did for work and the concentrated fury he attached to important matters. When he became president he began to taper off on the Scotch and within a year in his presidency, in order to keep his weight at a limit he deemed appropriate, he stopped drinking hard liquor altogether. He fastened onto Fresca, Tab, and tea, consuming them in large quantities during the day. He drank the tea with an artificial low-calorie sweetener.

As the day wore on, the staff became worn. Usually by 10:00 P.M. or later, Watson or I were the only senior members still on duty. The president, if he didn't have a social engagement, would sit at his desk working on papers, on the phone, having late-evening appointments that had been put aside during a busy day, or ones that were made on the spur of the moment. Often I would sit in the office with him, as we went over documents, he asking questions, me making notes of various points he had raised.

Mrs. Johnson would often call in, to remonstrate with the president that it was time to have a late dinner. He would joke with her, but if he wanted to work longer, he would evade the importunings. Then, Mrs. Johnson would soon show up in the office, quietly plucking at her husband's sleeve to detach himself from his desk.

By now, the hour was late. I had by this time assembled all the papers I thought he ought to see, and Juanita Roberts, the president's executive secretary, had also put together a stack of documents. They would be sent, neatly packaged, to the president's bedroom, put on the side table by his bed. This was his night reading, measuring inches in thickness and possibly 50,000 words or more to examine.

There would be staff memoranda; reports and memos from cabinet officials; messages, suggestions, and ideas sent in by governors, friends, members of the Congress; a sampling of letters received by the White House that day; surveys and polls that seemed relevant; CIA information; various messages to precede legislation the president wanted; Task Force reports (an assembly of picked brains in the country, gathered to illuminate vexing national problems with ideas and programs on matters ranging from fiscal policy to conservation, and everything in between); in short, the grist of decision-making and government-managing.

Some of the unrevealed sources of original humor during the LBJ administration came from the president's written retorts to various memoranda I sent him in his night reading about possible appointments for him.

On August 5, 1964, I passed on to the president a memo from one of his staff members which advised the president that a senior senator was anxious for the president to see a county commissioner from his home state who, according to the senator, was one of the prime moving forces in the re-election campaign of the president. The senator, in pleading tones, explained that the county commissioner could then go back to his hallowed ground in his home state having fulfilled a promise to see and talk to the president.

On the bottom of the memo the president scrawled a note to me: "Why don't you all try, *please*, to get this fellow to see Cliff Carter or Walter Jenkins or someone except poor old me all the time."

On September 30, 1964, another staff member wrote me a memo asking me to importune the president to see some New York political leaders. The memo said in part: "As you know, the president did agree to do something, but this invitation has been a long time coming. You might find out if he still wants to try to work this in if he is in New York sometime before November. If he cannot, let me know and we will understand."

On the next day, the president had written at the bottom of the memo: "Jack, see if you can work this blackmail into my schedule."

The president had a "thing" about staff members who wanted him to see someone and who said it would only be for a "brief moment." Once the president told me after I had ushered in a prominent visitor for a "brief visit" and the p.v. stayed for twenty minutes, "Hell," the president grumbled, "by the time a man scratches his ass, clears his throat, and tells me how smart he is, we've already wasted fifteen minutes."

On January 5, 1965, I sent the president a memo calling his attention to the fact that a former cabinet officer in another administration had just talked with General Eisenhower and wanted to come in and discuss this with the president. I wrote: "He will be in Washington on Thursday if you choose to see him for a brief moment."

Under the phrase "brief moment," the president scrawled: "ha, ha, ha!" He did see the former cabinet member.

On April 26, 1965, I sent the president a memorandum describing long conversations between myself, Secretary of the Treasury Henry Fowler and the chief of the Secret Service, James Rowley. The subject of the memo was the desire of the Secret Service to occupy 4,249 square feet in the Executive Office Building, the large, former residence of the State Department, right next door to the White House West Wing. The president was chary and cautious about the EOB bulging with too many staff members or ancillary offices. He wanted fewer bodies, not more, in the EOB. I had informed Rowley in no uncertain language that the Secret Service could not have the additional space. But both Fowler and Rowley demurred and I suggested they take their case to the president.

On the bottom of my covering memo which contained letters to the president from both Fowler and Rowley, LBJ wrote: "NO, HELL NO. Secret Service would absolutely have no hesitancy in occupying my bedroom!"

That settled that.

On March 30, 1965, I sent the president a memo informing him that Marvin Watson had told me that the president had agreed to receive the members of a high school band from Texas. I suppose the president received about 1,000 requests each year to visit with some high school group visiting the capital, and I sent him this memo only because Marvin Watson had pushed it.

The memo returned with the following LBJ comment: "NO, HELL NO. I never heard of this. Marvin must be smoking marijuana."

In late April, 1965, I sent the president a long memo telling him of various appointments I had scheduled for him. I usually didn't do this, because it was obviously a heavy schedule, and I rather liked to dole out appointments in small doses so that the president wouldn't feel cabined, cribbed, and confined.

On the bottom of my memo, the president wrote: "Why do you hate me? You must hate me else you wouldn't be trying to kill me slowly, like being nibbled to death by ducks."

When at last the president called it a day, he would walk to the Mansion, to his bedroom. Many times I was with him. He would begin undressing, and stretch out on a rubdown table. A Navy medical corpsman, standing by, would begin a methodical rubdown of the president. He would put his papers on a table at the head of his rubdown platform, so that as he lay on his stomach, groaning a bit under the expert kneading of the corpsman's hands, he would read his papers, noting with a pencil comments he chose to make.

I remember so vividly one evening after a White House dinner; the president invited Gregory Peck, Hugh O'Brian, and Vice-President Humphrey to join him in his bedroom for some talk. I was there also. We accompanied the president up to the second floor in his private elevator. Then as Peck, O'Brian, the vice-president, and I stood chatting, the president disrobed, planted himself on his rubdown table and as the corpsman began, the president, rummaging through his papers on the table in front of his face, would pick up a document and offer it to Peck or O'Brian to read. He grabbed a CIA folder and said over his shoulder to Peck, "Here is a report on what is happening in Laos." He handed the folder to the actor, who hesitated for a second. I intervened, picked up the document from the president's hands, saying, "Perhaps Greg would feel he couldn't carry this much top secret information around with him, he might get mugged."

It was a fumbling attempt at humor, but the president didn't buy it. "Now, Jack," he said, "we won't be violating national security too much if Greg finds out a little bit about Laos." Peck took the document tossed me an anxious glance and began to read. The president, over his shoulder again, suggested to Hugh O'Brian that he might read another piece of paper, also marked "top secret." The vice-president grinned hugely, enjoying the byplay. I shook my head in some wonderment and the president, noticing my discomfort, laughed. "Jack thinks everything marked top secret is really top secret. I am not as sure as he is."

For Peck and O'Brian, present for the first time in the bedroom of the president, with that august figure lying naked on a rubdown table, swaying to the rhythm of the corpsman's tugging and pulling of his back and legs, examining for the first time CIA and other top secret documents, listening to the good-humored talk of the most powerful political man in the world, with the second highest official in the land in rapport with the easy jesting of the president, it was, I am absolutely certain, an unforgettable moment.

* * *

From his first hour as president, LBJ reached out his arms for the Congress, knowing that within every congressman was a nature that would find a presidential entreaty hard to resist. LBJ knew that there is nothing so heady as a call from the White House. Most congressmen can go through a lifetime without ever having talked to the president over the phone in a conversation not initiated by the congressman.

When the call was done, whatever it was that the president was asking—short of denying access to constituents or cursing his contributors—the congressman, or the senator, was mighty willing to go along, or try to go along. The fact that LBJ thought enough to call was sufficient reason to bury a good part of their doubts.

I recall that one of my first instructions from the new president was a speech that went something like this (when the president installed me as his appointments secretary):

"You are going to get a lot of phone calls. People are going to court you and flatter you because you have access to the president. You are going to find yourself a social lion and a fellow with more charm than you ever thought you had and you will be all this because of the job you hold. But I want you to understand one thing more than anything else I will tell you. The most important people you will talk to are senators and congressmen. You treat them as if they were president. Answer their calls immediately. Give them respect. They deserve it. Remember senators and congressmen, they are your most important clients. Be responsive to them."

I made it my business, never breached to my knowledge, to satisfy that admonition by the president. He was right. My phone rang off the wall. Oftentimes I would receive 150 to 200 phone calls in one twenty-four–hour period. If I was out or otherwise busy, within minutes after returning to my desk I would sort out the incoming calls, and put the senators and congressmen at the top of the return-call list.

September 16, 1964, aboard Air Force One on a journey to Vancouver to sign the Colorado River Treaty and thence to Seattle, Washington. Left to right: Senator Warren Magnuson, senior senator from Washington state; General Ted Clifton, military aide to the president; the author; the president (reading a CIA report).

The author and Secretary
Rusk in the anteroom of
the Oval Room prior to
a cabinet meeting
on Vietnam.

Campaigning in Brooklyn,
October 14, 1964:
Jim Mangano, Democratic
district leader; the
president; the author;
and Robert Kennedy.

The author and Robert
Kennedy, October 31, 1964,
during RFK's campaign for
the Senate. At the airport
in New York City,
discussing arrangements
for a meeting with
the president.

Early in 1965,
now president "in his own
right," Lyndon Johnson
walking on the White House
driveway with Vice-President
Hubert Humphrey and
the author.

In the president's
hospital room at
Bethesda Naval Hospital,
October 7, 1965:
the president, the author,
and Bill Moyers.

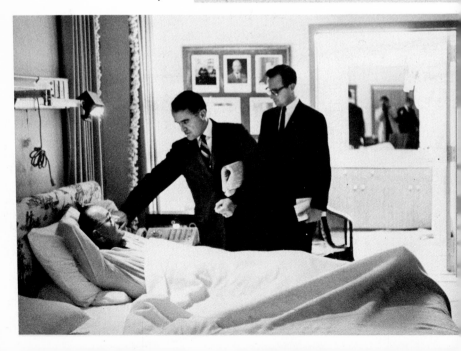

President Johnson
photographed on the South
Grounds of the White House
with the author and
Marvin Watson,
September 23, 1965.

At the south entrance
to the White House:
the author, the president,
Marvin Watson, Luci
Johnson, Lady Bird Johnson,
and Chief of Protocol
Lloyd Hand.

In the president's office:
McGeorge Bundy,
the president,
and the author.

Top right. In the
president's bedroom
on the second floor of the
Mansion: the author, the
president, and Bill Deason,
a member of the Interstate
Commerce Commission,
January 17, 1968.

At the president's desk
in the Oval Office:
the author and the president.

In the author's office at the White House in 1965: the president; Courtenay Lynda Valenti, age two and a half; in the background, the author's assistant, Charles Maguire.

Sometimes it would be late in the evening and I would still be at my desk, with too many calls still unanswered. And many times, I would place a call to a senator or congressman at midnight or later. When he came to the phone, I would say gently, "I'm sorry, senator, to call you so late, but I did not want the day to end without returning your call. May I be of assistance, sir?"

Usually, a sleepy-voiced senator would respond with a kind of special affection and satisfaction, emerging from the fact a presidential aide thought so much of the call he got the senator out of bed to ask what could be done. And usually, the senator would say, "That is very kind of you, Jack. May I call you in the morning when I get to my office? I want to discuss something with you."

The venom, if it was there during the day, had now been extracted. The senator was satisfied his wants were being handled. If ever he was before, he was now no longer angry or impatient.

Capitol Hill is too crucial to presidential plans to brush it aside with unthinking casualness. LBJ would have flogged any of his assistants whom he found lording it over senators and congressmen.

Invariably I spoke to every member on the hill, Democrat and Republican alike, with respect and deference. I used to challenge myself to see how quickly I could respond to congressional request. Many times within hours I would be back on the phone telling that senator or that congressman that the question he asked, or the request he sought, or the cause he favored, had been handled. I never glossed over the truth not because I could not, but because it is impossible to screen out falsities or inequity, for "foul deeds will rise though all the earth o'erwhelm them, to men's eyes." That is especially true in Washington. Moreover, I knew that if I was to be trusted by the Congress, I could not ever dissemble with them. I didn't. It was essential, beyond all doubt, to insert in the congressman's mind the sure conclusion that I would speak a plain and simple truth and that he could trust me. Therefore, if he trusted me, the president's word was bonded.

That is not easy to do. Often the truth has a harsh ring to it. Sometimes the request was ungrantable, the cause unwinnable. No man likes to be told he is wrong, or that he can't receive what he asked for. Here, a presidential aide had to prick the skin without drawing blood. I never shoved the lance in deep. I always remembered that it was not I who would be the legatee of the congressman's vengeance or humiliation but the president, and thus my footing rested on a very fragile edge.

I never forgot that the men at the other end of the line were elected officials. If nothing else this selection by their peers earned them respect from those who had only been plucked out by the choice of one man.

The availability of power is new to most White House aides, and therefore, gigantically exciting. They come to the palace of power so quickly (and in the case of the Johnson aides, abruptly) and put on their Olympian robes so swiftly they have no time to adjust, to take a deep breath and consider their new environment. Ergo, they are there and they are powerful because they speak and act with the looming shadow of the president always there, involved in every conversation they have, every meeting they attend, and from that ever-present shadow they draw their strength. It would not be strange, therefore, if in the exercise of this awful and beautiful instrument a White House assistant sometimes found himself believing it is his own peculiar talents, his own agile mind and charming manner that makes him welcome at social and official gatherings.

This is political bewitchery, masked and irresistible. So, when the aide talks to the congressman, there is ample opportunity for him to forget that the congressman must wait in dismal impatience for the accumulation of seniority and its attendant authority, while the aide's came so easily, so quickly. That is why the experience of running for public office is so important as background for an effective White House assistant.

My own personal judgment is that the U.S. invites a peculiar kind of disaster if it chooses as its president a man who has never sought and won elective office. General Eisenhower is the heroic exception of this century.

The point is clear: The politician, the vote-getter, the man who knows about "the slatternly foundations of public life," who understands the delicate balance of public priority and public choice, this is the kind of man suitable to the office of president and more likely to advance the public reach for quality.

It is also why presidents have to instruct their staff in the mystical aspects of elected leadership that sometimes to aides seem to be a God-given, inspired light that glows inside them as well. In truth, on closer inspection it is only the reflected shine of the Oval Office.

Thus it was that whatever else my faults may have been, I truly never forgot who had legitimate access to respect. Whether I spoke to the majority or the minority leader or to the rawest freshman representative from a rural constituency, I honestly felt what I gave him, which was deference to his having a vote in the Congress.

In the performance of one's responsibilities, one is apt to be negligent about human feelings and though the deed may be skillfully accomplished, the bruised sensibilities of those who ought to be allies sometimes become a larger loss than the gains advanced. What is so costly is that the sins of the lieutenant fall abrasively and heavily on the shoulder of the captain. In the White House this is a deadly business. The effective aide must never forget he serves the president and not himself, which, sometimes, does get twisted in some assistant's mind. To put it another way, the assistant sometimes forgets who it is that is running the country.

One of my unpublicized duties was to be the president's liaison with certain key figures in the government and to be available to them for quick conversation, so that their needs, suggestions, and ideas could be brought to the president's attention promptly after they had been proffered.

One of my most delightful senatorial contacts was the late minority leader of the Senate, Everett Dirksen of Illinois. He was a man of immense and persistent fascination. But Dirksen had more than fleshly charm. He had an inquiring, thrusting mind, with those finer tunings that only a keen intellect and depth of human understanding could achieve. He did not become Republican leader simply because he was a congenial, witty fellow. He was a tough, resolute commander. To this hour I can hear that voice over the phone, rumbling up from some vast ocean deep, flooding the receiver with its sonorous tones. The president had a splendid affection for Dirksen. They were old pros, they understood the ground rules and played by them, and never allowed combat in the press to obscure a hospitable regard for each other.

Neither did Dirksen and LBJ let their party roles clutter the practical matter of getting things done, though each was serving his own self-interests; the president disengaging Dirksen from thwarting his legislative march, and Dirksen extracting from the president some political coin in return.

I sat with the two of them many times in the West Hall of the living quarters of the first family, the president sitting in his wing chair and Dirksen on the couch, their knees almost touching. They would sip a bit of refreshment, though when the president drank Fresca, it brought a grimace to Dirksen's craggy features which resembled nothing so much as worn corduroy.

"Now, Mr. President," the organ tones would pour forth like melodic molasses flowing over tiled slopes, "there is that matter of . . ." And here Dirksen would mention some regulatory agency or commission, and inevitably the minority leader would have on the tip of his tongue the names of several people who were, in Dirksen's words "ably suited to carry out that responsibility."

"Dammit, Everett, if I am not careful you'll have a marker on every appointee to every agency in town." The president turned to me: "Didn't you bring me in some name Everett sent over the other day?"

I nodded. "Yes, Mr. President, Senator Dirksen had a nominee."

"Hell," said the president, "Everett is never without a nominee."

Dirksen would spread his mouth into that peculiarly engaging grin, wisps of hair meandering over his forehead.

"Alright, Everett, who's your man this time?"

Whereupon Dirksen would plunge into his coat pocket and out would come a list that nearly covered an entire page.

The president would pretend mock outrage, Dirksen would remonstrate that it was "only a suggestion list," and the two of them would then amble off into some reminiscence of a long-ago battle in which Dirksen would have put a shaft in the president's hide, and the president would recount another occasion where he caught Dirksen napping. More laughter, more sipping of the refreshment, and when they finally finished, a deal had been sealed. Dirksen would have an appointment of one of his friends and the president would have a commitment on some piece of legislation.

One time I put through a routine request to the FBI to run a check on a Dirksen-suggested appointee to some unimportant commission. When the report got back to me, I called the president.

"Sir, Senator Dirksen's friend to the so-and-so commission has been given a pretty bad report by the FBI." I read the relevant parts of the report. The president listened, chuckled. "Alright, you call him and tell him. And tell me what he says. In detail." The latter said with much relish.

I called Dirksen. "Senator, we have the following report on your nominee to that commission." I read him the report. There was silence. Then the Dirksen organ began to grind. "Jack, that's not a very good report, is it? Well, let us see. Perhaps we should pass that one. But wait a minute . . ." There would be a rustling of papers, sonorous whispers to an aide, more moments, and then: "Here is another name, a truly good man, from Chicago, and I am sure you and the president would find him eminently qualified. Possibly Mr. Hoover might confirm it also."

And so it went.

Often Senator Dirksen would call me to say, "Jack, tell the boss I intend to cut him up pretty good today. I just wanted him to know about it in advance." Sure enough, Dirksen would rise in the Senate and deliver a rousing, orotund speech in which the president would emerge somewhat in the shape of Attila the Hun. The next evening at a White House reception they would meet, and embrace each other in the manner of old warriors who had survived the blows of the other for many years on a dozen battlefields.

In the same manner did the president respond to the late Wayne Morse. At midday, the irascible senator from Oregon would rise in the Senate Chamber and in the most furious and virulent manner attack the president for a multitude of sins, and denounce him for an impressive number of shortcomings. The next morning, Morse would be sitting at breakfast with the president discussing, at the president's request, a labor problem, and giving counsel to the president on how it could be solved. Before the meeting would end, they would invariably chide each other in high humor about the quality of the bulls they raised and the offspring sired by their masters of the herd.

During the campaign of 1964, President Johnson went to Oregon. At a Portland dinner, Morse was by his side when the president told his classic story of his offer to Morse to help him in his election campaigns. Said the president: "I told Wayne, 'I want to do all I can to help you win re-election, so I am willing to come to Oregon and make speeches for you or against you, whichever will help you the most.' " Morse laughed loudly, and so did the audience for it was true. And Morse, of course, went on steadily denouncing the president whenever the mood stirred him, which was often.

In my role as confidential presidential conduit, I became close friends with the vice-president. Of all the political figures I have ever met, none surpasses Hubert Humphrey in flashing wit and innovative mind, and none endeared himself more completely to presidential aides. There was not a speck of hesitation in any White House assistant in his regard for the vice-president. As one man we joined in an open conspiracy to make certain he was privy to all that went on in the White House so he could at all times be armed with precious information necessary to him and his future. Humphrey is an unusual breed of public man, the decent fighter, the warm humane leader, whose brain fetches up more swiftly than any other little flecks of ideas and efficiently transforms them into public issues and public benefits.

While there was much public mystery about who would be on the ticket in 1964, to many of the White House aides there was never any doubt that President Johnson would choose Humphrey. The president knew better than anyone the imaginative resources of the man, and the lively, sparkling way he joined a battle, unaffected by fear or regret or the possibility of defeat. It is a curious piece of business that caused so many liberal and broad-minded commentators who knew better to cruelly torture Humphrey in the 1968 campaign. His great fault, the non-stop speech, was a kind of compulsion or rather affliction that was visited on him continually. Every man must be pardoned faults, for there is none without some. Yet it was my judgment that for twenty to thirty minutes, Hubert Humphrey was without peer as a platform speaker. Without the benefit of speechwriters, he could invest his talk with gay and spirited humor, guaranteed to defuse the most hostile of audiences.

Another public figure who was one of my special "charges" was the unpredictable, celebrated black leader, the late Adam Clayton Powell. In many ways, his life was one continuous escalation of waste—a waste of natural skills and a waste of purpose. In some bizarre fashion he chose to mock his talents by neglecting them.

Yet, it was impossible for those who knew him to resist liking him. Early in my White House job, President Johnson, perhaps noticing the quick rapport between Adam and me, assigned me the task of being Adam's White House contact. As chairman of the House Education and Labor Committee, Powell was a key figure in the vast and ceaseless flow of Great Society education measures aimed at the Congress. He and the president shared common objectives and it was the president's judgment that when Adam was at the peak of his form, there was no better chairman to shepherd the education legislation through committee. For my own part I was fascinated by him, his *élan*, his careless arrogance, his great gusto for living. I liked him enormously. He responded in kind.

He would call me at odd and irregular hours. No subject was too serious not to be garmented in his infectious comic cloak. Behind this jaunty mask was a spacious, shrewd intelligence. Life for the chairman was a continuing drama in which he was author, director, and actor. He chose to play many of the scenes in comedy but he was always in command of the dramatic continuity.

When he applied the full concentration of his intellect to his congressional duties, he was, as so many of his colleagues testified, a dominating captain. When he chose to, he presided over an efficient committee and guided the great educational advances of the Johnson administration.

One day in 1965, when a number of LBJ educational bills were languishing in committee because of the chairman's absence, the president, vexed and impatient, ordered me to find Powell, wherever he was, and get him back in the chairman's chair. I scoured the town. I called his closest aides, his friends, without success. He was simply out of touch, nowhere to be found.

Finally, in desperation, I talked to his chief assistant and said that if I couldn't find Powell within twenty-four hours I was going to call in the FBI. I said this jestingly and then continued my search. Late that night, about 10:00 P.M., the phone rang at my White House desk. Through the wire came that mellifluous voice, vibrant and light. "Jack, my boy, this is your humble parish priest talking to you." I almost embraced Adam over the phone. I put him on "hold," buzzed the Oval Office, and told the president our quarry had been located. The president picked up the phone when I had Powell transferred to his wire, and proceeded to admonish Adam in tones that were, shall we say, emphatic and firm. The essence of the conversation was that the president wanted him presiding over committee work the next day, or else.

After the president signed off, I returned to my office to talk further with Adam. The tensions had vanished, and the irrepressible Powell humor flooded back through my ear. "You know, Jack," he said, "that president of ours sure does know how to persuade, doesn't he?"

He was on duty the next day, brisk, attentive, knowledgeable, and the legislative flow in the Education and Labor Committee commenced again. The bills were reported out on schedule.

Somehow, it all seemed to crumble in the months that lay ahead. There was in Adam a suicidal rush toward some dim and unperceived (to me) shore whose reefs held nothing but tragedy for those who chose to steer that course. I cannot say why. I do know that he was unique, a dashing, handsome man with charm and wit and brains, all of which he negligently flung to the winds. I can surely understand the spell he cast over the Harlem community, for its mesmeric net caught me too.

Like so many colorful humans, his faults, so garishly exposed, so luxuriantly displayed for press and public to view, obscured the plentiful talents and intelligence of an unusual leader. I have thought so much lately about Adam Clayton Powell. He was my friend. I keep thinking what might have been.

The president did not stand aloof when one of his programs was threatened. One of his favorite expressions was to "shove it in my stack," which meant going all out to win the battle in which he was engaged. He did this in varying amounts, however, for he knew that if he shoved in the stack every time, both the threat and the shoving would become commonplace, and nothing wears so quickly as too often brandishing and using a presidential club.

Though he was accused of arm-twisting, this was not a worthy phrase, for it lacked precision. Arm-twisting has the taint of strong-arming while in truth the Johnson treatment, glorified in print and lore, was considerably more sophisticated than that. One does not really twist the arms of powerful, influential congressmen. They are usually men who have egos as enlarged as any president and they become sullen, intractable, and vengeful if too much explosive wrath or demands are put upon them. They didn't like this, and Johnson knew it. As a member of Congress for twenty-four years he knew exactly how much a congressman would take before rebellion set in. Moreover he was keenly aware that the best way to a congressman's heart is through his constituency. "Give a man a good reason for voting with you and he'll try. Try to force it down his throat and he'll gag. A man can take a little bourbon without getting drunk, but if you hold his mouth open and pour in a quart, he'll get sick on you."

Therefore, the classic Johnson approach, as revered by him as the Sicilian defense by the chess masters, was to create a mood and feeling within the legislator that the best interests of the nation and his district (or state) would be served if a particular law was passed.

When rent supplements, a Johnsonian doctrine important to him and crucial to his domestic program, was up for vote in the House, the president didn't rely just on the White House congressional office. As he often did, he called his entire White House staff into the legislative battle. Within the space of a few days, some eight to ten assistants would be roaming the halls of Congress, engaging in face-to-face conversations, and also making phone calls summoning the better angels of national interest and beguiling the congressmen with visions of re-election sugar plums and presidential embraces, as well as freighting him with vital information he could use in newsletters and back-home speeches to account for his vote.

Rent supplements was a dicey issue and a good many southern congressmen were as reluctant to be caught in the same voting booth with this one as they were to assault the local minister's wife.

At a staff meeting late one evening, LBJ admonished his staff. We were about to hear the bugle ring out "charge" as the commander addressed his field lieutenants. He sat in his rocking chair, sipping that damn Fresca and preparing his case.

"Now, the first thing you have to remember is these men have to go back home and get re-elected every two years. They're not going to be impressed if you ask them to vote for something that will give them political leprosy. They have to have a fall-back, something they can talk about in positive terms as to why they voted with us. It has to be something that Cousin Oriole can understand, not some fancy theory about life in the hereafter. Just telling them rent supplements is fine is not enough."

He held up a piece of paper he was writing on. "Now here is an argument you ought to make with those congressmen who tell you they want to be with us, but no chance on this bill. Most of them will tell you 'how can I explain that one?' and they're right. Let's get the facts from the Budget boys on all the subsidies the government pays to farmers, to maritime people, to every damn interest sucking on the public teat. Then we can figure out how much the subsidy costs per person in taxes. Our argument ought to be, look, we pay blank dollars per person to subsidize these various interests; and keep remembering that a lot of their constituents get some of these subsidies. So, tell them, why can't we pay much, much less per person to provide a poor family with a home. And then show the congressman how much less it will cost the government, rent supplements versus public housing. Keep it factual, keep it simple, make it all in dollars and cents. Of course, you can point out I sure as hell want this bill and I will be grateful. But give him information so that when he gets back home he can go on TV and say, 'Folks, I saved you a lot of tax dollars the other day when I voted for rent supplements. It's going to save the taxpayer blank dollars per person per year.' Now, few people will get upset if you tell them you are saving them money, if at the same time you are not taking anything away from them. The congressman knows that. Make him a hero. Then he will be with us."

Overnight, we organized a fact-finding group in the Budget Bureau, and by morning's early light we had our case. It was a tight one, simple and clear, and it worked.

I had been rebuffed by a good congressman friend of mine in an earlier conversation. He was from the South, and a canny, perennially re-elected legislator, so he was cautious and usually right on target with his district.

I rang him again in the morning and went over the figures we had prepared. I told him how much this meant to the president, and how rent supplements could be an asset to the congressman when he talked about how Congress saved money instead of spending it all the time. When I finished, he said, "Well, Jack, that's pretty convincing. I want to think about it for a while. Tell the president this does give me a good handle if I have to use it. I might be able to sell this back home. Let me give it some thought."

He voted for the bill. HR 7984, known as the Housing and Urban Development Act of 1965, was passed by the House on July 27, 1965, on a roll-call vote of 251 to 168. The president signed it into law on August 10, 1965, and became Public Law 89–117.

The first real evidence of the LBJ style and tenacity came within weeks after assuming the presidency. LBJ was caught up in a vicious congressional fight on the administration's foreign-aid bill. The Republicans in the House, led by a wily infighter, the House minority leader, Charles Halleck of Indiana, threatened to shatter the bill, and paste the president with a bloody defeat soon in his new responsibilities. President Johnson immediately took up the challenge. Congress was called back into session right in the middle of the Christmas holidays. He gathered his aides about him and we began the counter-assault on the phone, with the president calling in key congressmen to have private chats with them.

"If you want me to keep this world from exploding, if you want me to keep from calling up the young men from your district to fight in World War III, then you better back this bill. A few dollars won't break us, but the absence of those dollars might start a fire in some part of this world that I can't contain. This isn't just a crummy little bill, but this is a gut issue, and by damn, if you fail me here, I might not be able to save you later on."

That's the way the pitch went. Endless talking, ceaseless importuning, torrential laying on of the facts, it went on and on for several days. Christmas was looming up, and LBJ was absolutely resolved that if he had to keep the Congress in session on Christmas Day he was going to win this battle.

The vote was to be taken on Christmas Eve. The president did a typical thing. Through the Speaker of the House, the president invited the entire Congress to come by the White House for Christmas cheer before they took the crucial vote on Christmas Eve.

On December 23, hundreds of congressmen gathered in the State Dining Room, sipped their drinks, and mingled with the president and his family. The bitterness which had been devouring the Congress the last several days was now subsiding, and by evening's end it would have vanished.

The president, without ceremony, walked to the side of the room, picked up a gold damask chair, and personally carried it to the center of the room, brushing past astonished congressmen, unsettled at seeing the president move furniture. LBJ put the chair firmly down, and then proceeded to step on it, carrying his six-foot-four-inch height high above his colleagues. Mrs. Johnson stood beside him. "May I have your attention for just a minute," he said, and delivered an impromptu talk.

"We can disagree without being disagreeable," he said. "You have only one president, we have only one Congress and one judiciary. We're Americans first and your country is no stronger than your government." It was pure, undiluted Texas corn, but in this setting, in these hours before Christmas, the assembly of congressmen responded to what they heard.

"You're always welcome in your house," with emphasis on the "your," was the president's parting comment. "Thank you all so very much, and I hope you forgive me for delaying your Christmas with your family and your friends."

In the room were Charlie Halleck, as well as Otto Passman, congressman from Louisiana and a last-ditch foe of foreign aid, any kind of foreign aid, it didn't matter to Congressman Passman. He was equally opposed to every kind. Halleck and Passman sensed they had been "had." Not only did the president's White House Christmas party keep malingering members in town for the key vote the next day, but it also softened the ire of the opposition, and sealed the votes of the wavering.

The president went up to Halleck. "Charlie, I'm sorry if anyone down here said anything ugly about you," he said. It was a fair assessment of the president's mood and the truth of what he said. There had been a few, perhaps a lot of, remarks made by the White House assistants about Halleck's ancestry, and some other odd, assorted billy-club comments. Halleck grinned. He knew the president. He knew his fight was lost now, but he had to admire the gut-fighting instincts of his old congressional colleague.

The president was on the phone after his aid bill victory

to literally dozens and dozens of congressmen whose votes had been crucial to the passage, and he thanked them. Silvio Conte, a handsome, articulate Republican congressman from Massachusetts, recounted that moment to me several days after the president had died in early 1973. "You know," said Congressman Conte, "I was sitting in my office and the phone rang telling me it was the president calling. I damn near collapsed right on the spot. Sure enough, it was the president. He said, 'Silvio, this is Lyndon Johnson, and I just wanted to thank you on behalf of this nation for your vote. You stood up and you were counted at the right time. I am mighty grateful to you.' " Silvio Conte of Massachusetts, now an influential leader on the Republican side of the aisle, smiled nostalgically at the remembering of this moment. "It's the only time since I have been in Congress that a president called me. I will never forget it."

This was to be the augury of the Johnson style of Congress-treating and Congress-handling. His was the personal approach. Man to man. Phone to ear. Come let us reason together. This is Lyndon Johnson talking. Now, we don't have to be at each other's throat, do we? Your country needs your help and so do I. So it went.

The economy was always on Johnson's special priority list. When LBJ became president, one of his first long and exhausting meetings was with the Budget Bureau under Kermit Gordon and the Council of Economic Advisers headed by Walter Heller. They convinced him that the tax cut, offered by President Kennedy, was essential to the durable prosperity of the nation. But the tax cut had to be sprung from the Senate Finance Committee where it had been held up for many months, having defied all attempts by President Kennedy to bring it to the Senate floor.

All of President Kennedy's persuasions and power were baffled by the person of Harry Flood Byrd, senior senator from the sovereign state of Virginia. The late Senator Byrd was a uniquely fascinating man. He was a pragmatic patrician, whose family roots were fastened deep in historic Virginia soil; in fact, the Byrds of Virginia were as indigenous to that mother state of presidents (and as proud) as the Randolphs and the Lees.* Senator Byrd tended his power in the Senate as he tended his apple orchards, which lay blissfully productive on the beautiful acres of the Byrd estates. Both his power and his apples were ripe and fat and shiny.

Harry Byrd was neither an easy target nor an accessible one. Budging Byrd from his immovable position, according to the congressional liaison people who had managed Kennedy's Capitol Hill affairs, was well nigh a chore to be ranked with the Augean Stables task of Hercules. But Hercules had one advantage. He was divinely endowed. Alas, only mortals were available to deal with Senator Byrd.

On one issue there was no debate. No Byrd approval, no tax cut.

President Johnson pondered this dilemma for several days. He and Byrd had respect for each other. Indeed, it may even be said that Byrd liked the president as the president decidedly liked him. Surely, when Johnson was majority leader they worked together (when the issue and the outcome suited Byrd) with a congenial harmony nourished by the realisms of power and influence, for each had ample stores of both.

---

* The certainty of heredity is verified in the person of the elder Byrd's son, Harry, Jr., who is now the senior senator from Virginia with all the Byrd traits of public duty and private honor visible to press and constituents.

Johnson was a guest many times during his Senate days at Byrd's elegant estate in Virginia, and he felt comfortable with him. And so LBJ determined he must approach this most regal of the Senate proconsuls and he settled in his mind how it was to be done.

The president invited the Virginian to lunch with him on December 5, 1963. This was to be no ordinary luncheon. Its setting was the small office just off the Oval Office of the president. It was one of the few times, possibly the only time, the president would lunch there. He took great pains to make certain all was perfect, even selecting the menu himself. The president invited me in to sit with him through the lunch as working assistant and friendly observer. Senator Byrd was warmly courteous to me and I was personally grateful for this moment for I had been anxious to meet the senator.

The two of them ate leisurely, refreshing the meal with quiet reminiscences of Senate days and of the combat and the affection they had both engaged in and gave. Then as the president poked aimlessly at his dessert, he said easily, unhurriedly, "Harry, that tax cut is important, mightily important to me."

Byrd, impassive, his cheeks pink and cherubic, replied, "Now, Mr. President, you know that we cannot have a tax cut without serious decreases in the budget, substantial decreases."

"Yes," said the president, still easy and dispassionate, "but my latest studies tell me I would be fortunate, really fortunate, if I could get it down below $105 or $107 billion."

"Too big, Mr. President, too big," said Byrd, shaking his head.

The president continued to toy with his dessert, swirling a remnant of ice cream with his spoon. "Hmmmmm, well, Harry, just suppose, and I say just suppose because

I don't think it can realistically be done, just suppose I could get the budget down somewhere under $100 billion, what would you say then?"

The senator leaned forward, all those ancestral genes clearly on display, with an assured grace of movement and manner. He sipped a glass of water. "Mr. President, I would answer that if you got the budget under 100 billion dollars we might be able to do some business."

The president's face moved closer to Byrd, craning across the small table, until they were almost nose to nose. "Harry, I am going to try my damnedest to somehow get the budget under a hundred, and if I do, will the tax cut come out of your committee?" The voice was firm, the words clearly sounded.

Byrd moved ever so briefly backwards, possibly to escape the Johnson avalanche. He tugged at his earlobe. "Yes, I would say if you can bring in the budget less than 100 billion, I think it is quite possible the committee, though I can't speak for them personally, would surely consider this, and it is possible the bill could be brought to the floor."

The president knew that if Byrd was amenable, the committee would damn sure consider the tax cut, and if Byrd nodded, the committee would send the bill to the floor. The president got up quickly, shoved out his hand, "Harry, you have made a deal. It's been good seeing you. I don't see enough of you." With one arm under the elbow of the senior senator from Virginia, the president escorted Byrd to the door. The first step had been eminently successful. The president knew his man. Once his word was committed, Byrd would sooner die then renege. The Byrds value their word. They never defect from pledges given.

As Senator Byrd departed, the president leaned over to me and in a low voice said, "Get Kermit Gordon in here.

We've got a lot of work to do." Gordon was the scholarly chief of the Bureau of the Budget and a clear-headed, brilliant artisan of budget arithmetic.

However, when the president at a later news conference in his office announced a budget of some few millions under $100 billion, it astonished most of the press who, because of Johnson's former avowals he could not fashion a budget of less than $105 or $106 billion, did not expect this slim an accounting. Fast on the heels of their surprise came written versions of their displeasure in being bilked, as many of them contended. This later became their evidence of Johnson's lack of credibility and the president was rapped for his dissembling.

There was no way for the president to explain two very important facts. First, it was touch and go in constructing the under-$100 billion budget. When he made his pact with Senator Byrd, he did not specifically know he could perform. He thought he could. But the midnight sessions with Kermit Gordon that had been a dreary part of his life almost from the first hour he took office, were not illuminating any clear, open path to what he was seeking. And second, the figures he gave to the press, under questioning, were based on Gordon's own best judgments, as well as the president's searchings.

The spur of the Byrd commitment, however, sent the president and Gordon riding back over every department's estimates and this time they hacked away at even the tiniest outcroppings of waste. The issue of tax reduction was too essential to the future of the Johnson planning to let anything stand in the way, and if there was butchery performed on some departments' submitted budgets it was in a higher cause, as the president later proved.

Byrd kept his word, the bill came out of committee and went to the Senate floor and was passed. But the price of the triumph to the president was probably the first sour notes sounded of the so-called credibility gap, bitter echoes of what the press considered to be deception on the part of the president in his handling of the pre-announcement figures.

LBJ sensed intuitively that if his plans for the Great Society were to be realized he must have in his corner the business community of the nation. He would be hard-pressed to gather congressional support for the massive funding he was looking for if the business and industrial leaders of the country looked sourly on his course of action. A robust economy was the rock on which he would build his society. So he did what he always did when he began to construct his dreams for what he believed to be the right decision to be made; he "reasoned" with those he needed as allies. There came to the White House, in waves of meetings and dinners and luncheons and discussions, the premier captains of the American industrial empire.

There existed then, as now, the Business Council, composed of the proconsuls of American industry, in steel, oil, automotive, retail, heavy equipment, light industry, and other business activities. He sought them out, singly and together. He paid court to them, listened to them, persuaded them their advice was essential and their power necessary to the momentum of the economy, and of course, the Johnsonian legislative program. He paraded the highest officials of the government before them in briefings, not only on the economy but on defense, world affairs, and asked for questions from the floor. He made them understand that he cared about their opinions and that he needed their imagination and their ideas. He took their phone calls without hesitation and made a few himself.

It was an endless importuning, always delicately balanced between the power of the presidency and the egos of the men involved. The president talked numbers, finance, the arithmetic of the federal budget, as well as Dow Jones averages and balance sheets. He talked to the business leaders in language they understood. It was an embrace that these business tycoons had never experienced, even under a Republican president. It was warmth, affection, and courtship all blended together and even the tightest-fisted corporate executive was hard put to resist such blandishments on a scale never before imagined and with a ferocity never before confronted.

After one evening in the White House where some hundred business leaders had been wined, dined, and briefed, I walked out into the rotunda of the White House with a hard-nosed president of one of America's biggest companies. He turned to me and said, "I have never trusted a Democratic president, they are always figuring out ways to spend us into bankruptcy. And I never really liked Johnson before. But I'll be damned that I have to admit that I believe him, I trust him, and I think for the first time we have a president who isn't out to dismantle the business structure of this country. I am not sure I like everything he does, but he understands my problems, and he is smart as the devil, and I think I'll go along with him."

When the 1964 campaign got underway, it must have come as a shock to the Republican campaign managers to find their strongest legions and their firmest allies—the business leaders of the country—deserting in waves to the other side. It is fair to say that LBJ had captured, if not all the votes of the men who made the corporate ledgers sing, at least their support for much of what he aimed to do, and depleted their large pool of distaste for a Democratic chief executive. It was a singular performance, orchestrated with such splendor that even the diehards in the industrial community gasped out their amazement at what was going on. Never had the moneymen and corporate chieftains of the land been besieged with honey and warmth, and it proved to be the mixture that won their hearts. Well, not all their hearts, and not all their faith, but the remnants of opposition were too meager to hold back the tide.

*   *   *

The campaign for the presidency in 1964 was a classic case study of the power of the incumbency, and the quick, deadly reaction to issues offered by the opposition, issues that were tailor-made for a crushing counter-attack. The Goldwater campaign was decimated in the early days and had no chance to recover, though at the time we didn't know this with the certitude that later became so pleasurably clear.

The campaign really got underway in a halting, clumsy fashion on August 6, a Sunday. A meeting was called with what were to be the field commanders of the battle present: Ken O'Donnell, Walter Jenkins, Bill Moyers, Larry O'Brien, Cliff Carter, Jim Rowe, John Bailey, and myself. We met in Walter Jenkins's office to clear our strategy and assemble our tactics.

The convention was first on our agenda and the discussion was aimless. We fussed for over an hour on the festering issue, sure to surface like a ticking time bomb on the convention floor unless it was defused, of the Freedom party in Mississippi. This group contended with the regular Democratic organization for recognition as the official Mississippi delegation. A previous nose-count revealed that some ten to thirteen members of the Credentials Committee were keyed to vote for the seating of the Freedom party. These were enough votes to warrant a minority report and thereby haul it to the floor where the noisy conflict could be aired for all the country to see, and to the delight of the Republican party. The problem at hand: how to avoid a floor fight. Once this issue got in open convention it would be difficult to put a blanket over the debate, certain to be fierce and hostile.*

My own feelings, as I recorded in my notes of the meeting, were mostly dismay over the lack of pre-planning that allowed this issue to be so hot. There were no significantly practical solutions brought forth and if there was ingenuity present, it escaped me. Jim Rowe posted some legal questions which I thought pertinent, but no one seemed to have any answers.

It was quite obvious we had no plan. None. The Democratic National Committee leadership was supposed to have sounded out the delegations and smoothed over any rough edges. It was not done. John Connally had made it clear to me some days before that if the Freedom party were seated, and it might well have been their cause was solid, the entire South would take this as an affront, and the underpinnings of our campaign in the South would collapse before the campaign even got underway. The solution was for Cliff Carter and Larry O'Brien to go back to the drawing board for a new design of action.

---

* In early 1975, press reports surfaced about former agents of the FBI claiming they were ordered to wiretap Martin Luther King and Bobby Kennedy at the convention to relay vital information to LBJ. My only comment on this is the reporting must have been done by extra-sensory perception. I saw every piece of paper that crossed the president's desk. I was with him so much I heard almost every phone conversation he had during these convention days. I can certify without a doubt that I never saw or read one sliver of anything that resembled a wiretapping report from the FBI or anyone else. I don't know whether or not the FBI tapped King and Kennedy at the convention, but I am willing to declare it would have been a minor miracle for any of these reports to get to the president without me knowing about it. So what we have is a statement by a former FBI agent without any comment on its veracity from the one man who would have known. He's dead and can't comment.

However, we did put to paper our working organization so that lines of authority were clearly drawn. John Bailey was to be nominally in charge of the campaign and Kenny O'Donnell was to be his assistant. Larry O'Brien would be in charge of organization. I would be in charge of scheduling and coordination with the president; Bill Moyers would command the speech-writing operation; Bill and I would handle all advertising; Cliff Carter would direct all field coordinators; and Jim Rowe would be in charge of special groups. We settled on our responsibilities, after which Walter suggested we see the president.

The meeting with the president went about as I had anticipated. I knew, as did Walter, that the president would be scornful of half-laid plans, half-organized efforts, and mistily designed strategy. I was right. The president dismissed us within an hour, giving short shrift to our not-very-persuasive report. "Get these problems settled, organize yourself, get a sensible plan, and then come back to talk to me," was his parting shot to us.

I suspect the Republicans, closeted in their guarded meeting room, were fantasizing about the vast, immeasurable power of the presidency and of the legions of experts toiling over grand strategy, with mountains of volumes of fact books and tactical command directions. If they could have had this Sunday meeting under surveillance, they would have been slack-jawed witnesses to about as sloppy an operation as ever struggled to get off the ground.

But the president soon realized that even if we threw away all campaign planning, we would be far and away heavy favorites to win. The reason was that the Republicans threw us the heft we needed and threw it to us with an almost casual disregard for the hard realisms of the political marketplace.

Senator Goldwater spoke at Knoxville, Tennessee, assaulting the role of public power in America. This both amused and heartened LBJ. The senator was just warming up. He promptly took on the poverty program; savaged medicare; offered to abolish social security; suggested that the eastern seaboard be sliced off the rest of the U.S.; and to LBJ's uncomprehending surprise, let the notion surface that he would "nuke" the enemy if that was the only way available.

From those early weeks in September, our principal chore was to restrain our advertising agency from dropping the whole media load on the Republicans. Even the president thought Moyers and I (through the creative genius of Doyle, Dane, and Bernbach) had gone too far with the famous TV message of the little girl with the daisy and the exploding H-bomb in the background wiping out the soft picture of child and flower. He ordered it off the air. But it did not really matter. We had the issues now. Our speeches, advertising, and publicity were fat with facts, numbers, and the opposition issue positions. It was simply a question of how we would unloose them.

Nonetheless, seasoned old campaigners like the president, Abe Fortas, Clark Clifford, and Jim Rowe were uneasy. Things were going too swimmingly and they kept looking over their shoulder for monster mistakes, gargantuan blunders to overtake us and bring us down.

The victory seemed secure to me on September 28, 1964, when we set out on a campaign tour of New England that took us in one day to Providence, Rhode Island; Hartford, Connecticut; Burlington, Vermont; Portland, Maine; Manchester, New Hampshire; and finally, in the early hours of the morning, to Boston to visit an ailing Senator Ted Kennedy.

On this day, the president was greeted by over a million people. In every city his motorcade had to literally thrust its way through cheering, jubilant throngs, an outpouring of support and affection that overwhelmed us. While we expected something positive, none of us was really prepared for this unprecedented bear hug of a public embrace.

A Democratic president could expect love and excitement from Providence and Boston, but Portland, Burlington, Manchester, and Hartford? The effect was total. There was no diminution of the crowds as the night closed in around us. Portland at nine in the evening was as buoyantly alive as Providence in the afternoon. It was the damnedest day of the campaign. We never saw another like it, though we witnessed great movements of people in other cities. This six-city journey presaged the wholesale shift of the country, and gave prophetic measure to the November election.

I especially remember the motorcade in Providence. We were crawling at a snail's pace up a slight incline. I was riding in an open convertible with the president's physician, Admiral Burkley, one car behind the Secret Service security vehicle, which was following the president's car. Suddenly, without warning, the hood of our car began to smoke, and tongues of flame shot from beneath the hood.

The driver yelled, "Get the hell out of here," and leaped over the door frame. Dr. Burkley was clambering out the right door faster than any active admiral ever moved, and I, following the example of the sensible driver, jumped over the frame of my door. I ran to the curb—the car now bathed in flames and smoke—when I was jolted to a halt. In the rear seat I had left my briefcase carrying presidential documents, including several CIA reports and top secret information as well as some important documents the president wanted to read later. At that moment I considered my own safety and then I weighed the president's dismay at the loss of that material, and putting them on a scale, I wasted not one damn second. I ran immediately back to the car, high-hurdled over the back frame, glided onto the back seat, and then grabbing the briefcase in the same motion as I turned, I pole-vaulted with one hand onto the trunk, slid down the sloping trunk of the car and without breaking stride hit the pavement for the safety of the curb. Even as I was breaking the presidential campaign speed record for the fastest time into and out of a burning car, some practical soul was spraying the car with fire suppressant. Shortly, the fire was out, the car dragged away, and the doctor and I, ensconced in another car, proceeded on our way.

The president's comment to me later on Air Force One was: "How come you let that car catch fire?" For some time thereafter the president referred to me as the captain of fire wagon number three.

The most dramatic moment in the campaign came in the South, in New Orleans. It was night, the day had been long and the president was scheduled to speak in an auditorium to some 2,500 New Orleans citizens.

His staff was divided on what he ought to say. Some counseled caution. "You have the election going so well now, don't take chances, say nothing about civil rights." There were others of us, also cautious and more than fearful, who thought the president *had* to talk to this issue, right here in the heartland of the South. We had a prepared speech, with civil rights handled blandly, so as not to ruffle too many feathers.

Soon after he began speaking, the president, to our frozen and suspended senses, threw away the speech and began, in evangelical fashion, to pour it on, *sans* notes, *sans* text, *sans* everything except that remarkable instinct that served him so well. He told them the story about Joseph Weldon Bailey, a Mississippi lawyer who came to Texas, and achieved fortune, fame as a Texas congressman and U.S. senator, and finally political disaster. Senator Bailey was talking one day, said the president, to Sam Rayburn about the economic plight of the South, and its inability to plow a straight furrow of prosperity. "I wish I felt a little better, Sammy," Senator Bailey said. "I would like to go back to Mississippi and make them one more Democratic speech. I feel like I have at least one more left in me. You see, Sammy, in poor ole Mississippi, they haven't heard a Democratic speech in thirty years. All they ever hear at election time is 'Nigger, Nigger, Nigger.' "

Over that audience there flowed a consternation that could be felt everywhere in the auditorium. It was a physical thing, surprise, awe; ears heard what they plainly could not hear, a cataclysmic wave hit everyone there with stunning and irreversible force.

And the president went on: "Whatever your views are, we have a Constitution and we have a Bill of Rights and we have the law of the land, and two-thirds of the Democrats in the Senate voted for it and three-fourths of the Republicans. I signed it, I am going to enforce it, and I am going to observe it, and I think that any man that is worthy of the high office of president is going to do the same thing."

Of all the speeches LBJ ever made, only his monumental "I shall overcome" speech to a joint session of the Congress compares with this one in effect on an audience, and in the courage that compelled the president, that drove him to say what he did. It seems effortless these days. But in that time of southern political life, this speech was an electrifying discovery, the shattering visible evidence that the president of the United States would not pussyfoot around the hottest, most volatile issue in the South. When he came down from the rostrum the applause was there, not dominant, not of a total enthusiasm, but it was there in sufficient quantity to allow the president to believe that enough southerners were with him.

Later that night, in the crowds jostling around the president, one man came up to me and said: "You know, I never really liked Johnson. I always thought he didn't really have it here," he pressed his heart, "but tonight, gawd-damn, he shoved it right up us and made us like it. That takes a fair amount of guts and I got to say Johnson showed us that tonight, that he did."

It is easy for liberal public men from liberal public states to rise to testify as to their concern for blacks or whatever. On Manhattan's East Side, or in some other urban centers, to be very liberal about human rights is chic and popular and risk-free. But to nail it down, with the bark off, with neither equivocation or fear, with no promise of political capital to be gained and the specter of much to be lost, to speak his beliefs to an audience and in an area where his allies in this cause were few in number and where the opposition was powerful, urgent, and demanding, was an act of sublime courage.

One particularly funny event took place late in the campaign, in the waning days of October when the president, at the request of the Bobby Kennedy campaign people, spent the entire day in New York, roaming the state from top to bottom. The day had started early, very early, and we never stopped, motorcading, speechifying, ministering to the crowds—LBJ and Bobby side by side, inciting the large and enthusiastic throngs to a fever pitch.

As the night came on, we held the final motorcade through Brooklyn. By this time I was physically exhausted and I settled down, privately I thought, in a spare Secret Service car back in the motorcade. I fell asleep. Suddenly I was being rudely shaken. It was Rufus Youngblood, chief of the White House Secret Service detail. "Get up front right away. The boss wants you."

Wide awake, I climbed out of the car, and ran to the front of the motorcade. The president and Bobby had changed cars, from the closed presidential limo to the open Secret Service "black maria." They were both standing on the rear seat of the stopped vehicle, with what I would count as several hundred thousand people screaming and yelling joyously at them. The president saw me and beckoned vigorously for me to join him. I got in and at the president's direction stood between him and Bobby. To the president's right was a smallish bald-headed man, whom I later learned was Jimmy Mangano, Democratic leader of the predominantly Italian-American district through which we were now passing. Suddenly I found myself caught up in the fervor and I was waving and gesturing to the crowd as if I were also on the ballot.

The president nudged Mangano and said, "Okay, Jimmy." Mangano lifted his hand mike and his voice rose raucously over the crowd. "And now, let me introduce one of our own, the closest confidant to the president, our own Jack Valenti."

The sound from the people was deafening. Bobby and the president each took one of my hands and lifted them skyward, in the traditional gesture of victory. I was grinning and frankly enjoying the hell out of it all. Mighty fine thing, this public affection. I continued to smile widely, bowing slightly. Mangano continued, "And now, the next United States senator from New York, Bobby Kennedy." Again, the screams, Bobby waving and grinning, and the president and I applauding. "And now," said Mangano, the excitement cracking his voice, "the great man who leads us, the president of the United States."

The president spoke a few words, the usual back-of-the-car-standing-on-top-of-the-seat presidential words, and the crowd went mad. Then, Mangano got out and the car, with the three of us still standing, crept forward.

We navigated another few blocks and we stopped again. Another man got in the back seat, and someone, I forget who, probably the advance man, whispered to the president that we were going through a heavily Jewish district.

The president nodded to the advance man and then leaned down to speak to me. Ah, I thought, now the president is going to ask me my advice on the night's campaigning and I was ready to respond with wise counsel. Confidently I leaned toward the president and he said to me, "Okay, Jack, you can get out now."

Thus, my hour in the limelight, or rather the moonlight. With the noise and jubilation of a mass of very wise New Yorkers ringing in my ears, I returned to my comfortable spot in the rear of the motorcade. I used to think if I had been born in New York I might have made it to Washington on my own.

One of the oft-repeated charges by Republicans after the 1964 campaign was the presence and force of a sinister LBJ campaign group, operating in darkness and involved in all sorts of political skullduggery (during the Watergate scandals, this canard surfaced again, even more darkened by even more evil deeds).

The truth is that, on September 3, 1964, I wrote the president the following memorandum:

MR. PRESIDENT:

This is a thought for beefing up our work at the National Committee.

Mike Feldman is one of the brainiest men in the White House. He was one of the key men on Kennedy's 1960 campaign staff. One of the voids we have at the Democratic Committee is someone to take charge of the day to day refutations of the Goldwater-Miller charges—to organize on an effective basis an instant rebuttal to every accusation—to handle regional and state answers to Republican charges as well as on a national basis.

My suggestion is to put Mike Feldman fulltime at the Committee in charge of this aspect of the campaign. He would be responsible for the day to day refutation, as well as "truth squads" around the nation and would be a great help to us in the substantive issues of the campaign.

He is too valuable and too experienced not to be involved in the campaign in a responsible position.

Jack Valenti

The president wrote on the bottom of this memo: "This ok by me."

As a result, Mike Feldman became the foreman of a small group that met weekly to plot rebuttals to Goldwater charges and to steward our so-called truth squads organized to either precede or follow up on the candidate with refutations of the accusations he made. (In politics an "accusation" or "groundless charge" is something your opponent says about you, and "truth" or "facts" is something you say about him.)

Feldman and his committee did not go beyond this mandate for some very simple reasons: first, it was a fulltime job to construct an apparatus of rebuttal and travelling truth squads; second, we never really needed to go beyond this. The campaign was going so very well we might have mucked it up if we tried to get cute or skid too fast around the turns.

* * *

I was constantly alert to men of brains, energy, and judgment who could be brought into the Johnson administration. Almost every week the president would solicit, in conversation, any ideas I had about possible appointees. From the very beginning of my entry into the White

House staff, I was never far from thoughts about new people to run the government.

On November 19, 1964, I sent my first memorandum to the president on this subject:

November 10, 1964

FOR THE PRESIDENT
FROM: Jack Valenti
SUBJECT: Possible Appointees

1. Carl Sanders: Embodiment of the New South. Articulate, attractive, young. Only drawback is possible irritation of pro-Russell people—but it could be worked out so that Sanders does not oppose Senator Russell in 1966.

2. Lew Wasserman: President of Music Corporation of America. Independently wealthy. Ed Weisl called him "the best business brain I have ever known." Brilliant organizer and administrator. Tough, smart, full of common sense. Goes to heart of problems—practitioner of the art of the possible. A "can-do" man who could work miracles, if anyone could, as Secretary in a Department like HEW.

3. L. F. McCollum: Two years away from retirement as Chief Executive Officer of Continental Oil. For many years considered spokesman for the industry although his company is not the largest. Republican who voted for and supported LBJ. Not a good speaker, but exceptionally able administrator.

4. Gov. Harold Hughes: Rugged, handsome, with appeals that cut across party lines. Bi-partisan mid-west flavor. Secretary of Agriculture?

5. John Swainson: Friend of labor, popular with liberals. Wants to serve in some capacity in the government. Young, attractive; lost both legs in World War II.

6. John Connally: Could bring John in as Undersecretary of Defense or as head of CIA or as senior Assistant to the President. Thereby have benefit of his counsel as well as have him perform useful and valuable function. He could become the assistant President.

7. Thomas J. Watson
   John Loeb
   John Connor
   All three of these businessmen would be assets to the Administration.

8. Suggest Marty Underwood, who was one of our ablest advancemen as possible assistant to this congressional liaison section.

9. Lloyd Hand: Devoted to you and your purposes—loyal—has matured greatly in judgment and in focus. Excellent possibility for Director of Peace Corps. Only 36 years old—fits well into youthful image of the Peace Corps as the instrument of good around the world.

Most of these men, I am pleased to say, did receive a presidential importuning to join the administration. Both Lloyd Hand and John Connor did, the former as chief of protocol and the latter as secretary of commerce. I regretted deeply that Lew Wasserman declined because of his business responsibilities, as did Tom Watson and John Loeb.

The president was continually disturbed about the scarcity of ideas. His value of an assistant was measured in two precise and unvarying ways: how many ideas did he submit to the president, ideas that concerned lighting up new possibilities for doing old things better or devising new ways to do new things; and how sturdy was the judgment of the assistant when put to the test of an issue or problem.

He was amazingly open to anyone on his staff providing him with a new idea, something that had the glint of imagination in its substance and the potential for success in its implementation.

It was in this environment that I became fascinated with the prospect of the lifeline of Indochina, the erratic but durable Mekong River. George Woods—president of the

World Bank and one of the most influential world statesmen, though too few Americans ever heard of him— captivated me with the inexhaustible flow of projects that he generated through his ideas. It was Woods who prompted me to go to the president with the idea of fertilizer plants in India; plants to give them the chemistry to nourish and refurbish their land. It was also Woods who pushed the idea of a desalinization plant in the Middle East so that fresh water could transform uninhabitable desert into habitable land.* It was also Woods who ignited my imagination about the Mekong River.

On March 29, 1965, I wrote the president a brief memo. I did not go into specific detail, because I knew if

---

* I was the prime prodder for desalinization in the White House, persistently pushing the president with a flow of memoranda. My co-conspirator in this matter was Frank C. DiLuzio, who was then a key official in the Office of Saline Water in the Interior Department. Frank furnished me with piles of data and statistics and background material through which I sifted to draft my importunings to the president. Soon after I left the White House in mid-1966 to join the American film industry, the president called me to tell me he was going to give me an assignment. "I am going to appoint you head of a presidential desalinization commission to go to the Middle East and work out through negotiations a pact that both the Arabs and the Israelis will buy because it will be in their best interests to have a desalinization plant all those countries can use," the president told me. I said fine and I would await further instructions. About two months later I was summoned to the president's office. He looked tired and disconsolate. "I am not going to fight State any longer. Rusk and his people tell me you would not be the right choice to put in this job. Your leadership position in the movie industry will turn the Arabs against you and blunt your efforts, or at least that is what State has told me ten times now. So, let's shelve it for a while." I nodded, "I think they are all wrong, Mr. President. The very fact I served you in an intimate relationship would counter that apprehension."

The president shook his head wearily. "I know that, but I have too many problems not to take on the whole State Department and they feel pretty strongly about this." I said nothing more and that was the end of my chairmanship of the desalinization commission.

the idea was at all worthy the president would be sparked
in a few paragraphs.

March 29, 1965

REPORT TO THE PRESIDENT
FROM: Jack Valenti
SUBJECT: Lower Mekong Basin

Here are some simple facts about a massive and imaginative
project which could have untold benefits for that weary part
of the world.

1. *For seven years, Cambodia, Laos, Thailand and South Vietnam
   have been working on this huge development*—with little publicity and little disagreement.

   Diplomatic relations may be strained, and hostile moments
   may occur, but when all else is shut down the Lower
   Mekong project keeps going.

2. The Basin below the Burmese and Chinese borders includes virtually all of Cambodia and Laos, the Korat Pla-
   teau in Thailand and the Delta and SW portion of SVN.

   Half the population (20 million) of these countries live in the area.

3. More than $14 million has been spent to date—involving
   20 other nations and eleven international agencies.

   Chief supervisor: United National Economic Commission
   for Asia and the Far East began the project in 1957.

4. *The work:* gauge streams, explore dam sites, chart soils,
   study farming and all the other tasks needed to be done to
   design a program of managing water and land for the wel-
   fare of 20 million people, mostly rice farmers.

5. U.S. involvement: *Less than the cost of four days of military aid
   in South Vietnam, reported to exceed $1.5 million per day.*

6. *The planning so far:* Centers on improvement of agriculture
   to supply water for irrigation of a second crop in the dry
   season and by preventing drought loss. Massive opportu-
   nities to increase output of rice and to diversify crops in
   the Delta, around the Grand Lake in Cambodia and in the
   alluvial valleys upstream. Hydro-electric power plants on

the tributaries would provide cheap power. But this needs development of industrial complexes. The Japanese are very interested.

7. *What is needed:* Heavier investments are needed—and more security.

Needs of growing population need to be met and the raising of the level of living above present per capita rate of $60–$100. The big main-stem projects will take time (projects the size of Hoover Dam are on the drawing boards). *But expenditures of $100–$200 million per year may not be unreasonable over the next 20 years.* Much of this would be on village improvement schemes that benefit farmers directly and promptly. *The Mekong countries ought to have a central financial agency to receive and supervise the money.* Possible that the International Bank for Reconstruction and Development might play this role—or some agency of the UN. But the commitment to finance a long-term program would be the best display of good faith by the donors to support this kind of growth in this area.

The North Vietnamese and the Chinese have raised no objections. They know already what this kind of giant dam-building and river-controlling can do.

Moreover, none of the important field work has been halted by the guerrillas.

8. *Prime benefit from the Mekong:* It could be the one focus to which all the nations, including the North Vietnamese could be drawn. Its value would be so enormous and the potential so vast, it could possibly become the central task of the entire area, and the one project which could divert them from war and subversion.

Within an hour after reading this memo, the president called me to his side, questioning me about it. He had written on the top portion: "Get this to Goodwin this A.M." (Goodwin was preparing the first draft of an important foreign policy speech scheduled for Johns Hopkins University.) His face was alive with interest, I knew the signs well—he had leaped onto the idea of the Mekong as a linchpin on which could revolve the post-war efforts of both North and South Vietnam.

Within another hour he was on the phone exploring the idea further with Dean Rusk and Bob McNamara. He talked to Eugene Black, former head of the World Bank, an establishment figure who had been in the forefront of other vast and difficult-to-organize enterprises for other presidents. Before the day was ended, the president had inserted this in his speech before Johns Hopkins University as the set-piece for his announcement of a towering peace effort.

When he stood on the rostrum in Baltimore—on April 7, 1965—this is part of what he had to say:

A COOPERATIVE EFFORT
FOR DEVELOPMENT

These countries of Southeast Asia are not simply pawns on some giant chessboard. They are homes for millions of impoverished people. Each day these people rise at dawn and struggle through until the night to wrestle existence from the soil. They are often wracked by diseases, plagued by hunger, and death comes at the early age of 40.

Stability and peace do not come easily in such a land. Neither independence nor human dignity will ever be won by arms alone. It also requires the works of peace. The American people have helped generously in times past in these works. Now there must be a much more massive effort to improve the life of man in that conflict-torn corner of the world.

The first step is for the countries of Southeast Asia to associate themselves in a greatly expanded cooperative effort for development. We would hope that North Vietnam would take its place in the common effort just as soon as peaceful cooperation is possible.

The United Nations is already actively engaged in development in this area. As far back as 1961 I conferred with authorities in Vietnam in connection with their work there. And I would hope that the Secretary General of the United Nations could use the prestige of his great office, and his deep knowledge of Asia, to initiate, as soon as possible, with the countries of that area, a plan for cooperation in increased development.

For our part I will ask the Congress to join in a billion dollar American investment in this effort as soon as it is underway.

And I would hope that all other industrialized countries, including the Soviet Union, will join in this effort to replace despair with hope, and terror with progress. . . .

The task is nothing less than to enrich the hopes and existence of more than a hundred million people. And there is much to be done.

The vast Mekong River can provide food and water and power on a scale to dwarf even our own TVA. . . .

*   *   *

I was often amused and always impressed, with the president's constant exertions to find new ways to do old things better. There was, for example, the matter of foreign ambassadors—how to best utilize presidential time to see them and talk to them. It is quite possible for an ambassador from a small power never to speak with the president except when he offers his credentials (a brief, fleeting moment at best) and at no other time.

The president wanted to change this. One morning he abruptly turned to me: "Put your mind to work. Figure out how we can talk to ambassadors without it being a long line of them waiting to see me, or having more big receptions."

I immediately sat down with Lloyd Hand, chief of protocol. Lloyd was, and is, a man of splendid charm and intelligence. He was never happier than when confronting a challenge, and this was a beauty. He relished the prospect of helping to devise new rapport between the president and foreign envoys.

Together we brought the president a suggestion—a simple suggestion. Hand and Valenti, as hosts, would invite five or six (no more) ambassadors to lunch in the Fish Room in the White House (that room, so called from the FDR days through the LBJ administration because of a large sailfish mounted on the wall, has now been renamed the Roosevelt Room, after the Republican Roosevelt, naturally). Understand, that for an ambassador to be invited to lunch at the White House is an enticement of substantial heft. This invitation would give for the first time up to 95 percent of the envoys an opportunity to break bread in the president's office quarters. It would be an invitation they would take seriously, very seriously.

Ambassador Hand, as part of our plan, would provide me with detailed memoranda on all the ambassadors to be represented at each specific lunch, what problems their country was experiencing, what issues individual envoys would be interested in discussing, and so forth. I would capsule all this and put it into a briefing paper for the president.

We would set a handsome table in the Fish Room (just adjoining my office, and a few steps from the president's Oval Office). Sometimes we would invite the assistant secretary in charge of a specific geographical territory if the ambassadors came from that area. Ambassador Hand would greet the envoys at the Diplomatic Reception Room at the South Grounds entrance to the Mansion and escort them to the Fish Room. After the main course, with Hand and Valenti asking questions about their countries, seeking their opinion about what potential there was for programs they were endorsing, the coffee and dessert would arrive. At this point, I would signal my secretary, who then alerted the president's office. Some minutes later the president would appear.

For forty-five minutes to an hour the president would answer questions. Often he would brief them on issues of the moment or recount for them the meetings he had just been involved in if what had been discussed had a bearing on the countries at the luncheon.

In the intimacy of the luncheon table, these ambassadors had the opportunity, unique to them, to speak directly to the president of the United States on any subject of their choosing. None of them, with rare exceptions, had had any such experience before—therefore you may be certain this encounter was a welcome one to every envoy present.

I suspect the coded cables burned the air at each of these embassies as the reports of this unusual meeting flew from chancery to chancellory all over the world.

That these sessions were a smash hit in the foreign community in Washington was obvious. LBJ also found them extraordinarily interesting. He enjoyed them, as well as savoring the thrifty way his own time was being used, yet with substantial results readily apparent.

At the time of my resignation from the White House, we had luncheons for a total of some sixty ambassadors, about half of the foreign diplomatic community.

* * *

In November 1965, the president began to turn his mind toward some dramatic move which would loosen the grip of indecision in Vietnam. Hanoi was seemingly impervious to all entreaties by the president. He brooded about this, convinced that if the war could be brought to a conference table, with the fighting either stopped or greatly diminished, there would be a chance to find some solution. He hungered for peace talks, and they eluded him because the other side, obviously, believed it was to their advantage not to talk. So he probed and searched for some special means. It was during this period of reflection that the idea of a long, sustained bombing pause began to surface.

On December 17, 1965, the president was to light the huge Christmas tree on the Ellipse, just across Executive Avenue from the White House. This annual festive occasion could be, the president thought, a good occasion to announce some new initiative. Prime Minister Harold Wilson of Great Britain was to sit with the president on the rostrum on that occasion.

The president asked George Ball, Mac Bundy, Bill Moyers, and me to sit down and privately thrash out the bombing pause idea, pro and con, and see if we had agreement on one, the pause itself, and two, if it could fit within his speech on the seventeenth.

On Tuesday, December 14, 1965, the four of us met for several hours. As soon as the meeting broke up, I wrote the following memorandum to the president:

December 14, 1965
7:15 P.M. Tuesday

TOP SECRET—EYES ONLY

MR. PRESIDENT:

I sat with Bundy, Ball and Moyers in discussing your Friday night speech—and the possibility of a pause or a cease-fire.

Ball was for a pause. Bundy leaned the other way. I side with Ball.

I favor the pause for the following reasons:

1. We are in quicksand. The war is going to be hard and bitter and bloody days are ahead. The longer the war goes the deeper goes the bitterness and higher go the walls of hate. Thus, we need to do all we can NOW to end the fighting before we are in so deep we can never get out.

2. As long as the bombing in the North continues, it seems only to harden the will of Hanoi. Though the military disputes this, they have no solid alternatives to offer, only more and harder fighting.

3. Once we pause, it gives the Soviets more flexibility. I asked Ball how Ambassador Thompson felt about this. Thompson feels with certainty a pause would be received with relief and hope in Moscow. Thus, the Russians would be extricated from the painted corner they've been in and possibly may move toward helping in a settlement.

4. However long we pause in the North, we pursue the fighting with vigor in the South. The claim our boys would be murdered because of the pause would bear little weight. Moreover, the military knows that the war, if it is to be won, must be won in the South. Also, isn't it possible to use the latest methods to interdict the supply lines from the North into the South, and from Laos into the South.

5. We always have an option to begin the bombing again if after an appropriate pause we have had absolutely no peep of a response from Hanoi.

6. A pause would take some heat off the Chinese—and possibly deter them from moving in greater weight to Hanoi. Moreover, it would give Hanoi less dependency on the Chinese, and thereby allow the North more freedom of negotiating movement.

7. It would relieve, though to be practical only for a short time, the wails from the left. They will no doubt find ample reason to denounce us again, but the fact is their spear will have been blunted a bit.

8. It would allow third countries, both friends and neutrals, more breathing room, and possibly edge the thrust of world opinion in a direction more congenial to us.

9. But, above everything and all else, the largest logic for a pause is simply that it is the best alternative we have now to an endless, bloody war where there is no light in the tunnel.

10. Our biggest hurdle will come from Republican and hard-liners who are urging the blockade and quarantine of Haiphong. There is logic here, as Bundy pointed out, and we'll have to find some sound reason for not doing it—though if the pause is ineffective after a time, it is always there for us to do.

Simply stated, sir, the pause doesn't disallow us any later alternatives for a harder push. But it would give us an opportunity for possible talks. And the hope is worth the try.

Jack Valenti

TOP SECRET—EYES ONLY

The president talked to me about the memorandum. He grilled me for over an hour to see how firm my own recommendation was.

At 9:15 A.M. on the morning of December 17, LBJ ordered a meeting in the Cabinet Room. The president, Rusk, McNamara, Ball, Bundy, and I were present. Prime Minister Wilson was in Washington on this day and the first part of the meeting concerned a summary of talks with Wilson, and his attitude toward Vietnam. After a lengthy discussion of Wilson, as well as the United Nations, the president spoke.

"The Vietcong atrocities never get publicized. Nothing is really ever written to let the American people know of the VC tortures and killings, nothing to make you hate them. Everything that is being written is done to make the world hate us," he said.

"There is something of a racial element in what we do to the North, but it is not there when the North hits the South," Ball said.

The president nodded. "They do such a better propaganda job than we do. On NBC today it was all about what we are doing wrong. We must find a way to construct another Baltimore speech, not a desperate speech, but an appropriate one.* Harold Wilson told me his line has been steady since my Baltimore speech. Wilson is telling his opposition to bring the VC to the conference table and he will produce the president."

Here the president clasped and unclasped his huge hands. He leaned forward. "I am willing to take any gamble on stopping the bombing if I think I have some hope of something happening that is good. We must evaluate this very carefully. You have no idea how much I have talked to Fulbright and Lippmann and their followers. They are not coming aboard, but we must listen to what they are saying."

"Mr. President, we will increase bombing. It is inevitable. We must step up our attacks," McNamara said.

The president pulled out of his jacket pocket a folded piece of paper. It was an editorial in the *Saturday Review* by Norman Cousins. The president read aloud portions of the editorial which cited reasons why the U.S. must take initiatives in finding peace, and the failure of bombing.

Ball interposed, "I am holding a heretical view in Washington, but I think the bombings in the North are having a negative effect. If we look hard at bombing in North Vietnam it is not producing a salutary effect. We started bombing one, to raise morale; two, to interdict supplies; and three, to get Hanoi to change its mind.

"The first is not needed anymore. Bombing hasn't served the other two reasons. We can restrict supplies only to a critical level, no lower. Obviously we are not breaking the will of the North. They are digging in, taking a hardening line. I was in charge of bombing surveys in

---

* Here the president was referring to one of his most important public statements, "Peace Without Conquest," given at Johns Hopkins University, April 7, 1965, in which the president called for massive and compassionate peaceful reconstruction of Indochina.

World War II and bombing never wins a war. We are driving North Vietnam into a greater dependency on China and we are boxing in the Soviets.

"We are also making plans for negotiation much more difficult. I think the risks of escalation are great, and the risk is in the North, not the South. The one hope we have is to stop the bombing and seize every opportunity not to resume. Meanwhile conduct the war in the South with redoubled effort."

The president sat back in his chair, listening intently to every word from Ball. He snapped to attention as Ball finished.

"That has great appeal to me," the president said. He looked troubled. "The big problem is the chiefs. They go through the roof when we mention the pause."

McNamara set his jaw sternly. "I can take on the chiefs," he said.

"Can we sell the American people on the merits of stopping the bombing?" the president asked.

"The Navy and the Air Force are conducting 3,000 sorties in the North," McNamara said. "There is no way to stop the bombing in the North except as a part of a political move."

Rusk spoke next. "On George Ball's remarks, I don't think the bombing has caused the North to escalate. They are determined to do so, regardless of bombing. We tell the Russians, you ask us to pause, and we pause, now what will you do for us?"

"You really need several of these moves. We have one pause, we need more," McNamara said.

"I have no objection to stopping the bombing. What are the objections?" the president asked.

Rusk joined in with: "The Russians need more time to get something on with the Chinese."

"If the press asks why we are not bombing in the

North, we answer that we are increasing our effort in Laos and the South," McNamara said.

"Only 40 percent of our missions are going now. Let us concentrate on the South," Ball said.

"Should we not have someone moving throughout the world," queried the president, "trying for peace with other countries?"

There was not a quick answer to this, and the president seemed to be in deep, solemn thought. He stared momentarily into space, and then asked, turning to McNamara, "Is this something you want to explore with the chiefs?"

McNamara answered, "No sir. I need to know what you want. The chiefs will be totally opposed. We will decide what we want and impose it on them. They see this as total military problem. Nothing will change their view. They will answer we are better off now with bombing than we were without it. I know exactly what arguments the chiefs will use. Before you decide, I cannot deliver. After you decide, I can deliver."

"Why don't we work on specific suggestions and get back to the president later?" Rusk asked.

The president broke in, saying, "If we were to decide for a pause, I am opposed to announcements of a pause. We can pick weather as an excuse and Christmas as a factor. But we must try to sell our enemy that we want peace. We owe this to the American people. Now, we can't do this if we are dropping bombs on the enemy, as we did when Kosygin was in Hanoi, dammit. Anything with bombs is bad for our peace effort. Let us put off bombing until we can talk to others."

The president turned to McNamara. "Bob can say to the chiefs that we have a heavy budget, and the possibility of a tax bill, controls on the economy, the danger of inflation, the killing of the Great Society. Therefore we need to make sure diplomats talk before the roof falls in on us in

Congress and the diplomats tell us they can't talk with bombs dropping.

"They are right. The weakest chink in our armor is American public opinion. Our people won't stand firm in the face of heavy losses, and they can bring down the government."

Then the president said something very prescient: "We are going to suffer big political losses, every president does in off-years, but ours will be bigger."

He talked bitterly of liberals who constantly sniped at him, and he lauded James Webb, the NASA administrator, and Secretary of Agriculture Orville Freeman as two high officials who were making valiant efforts to reduce their budgets.

The decision was well nigh made now, almost locked in, but the president, ever cautious, always eager to be fed additional viewpoints, more information, said, "Let us meet again tomorrow and inspect what we have said today."

We all stood up as the president left the room. The others left by the corridor door of the Cabinet Room. I trailed the president into his office. He sat wearily in his chair. I stood beside the presidential desk. He looked up at me. "What did you think?"

"I think you are on your way to the right decision, Mr. President. So long as we bomb we will never get the North to a conference table. We just don't know enough about the Vietnamese mentality. What may seem logical to westerners is possibly twisted and distorted to them. What seems right to us may not seem right to them at all."

He nodded. "You are right. Every night I try to put myself in the shoes of Ho Chi Minh. I try to think what he is thinking. I try to feel what he is feeling. It's not easy, because I don't know him. I don't know him or his ancestry or his customs or his beliefs. It is tough, very tough." He leaned back in the chair, staring up at the ceiling.

Murmuring, almost to himself, he said, "God, we have got to find a way to end this war, we've got to find a way. We must keep trying." Then he swiveled the chair around to face me squarely. "Set the meeting tomorrow at midday. Ask Abe Fortas and Clark Clifford to sit in. And have Alex Johnson there. Keep it small, no others." I nodded to him and when he put his attention to the papers in front of him, I quietly left and went to my office to prepare for tomorrow's session.

At 12:35 P.M., on December 18, 1965, in the Cabinet Room, the president, Rusk, McNamara, Bundy, Ball, Johnson, Fortas, Clifford, and I gathered to begin the discussion. In front of each man was a summary of the discussion of the previous day and the possibility of the bombing pause was laid out.

The president opened the discussion. "Guard these papers we are reading. We simply cannot allow this information to get out. I had a conversation with the chairman of the joint chiefs and I can understand what McNamara is going through. The chairman gave me reasons why the chiefs are against a cease-fire and bombing pause. It would make it impossible for them to attack. The military says a month's pause would undo all that we have done."

McNamara spoke rather sharply. "That's baloney," he said, "and I can prove it."

The president answered in that curious way he had of always probing strong statements by any aides. He was endlessly suspicious of flat declarations of fact on subjects that denied tangible proof. He said to McNamara, "I don't think so. I think it contains serious military risks. It is inaccurate to say that suspension of the bombing carries no military risk."

Rusk seemed to agree. "I don't believe the suspension will last to January 22 unless we are well on our way to peace," he said.

The president nodded. "I agree. It could be short duration."

Bundy spoke. "It would be better to start the pause the twenty-third or the twenty-fourth."

McNamara shook his head. "It will leak if we give Lodge longer than the twenty-third. I would start it Wednesday, the twenty-second."

"What does Max Taylor think? How would he vote?" the president asked.

"On balance, he would say no. But he would vote with the president," McNamara said.

Bundy interrupted. "This is not what he considers his arena."

"Max thinks the military program and pacification is going better than it is," McNamara added.

The president was silent a moment and then said, "Incidentally, do we want a personal state of the union message? Clark (speaking to Clifford), I want you to think about this. My inclination is not to speak in person. We wrote an eight-year program in our first state of the union message. We've got all of it in the first year. John McCormack thinks personal delivery of the speech will help elect some congressmen. I don't agree."

Clark Clifford now spoke up. In a town filled with legends, Clark Clifford held his own. He was tall, still strikingly handsome, with a face cast by some skilled sculptor. He wore—no matter what the fashion or fad—the same carefully, expensively tailored double-breasted suits with wide lapels and wide, boxed shoulders. No matter how passionate the discussion or how crucial the issue, Clifford always spoke slowly, as if each word was being minted specially for that occasion. His voice was sepulchral, his words unhurried, precise. One had the feeling that one was listening to dogma lately sprung from a prophet's deeds, and even the most confident foes hesitated, that bare second or two, before taking on Clifford. He *had* to be right, because he *sounded* so right. He had a habit of holding his hands in front of him, palms facing, fingertips pressed against each other, the two graceful hands forming a billowed tent. I never failed to be impressed with Clark, for I was sure that behind the carefully architectured words there was also some master builder at work in that mind of his, measuring, making sure that what was being constructed was stout and accurate. In all my contacts with Clifford I never saw him once ruffled or confused. In almost any crisis, Clifford, brow unfurrowed, would carefully dissect the action alternatives with neither haste nor anxiety.

Clifford is that *rara avis*, the durable public man who privately advises presidents (Truman, Kennedy, Johnson) and whose durability is measured by the wisdom of his counsel, whose principal worth, it seems to me, is the objective and intellectual coin which he offers, coin which is rarely subject to devaluation.

"I think it would be a serious error if you didn't go in person. Last year you laid out a domestic program. This time you report on the shape of the program. I think after your illness, your failure to appear would be injurious to world leadership. To break a long-standing custom would be serious," Clifford said.

"If we were at peace in Vietnam it might be alright, but not right now," Rusk concurred.

The president addressed Rusk. "Dean, tell me what you sense in what Clifford says." Now the president turned his attention again to the position paper on the bombing pause. He looked at his associates and said, "It rankles me that we have to prove again to the Congress that we are striving for peace. We've done it again and again."

The president addressed Rusk, "Dean, tell me what you think will be achieved by execution of this recommendation of a pause?"

The secretary of state replied, "First, there is the underlying question of the American people. They are probably isolationist at heart. I am convinced the people will do what has to be done in a war situation if they are convinced there is no sane alternative. You must think about the morale of the American people if the other side keeps pushing. We must be able to say that all has been done."

The president frowned. "Haven't we said this and done this before?"

"To my satisfaction, yes, but perhaps not to the satisfaction of the American people," Rusk answered. "Second, it's our deepest national purpose to achieve that purpose by peace and not by war. If there is one chance in ten or twenty that a step of this kind could lead to settlement on the Geneva Agreements and the Seventeenth Parallel, then we ought to do it. One chance in twenty is my guess. We must try to create a heavy obligation on the Russians' part to settle. If we pause, they will owe us something. The Russians, the Yugoslavs, and the Hungarians have all pressed this with me. Of course, there is the possibility of deception. If there is a chance that Russia would take advantage of the suspension to start a movement toward peace, it is good. If it fails . . ." here his voice trailed off.

"I am influenced," continued Rusk, "by the fact that Russia and the Iron Curtain countries acted in the Indo-Pak crisis.

"Also, the Russians don't want China's policy to win. They don't want a confrontation with the U.S. over Southeast Asia. If it moves to the U.S. and China directly engaged, they have deadly problems. This worries them. One minor point. We must make sure that the world knows the U.S. is not an obstacle to peace. Those who support us will find it easier to support us."

"Then you believe from a propaganda point there is a long shot chance that one, the Russians will owe us something; and two, it will give our supporters further reason to support us?" the president asked.

Rusk nodded. "There is the possibility of a trap, by prolonging the pause into a unilateral peace."

"Do we eliminate this by keeping the pause on an indefinite time limit?" the president queried.

Rusk nodded again. "Right. Another concern is the pause that fails."

The president turned to McNamara. "Bob?"

McNamara replied, "The Soviets have not applied all the pressure they could."

The president asked, "Have they applied any pressure?"

"Yes," answered Rusk. "During the first pause they said they didn't have time."

McNamara said, "My point is I don't think they have made all the effort they are capable of."

The president asked, "How do we know that, have you talked to the Russians?"

"No, no contacts. This comes from State. The pause may give us some leverage on them. It would stop them from any precipitous action. I think there is some movement from DRV (Democratic Republic of Vietnam). We really don't understand the DRV reactions. We don't really know. We are out of communication. There is danger because of that. There is a chance the pause will help them move toward us," McNamara answered.

"What does Thompson (ambassador to the Soviet Union) say about the Russians?" the president asked.

George Ball broke in here. "It would relieve them of intense pressure to respond to our actions. There is more danger of a Russian response than a Chinese response. We must not push them into a corner."

The president was interrupted by a buzz from his secretary. He spoke in muffled tones into the phone, and then left the room, saying he had a phone call he must take. He was back in his chair in ten minutes.

McNamara was speaking. "The Soviets have not applied all the pressure they are capable of applying. This action on our part would stop the Russians from responding forcefully to our attacks. The North might then make some favorable movement. We don't know enough of their reactions to judge. The suspension of the bombing would, in my view, widen the gap between the Chinese and the Soviets. Moreover there is a strong feeling on the part of the American people that our efforts toward peace have been superficial and inadequate. The military solution to the problem is not certain, one out of three or one in two. Ultimately we must find alternative solutions. We must perforce find a diplomatic solution."

"What you are saying is that no matter what we do militarily there is no sure victory," the president said.

"That's right," McNamara said. "We have been too optimistic. One chance in three or two in three is my estimate. What I am saying is we may not find military solutions. We need to explore other means. It is impossible to negotiate on uneven terms. Our military action approach is an unacceptable way to a successful conclusion."

Bundy spoke up. "I am for the pause. I share Bob McNamara's view that settlement must be a political one. This will be in the form of a diplomatic initiative."

"I am not in a position to quote General Wheeler on the pause, pro or con," the president said. "He is a soldier and he will follow his commander in chief. I don't think his views are emotional at all. He is loyal to McNamara and to me, but he does have his convictions. He did point up his views to me, rather systematically."

"Whatever decision you make, Wheeler will follow," McNamara said.

The president turned to Abe Fortas. "Let me hear your views, Abe."

Abe Fortas sat very quietly. He had come to the capital a young lawyer, caught up in the frenzy and the dazzle of the FDR revolution. He quickly rose to the sight and confidence of President Roosevelt. He is deeply read in many fields, and culturally was probably the most aware of FDR's aides and of the LBJ counselors. He is an accomplished violinist, is comfortable and at ease with the best musicians of the era. In all their long years of association, President Johnson reached out for him and his counsel automatically, whenever a crisis or problem arose. He is soft-spoken, charming, erudite, warm, and companionable; a gentle man and yet there are those times when he can turn to ice and steel. But invariably, when a problem is brought to him he gives off the sure impression that he has taken the weight from your shoulders and put it on his. It would be my judgment that if the president could have only called on a few men to give him advice, one he would instinctively turn to would have been Abe Fortas. As he did now.

Fortas answered the president. "I would divide the problem into two parts. One, the military effects of the pause. Two, the psychological and political aspects.

"First, then, the political effects on the country. The case is not proven. I believe this action will be good, if it results in some kind of conference or cessation of hostilities.

"I think the public reaction will be negative, showing uncertainty. I always think there is the possibility of error in assessing public opinion. What they really want is cessation of fighting. Not very much point in responding to manifestation of public opinion that says 'you are not doing enough.'

"Any time there is evidence of a lack of certainty on the part of the government, it leads to negative thinking in the public mind. It will cause people to worry about depth of conviction in the government's objective. Thus, there is a negative net balance. But the real question, on whether this action should be taken, is whether this action results in actual accomplishment.

"As I understand, this action will not be done with pre-arrangement with the Russians. This is an action which is ambivalent and ambiguous. We use the Christmas season and by that fact and presentation, we are diluting the effort in its hoped-for psychological and political results. Also, we are diluting its effect on the Russians, and any bringing about of peace negotiations.

"I am concerned as to what happens if this fails. If we fail, we don't get credit for it. There will be renewed pressure for drastic action. We will have obstacles to negotiations because of the failure of a major and spectacular effort."

The president asked Fortas, "What do you think would be the value?"

Fortas replied, "If we could do this by pre-arrangement with the Russians. If we would say to the Russians, 'if we would favorably consider a pause, would this give you an opportunity to get the VC to the conference table?' "

"We have already done this with the Russians," the president said.

"We don't think we can put them in a corner. The paper to the Russians is drafted carefully to go as far as we can with them," Bundy said.

"We have tried to engage the Russians in the VN (Vietnam) settlement. But Moscow can't deliver Hanoi," said Rusk.

Fortas replied, "This venture depends on the Russians using our actions for some useful purpose with the North Vietnamese. All I do is raise the question as to whether we have an adequate reason for resumption."

Ball spoke up. "This assumption is not based on one

conversation, but on a number of them. Very often the means used by Communists is not direct. Also this assumption is based on direct conversation with the Soviets. If we paused, the Soviets tell us they will do the best they can, and this is based on twenty-plus conversations."

"There is danger that Hanoi would greet the pause as visible evidence that the protests in this country have had an effect on the government," Fortas said.

"What offsets that is heavy deployment in the South," replied Ball.

Alexis Johnson now spoke. "We can't have it said by Hanoi and China that Russia is conspiring with the U.S."

Now it was Clark Clifford's turn. He had sat quietly throughout the previous discussion. Now he spoke. "The arguments of the pause are well presented. Even if I accepted them, I still feel deep concern over this move.

"One, I have tried to figure out the circumstances under which Hanoi would talk. It is only their belief that they are not going to win the war in the South. I don't believe they are at that stage now. I think they believe they are *not* losing. They are sending large numbers of men down. They have the example of the French before them. They believe that ultimately the U.S. will tire of this and go home and the North will prevail. Until they know they are not going to win, they will not talk and the Russians cannot convince them.

"Two, I believe the president and the government have talked enough about peace. I don't believe any more talk will do any good. Any objective citizen knows the government position. Talk of peace is interpreted in Hanoi as a sign of weakness. This pause would encourage North Vietnam. They will take this to be a step backward, in response to U.S. protest opinion and world opinion. Anything that hinders the North from figuring they can't win, hinders the close of the war.

"Three, when the time comes to resume bombing, and it will resume because chances are only one in twenty or more, those who want peace at any price, who want us to get out, will demand that we not resume. They will urge enough fluid events to happen to encourage the pause to go on.

"Four, if you accept the hypothesis that there is no chance of success, others will know it too, and I don't like the president to take a posture that is clearly unproductive. It might end up being viewed as a gimmick. Timing during the Christmas holidays is inopportune.

"Fifth, I don't believe Vietnam is going to be settled publicly. Humphrey's and Harriman's trips will not settle anything. Only when Hanoi feels there is nothing to be gained by further fighting is the war going to end.

"Sixth, if the Soviets believe it is to their best interest to take favorable steps, they can do it any time. Simply because bombing is going on will not stop them from intervening.

"Seventh, time might come when the pause would be valuable. If we thought there was a chance of it being successful, then and only then would I do it."

Ball said, "I think we make a mistake in feeling Hanoi has freedom of action. They can no more give up this war alone than we could let Saigon fall. It's what the Communist powers believe is the right course. The bombing immobilizes China and the USSR."

"Should we pursue the military estimate of a fifty-fifty chance of victory, or what should we do?" McNamara asked.

"In carrying the political battle I need something more than we have at the present time. We need to make it clear that the U.S. is honorable and has been given no alternative. We strengthen our position by proving we want peace," said Rusk.

Fortas replied, "It seems to me that we have already made your case for peace. Perhaps it looks different on the inside than it does on the outside."

McNamara now pursued a different line of reasoning. "If we put in 400,000 men what will they do? They will match us. We are going to be bombing assets of North Vietnam dearer to them than the ones we are now bombing. China is beginning to ready planes to meet us in the skies. It appears that MIGs are being introduced in the North. They are getting ready for escalation and will call on Russia. They don't want to confront us in Vietnam. They want a way out."

"The way we are doing it is too little to get the Soviets to do anything," Fortas said.

"But North Vietnam would know a diplomatic offensive is going on on behalf of the Russians," Ball said. "If the North says no to the Soviets they (the Soviets) have a way out when the North calls on them for arms and men."

"Have we any other diplomatic moves we can make, any approaches with any other government?" the president asked.

Thus, the president showed again his probing instincts. It was clear to everyone around the table that the president was searching, almost hungrily, for some means to get the North Vietnamese talking. There was silence around the table.

Then Rusk spoke. "We could take it to the Security Council, if Russia wouldn't veto, and ask the secretary general to go to Hanoi. We could press the Hungarian channel pretty hard. They are in touch with Moscow. I worry about bringing this to the General Assembly in view of the Rhodesian question. We could continue these discussions of which we have had a lot."

"We have just about exhausted third party contacts based on what we have given them about our position," Ball said.

The president frowned. "But the VC haven't done any-thing."

Bundy broke in with a laugh. "If we had a newspaper in Hanoi not under their control we could do more." The president smiled at this.

"One of the pitfalls is that a new situation can always turn out different," Rusk said. "For example, lifting of the Berlin blockade came as a surprise. In the Pusan penin-sula, we thought we couldn't hang and we did. I have a feeling that the other side is not that tough, and it does not follow that in a year or two we won't be in far more favor-able a position than we are now. I think the other side is hurting just as we are hurting."

Clifford spoke up. "We could make quite a case that our stand is producing good results by preventing the VC from achieving their objective. Perhaps we can connect beneficial events in Indonesia with our presence in Viet-nam. At least we are preventing a Communist takeover in Vietnam and that is to your credit, Mr. President."

The president turned to McNamara. "What do you think we should do if we don't have a bombing pause, Bob?"

McNamara replied to the president's question. "As a minimum, carry on a military buildup. We should study the possibility of a cease-fire which I would recommend in a few months, or a military standstill."

The president asked, "Is there any solid information of an increasing of NVN (North Vietnam) activities?"

"They have stepped up infiltration to about 1,500 a month through Laos, and this will soon probably be up to 4,000 a month. This has not been proved, however. About a year ago, they began bringing up regular troops instead of cadres. About nine regiments of regulars are there. They have substantially expanded facilities," McNamara answered.

The president asked Johnson, "Alex, do you have any

strong views? If you were president what would you do?"

Alex replied, "I'd take the pause, if for no other reason than to engage the Russians."

"Can't we engage them by saying we are ready to stop if the VC are ready?" the president queried.

"No, sir, I don't think we can without bombing."

The president leaned back in his chair. "What troubles me more is their doubt as to our will to see this thing through. What problems do we get into if we don't bomb during Christmas, and tell the Russians we are willing to go farther? You say the Russians won't and can't do any more unless we stop bombing, and yet, they probably won't do anything."

The president sighed and stood up, stretching himself to his full height. He looked solemnly at the men around the table. Then he casually addressed McNamara. "We'll take the pause." With a slight wave of his hand, he strode from the room.

The bombing pause began. But as the president dismally feared, nothing came of it. The war continued.

* * *

I continued to bombard the president with memos about Vietnam.

One memorandum which I flung at him did strike some fire for he seized on one suggestion, a Honolulu conference, and within hours began to give it shape. The memorandum was as follows:

January 22, 1966
3:50 P.M. Saturday

MEMORANDUM FOR THE PRESIDENT

I think that your statement of today makes it all the more important to begin immediately on one peace move right after another. Meanwhile, at the same time, we keep up our military pressure.

Here are some suggestions about peace initiatives:

1. You write a letter to the Pope in which you thank him for his efforts and suggest your readiness to dispatch Goldberg or someone else to the Vatican to discuss with the Pope his idea about non-aligned nations taking an active role in peace-making efforts.

2. Brief the members of the House and Senate in small sessions as you did in the early days of your Presidency. As Senator Clinton P. Anderson told me, there are many Senators and Congressmen who have not had the opportunity to hear the briefings of Secretaries Rusk and McNamara.

3. Begin almost immediately the series of task forces on-the-scene in Vietnam—Secretary Freeman and agricultural experts—Dr. Hornig and health experts—Secretary Gardner and education experts—some well-known U.S. Mayor and public administration experts. As I outlined in an earlier memorandum, these task forces could go into Vietnam at two-week intervals to do substantive studies of how to increase the civil effectiveness of South Vietnam.

4. Have Walt Rostow gather a group of political scientists like James McGregor Burns, Dick Neustadt, and others to develop a viable political party system in Vietnam.

5. The President travel to Honolulu and meet with General Westmoreland and Prime Minister Ky. Here the President could get first-hand information on the military campaign. But most important, the President could appear with Prime Minister Ky and stress the political, economic, and social future of South Vietnam once the fighting has stopped. Perhaps economic news could be announced here—some specifics on the Mekong River project—housing projects—land reform—such a meeting could serve as a focal point for showing how bright the future for South Vietnam could be—and indeed a future for all of Southeast Asia.

Moreover, it would be very helpful for the world to see the cordial relations between Ky and the President and their combined faith in the kind of world that can be built without fighting in South Vietnam.

6. Why can't the President write a personal letter to the heads of governments all over the world telling them why we are in Vietnam, what we hoped for in Vietnam and how the fighting can be stopped in Vietnam?

These are some ideas which may or may not be worthwhile.

Jack Valenti

While we were preparing the agenda and the schedule for the Honolulu Conference, the president talked to Vice-President Humphrey and suggested that the vice-president, Governor Harriman, and I continue on from Honolulu, taking General Ky and his entourage back to Vietnam and then proceeding on to a nine-nation Asian tour. He wanted Humphrey to talk firsthand to the leaders of the Asian world, to brief them on our Vietnam aims and to extract from them their views about their own involvement and their commitment to the cause that was in their interest and to which we were devoting so much money, men, and blood.

A month before the president's state of the union speech to be delivered in January, 1966, I pondered the problems we faced and what possible alternatives were available to us.

I talked at length to Mac Bundy, Walt Rostow, and George Woods, president of the World Bank; and I spent several late evenings trying to sort out my own thoughts so I could put them on paper for the president to consider. I was particularly keen on a program of fertilizer plants for India, suggested to me by George Woods, as well as a carefully planned venture in desalinization. I was also eager for him to include an exploration of regional groupings in the economic arena, such as the Asian Development Bank. It was my judgment, so often expressed to the president, that without stable national economies there could be no real peace in the world, and that should be his foremost foreign aim.

But Vietnam was too scouring an issue for the president to dwell much on anything else, abroad. As I recall, Bill Moyers was the principal writer of this 1966 state of the union message, and it bears the imprint of Moyers' sensible and readable prose. The president chose not to make this forum the site of an announcement of a cease-fire, a piece of advice that floated in the White House from time to time, like a paper glider flung across a room, soaring momentarily and then falling to the floor.

If ever I had any doubts that the war was a plague, they began to leave me after this state of the union speech. Gloomily, it was apparent that Vietnam was a fungus, slowly spreading its suffocating crust over the great plans of the president, both here and overseas. No matter what we turned our hands and minds to there was Vietnam, its contagion infecting everything that it touched and it seemed to touch everything. At that time hope still was alive within me that the president would be able to dig his way out, without injuring the Great Society programs, and without polarizing the country beyond the redemption for which most of us in the White House so devoutly prayed.

I was particularly unhappy that the George Woods plan for fertilizer plants also got lost in the need to expatiate on Vietnam. And of course, my own pet project, to construct desalinization plants, also failed to be included.

What did get in was an LBJ recommendation to extend the term of service for a member of the House from two to four years. The president felt, and I surely agreed, that two years was too short a span for a congressman to serve. Elections came too swiftly, they were expensive and time-consuming and the length of the term ought to be expanded. The president told me that if this succeeded, he would push for the six-year term for a president. On this subject he and I were in total agreement.

During April 1966, the president was besieged with doubts about the viability of the Ky government and whether or not it could withstand the enormous pressures being brought to bear on it. The Buddhists were restless, motivated by their own special anxieties and their encroachments on Ky and his government were beginning to stir misgivings among the president's advisers. Since I had just returned from accompanying the vice-president on his nine-nation Asian tour, I had my own queasy feelings about what might happen. I surely was no expert on Vietnamese affairs, but I was comforted by the thought that the experts had all, one by one, been proven wrong in their own assessments and so I gained the courage to broach my own specific ideas to the president. We could not do much worse than we were doing then, and possibly an innocent could tread and survive where the experts had already foundered.

I sent the following series of memoranda to the president:

April 4, 1966
8:30 A.M. Monday

MEMORANDUM FOR THE PRESIDENT

You are being counseled by those far wiser than I, but I pass along these thoughts to you for whatever value, if any, they may have. These are troubling times for you and I am only trying to help clear the dark alternatives that seem to be available.

Where are we?
1. The Ky government will hold on or
2. The Ky government will fall and
    a) either another government takes over that will choose to continue both the fight and the peaceful reconstruction

or
  b) another government will determine to strike a
     bargain with the Viet Cong.

Two questions present themselves:

  1. How can we help preserve Ky?
                    and
  2. What do we do if Ky falls?

I. Preserve Ky:
  1. We can help with the use of United States force. This
     would be dangerous. It would erode our moral, even our
     treaty obligations. It would smack of colonialism.

Thus, the decision is how to preserve Ky without the deployment of United States force.

A.   Elections Now.
     This is hazardous. The Viet Cong may win in the heat
     of the anti-government demonstrations; a public
     whipped up to march against the government is likelier
     than not to vote against that government.

     But if Ky were to set a date—say June 1—for a national
     election, it may take the starch out of the demonstrations.
     At least it would give Ky some breathing room to present
     the case for a unified central government whose objective
     is to defeat the Viet Cong, not commit suicide.

*B.   Bring in four to five Buddhist, Catholic leaders as part of the
     directorate.*
     This might ease the pressures, if this move were coupled
     with a definite election date.

*C.   Surface Viet Cong agents as provocateurs—and link them to
     the demonstration leadership.*
     The drawback to this is the lack of time available to
     make the case. Communicating with the Vietnam public
     is not as easy as in this country.

     *But suppose we airlifted 100 soundtrucks to Vietnam (or sound
     gear to put in South Vietnamese trucks)* and the government
     put on a campaign (U.S. style) to convince the people
     the Viet Cong were inciting the demonstrations? Sup-
     pose we didn't indict the Buddhist leadership, but fo-

cused on a known enemy (the VC), and the perils that would come if the VC intrigue won (i.e. if the central government fell). It is a long shot, but it might work.

D. *Split the Buddhist leadership*
This has possibilities. There is no durable cohesion in the Buddhist leadership. Can we pit some of the leaders against Tri Quang? Can we use the Dalai Lama and Buddhists outside Saigon, Hue and Da Nang to our advantage?

As a corollary to this—why can't Ky ask that all the Buddhist factions—indeed all religious factions—gather together for a meeting to discuss the future of the government? Perhaps Ed Lansdale and his group could be useful in getting this meeting together. *Object of the meeting:* To try to drive a wedge between the leadership groups—and to bring to bear the argument that the real enemy is the Viet Cong and if the leaders would allow the government to have an orderly free election all groups would benefit. It might be worth a try.

E. *Urge Ky to use force*
Only those on the scene can assess the value of this. It looks like this would not work for the demonstrators have seemingly gathered too much momentum. Before it would work, Ky must restore the usefulness of the 1st Corps soldiers.

Is it possible to restore Thi—and back him in efforts to retrieve the sagging loyalties of the 1st Corps? This is admittedly dangerous, but as a final, totally last resort, it could be tolerated.

II. *If Ky Falls:*
  1. We would wait and see what a new government would bring. Past history indicates it would have the same durability as Quat—or even worse.

    A new government will
    a) Be a weak reed, but insist that we stay. At least we retain our credentials as an invited guest rather than an interloper.

b) Demand that we leave—which is unlikely since the Buddhists have an irrational goal of destroying central governments but under our over-all security.

c) Be satisfactory to us for the moment, but leave a sour taste in the domestic mouth. Our antagonists would seize this change-in-government as final evidence we are fighting windmills and pour the steam on for us to get out. It would be a cheerless several months in the White House.

2. We could announce we were going to leave Vietnam because of a lack of national will to secure stability and freedom.

If we did this, our reasons are, as follows:

a) We adhere to our beliefs in self-determination—and in our resolve to protect a small country from being chewed up by its neighbors, but we cannot force anyone to choose stability and liberty. We can only aid when the people are determined to help protect themselves.

b) We would, if the Thais invited us, assist them, for as long as they chose to have our aid, to help them resist intrusions on their national sovereignty.

Thus, we would withdraw from Vietnam, not because our resolve or our objectives are shaken, but because there existed no longer a central authority with a desire to remain free of aggression.

This would have the following effects:

1. The Vietnamese might be so shocked it would cause even the erratic Buddhist leaders to sober up. Perhaps a really stable government could then be formed. Thus, we could turn political catastrophe into a hopeful direction.

2. We could rid ourselves of the Vietnamese bone-in-our-throat and at the same time give sustenance to those allies and friends where a truly nationalistic spirit and tradition exists.

At the same time, we would call for a neutral zone

along the Mekong to get on with the development of that region. United Nations authority would be asked for—with our troops supporting much of the force. In this way, we get rid of the South Vietnamese albatross, secure the rich Mekong, and hold the Thai resolve to resist. We would have demonstrated that we will stick with an ally and a commitment until the one becomes insane and the other no longer has real meaning.

Jack Valenti

*   *   *

April 4, 1966
10:20 P.M. Monday

MR. PRESIDENT:

More advice.

All that you said in tonight's meeting on Vietnam had the tough truth in it.

Let me add this:

The first thing we ought to do, in my judgment, is take the starch out of the demonstrations. Until we do that, Ky must fall and it would be greatly difficult to pick up any pieces without showing your hand.

Suggestion:

Could we not explore the path toward some quieting of the street explosions by bringing in Thi to the directorate again—hoisting Thieu alongside Thi as the rulers of the directorate. You'll have a Buddhist and Catholic—with Thi's obvious popularity among the 1st Corps as a stopgap measure.

(Note Brom Smith's recount of a conversation with one of our people with Gen Thieu about Thi—Thi shows up with some guts and some national patriotism.) Then, have the directorate announce a constitutional convention—to take further heat off the demonstrations.

We have to do something to hold this together while we gather our own strength. I felt that tonight our wait-and-see attitude might wash us down the drain and allow events to guide us instead of us guiding the events. That's why I fervently believe you are right—we have to take the initiative which, in the past, we never seem to do. We have to sacrifice Ky, but we could placate him in doing this, I judge, in the larger interests of a free Vietnam.

Jack Valenti

* * *

April 6, 1966
6:30 P.M.

MR. PRESIDENT

A note about the meeting at 5:00 today.

1. Why can't every Buddhist expert in this government be asked to give his opinion of Tri Quang and general assessment of the Buddhist way of thinking?

2. When I was in Saigon I was introduced to a young man who worked for Phil Habib (the political officer) who spoke Vietnamese and had daily conversations with Tri Quang. He was described as the "closest man to Tri Quang among the Americans."

   What is his assessment of Tri Quang's motives?

3. Attached is a document from General Walt (sent to General Greene) of the general's evaluation of General Thi (the deposed commander of the I Corps.) The Vice President gave me this—he got it from Greene.

Your admonition that "a man's judgment is no better than his information" came to mind in this meeting.

There is such a poverty of information. We really have nothing substantial on which to base hard decesions. Why not, during the next 48 hours, set in motion a governmentwide project to bring in and sift every shred of information to widen our knowledge about the people and the events.

Jack Valenti

The president thought these ideas made sense, but I found out later that Saigon headquarters had little hospitality for the views I put forward. It made Saigon policy planners look deficient. It occurred to me some years later that perhaps this kind of intimate searching right on the spot would have, possibly, been useful to the president. It may have exposed to him information he did not have at the time. Yet it is true that any assistant of the president without long years of experience in the foreign policy field was apt to be waved aside as one who "doesn't really know or understand Vietnam." In a crunch, I suppose the president had to go with the older, more experienced hands.

*   *   *

By the spring of 1966 I began to chafe under what I thought was a stalemate in the president's communications with the public. The president had seemingly been responsive to my suggestions that we aggressively begin to show initiations in the White House, both in the manpower deployed to cope with current problems and in the approaches we took to solve those problems. So I continued to prod him. He knew my own misgivings about the lack of the LBJ brand on the White House personnel. It was not that the holdovers from the Kennedy administration were not excellent men. On the contrary, they were of unusually high caliber, but it wasn't the specific men I had in mind, it was the public notion that they weren't Johnson men. I suggested we needed to start afresh in the redesign of the apparatus, though we could surely retain the best of those who were already on board.

The president had already told me he was leaning toward Walt Rostow as his choice to succeed McGeorge Bundy in the slot of special assistant for national security affairs. The choice to replace Bundy produced some palace guard infighting in the West Wing. Bill Moyers was keen to have the job and he did some campaigning to get the appointment. I joined that campaign and on several occasions when I was closeted with LBJ and thought the timing was right, I put forward Moyers's name and with some enthusiasm certified his assets for the job.

LBJ was a little vexed at this and made it clear to me that he was not going to name Moyers. "He doesn't have the experience and the background for the job" was LBJ's comment to me. Later, when Rostow's name began to float, Ken Galbraith called me for an "urgent appointment" to see me and talk about the vacancy. Galbraith came to my office and eloquently, possibly desperately, cited a catalogue of laments about Rostow in that spot. It was pretty clear that Ken and Walt Rostow were not what one could describe as *en rapport*. Ken left my office in an unhappy frame of mind.* With the Bundy replacement

---

* There is a bemused grace about John Kenneth Galbraith that celebrates the elegance of everything he says or writes. I rejoiced each time I was in his presence, mainly because he is one of the few non-Xeroxable beings; originals that defy duplication ought to be considered national treasures. Galbraith was a favorite of LBJ in those early days of his presidency. LBJ admired his facile pen and scalpel wit. I called Ken one day, at the president's urging, to ask him to write an economic speech for LBJ. Ken had only a Sunday free and on the Sabbath he came down from Cambridge and he and I closeted ourselves in my office in the West Wing of the White House. Ken sat at my secretary's desk. His fingers flew across the keys clacking out celebrated Galbraith copy. As each page came out of the typewriter I collected it and bravely but cautiously made minor editing changes. Ken, with that grayish forelock dangling over his right eye like a rumpled flag on a windless day, bore with great fortitude my mangling of his emerald prose. Within a few hours, the draft was done, edged with traces of Galbraithian spice. Ken positively bloomed in those passages which claimed for LBJ-Galbraith the full truth, guaranteed to stir the right-wing Yazoos whom Ken adored to smite. Ken wore his certitude with dazzling assurance. When LBJ read the completed draft he glowed with satisfaction. "Ken, this is a great speech. But I have to tell you that whenever a man makes any

as the prod, I wrote the following memorandum to the president:

MEMORANDUM

THE WHITE HOUSE
WASHINGTON

March 21, 1966
7:45 P.M. Monday

MR. PRESIDENT:

If we have fallen down anywhere it is our inability to dramatize and communicate the fantastic strikes and breakthroughs of the Johnson Administration—that contribute to a higher quality of life everywhere in the world.

With a theme of "how to dramatize" our achievements these are some thoughts:

1. We might want to clean house and start afresh in the ex-Bundy operation. Why wouldn't it be beneficial to let it be known that a new, hard-striking, imaginative, creative brain-team is working for the President in the foreign field in the White House:

   a. Bring in *Rostow*. Rostow would be your representative on SIG (State Department). Let him bring with him some truly outstanding people—

   Adam Yarmolinsky to handle defense matters. *Robert Scalapino*, professor at the University of California—who has been with us on Vietnam—and who testifies Wednesday, March 30, before the Fulbright Committee.

   John Roche, another professor who has been with us. In the Bundy shop now, there are three really brainy men, *Jim Thomson* (China), *Ed Hamilton*, (economics, AID), *Rick Haynes*, the brilliant young negro working on African affairs. Also *Francis Bator*.

   This would be a Johnson team—and it ought to be advertised as such.

---

kind of economic speech to any kind of audience, it's like pissing down your leg; it makes you feel warm, but your audience is colder than a Texas norther."

2. If Bob Komer is to take on the Vietnam job, he ought to be given a title that bespeaks exactly our aims so that everytime his title is mentioned, it becomes a slogan: *Special Assistant for Peaceful Re-Construction in Vietnam.*

3. I believe the reason why the Asian Development Bank has not really been illuminated as a great step by the Administration is because it hung by itself—not seemingly as part of a glittering whole. Could Eugene Black be named Special Consultant for Asian Development—and all matters pertaining to the Bank, to the Mekong project to come under his aegis. In time, if we can, put together a meaningful plan that could be brought forward as the Johnson Asian program.

Jack Valenti

Unfortunately, I was not able to follow up the implementation of these ideas, because I had begun to think seriously about the offer made me to become president of the Motion Picture Association of America.

When I was first approached by Lew Wasserman, president of MCA, and Edwin Weisl, Sr., the president's lawyer and longtime confidant, I had mixed feelings. At some point soon I had planned to leave but leave-taking is difficult. White House assignments are transient duties. Even presidents must leave after eight years. The president had discouraged the entire idea of my resignation saying that he needed me and besides, he said, I should stay in the public arena and not go back to private enterprise. He chose not to discuss the matter further and so I thought the movie offer had collapsed. But Weisl and Wasserman persisted, and indeed, Weisl took it up personally with the president. Weisl called me after one meeting with the president to say gleefully, "The boss hasn't closed the door."

Wasserman had convinced me that the presidency of the MPAA would give me spacious opportunity to continue my interest in global politics and international affairs. Wasserman, a lean, taciturn man, was the most impressive and successful executive (with Arthur Krim) in the entire movie world. The president liked him and offered him a cabinet post, which Wasserman declined. Wasserman had that quickness of thought and that curious anticipatory instinct that is the baggage of the great political and industrial captains. He spoke quietly and seldom, but when he did speak, everyone in the movie world listened. I was impressed by him, by both his intellect and his exposition of what lay ahead in the international film marketplace that needed my services.

By April, Ed Weisl had more or less cleared the way with the president, and one evening that month Mary Margaret and I dined with LBJ. I went into some detail of why I thought I ought to leave (family economics), and the pledge of the movie industry chieftains to insert into my contract a clause that gave me the right to take time out whenever the president wanted me to serve him on specific occasions. LBJ nodded at that, pleased. (In October, 1966, I was on my movie job, meeting in Rome with Italian government officials on industry problems, when I received a call from the White House informing me that the president wanted me to fly to Manila immediately to join him and participate in the Manila Conference. That was one of many times when I fled my film duties to do special presidential chores.)

The negotiations with the MPAA moved swiftly. I asked Paul Porter, a prime mover in the Washington political scene and senior partner in the law firm of Arnold and Porter, to handle my affairs in that direction. By the end of April, we had sealed our agreement and by June, 1966, I resigned from the White House and assumed my new duties. Thus, I never was able to finalize my suggestions about a new team in the White House.

The president was never completely happy about my leaving to accept a job in the film industry. He wanted me to stay in public life. When I pressed him for his "blessings" to leave, he had the notion that I was unhappy in the White House and abruptly he suggested one evening that he would make me ambassador to Italy. Unbeknownst to me, he had already informally sounded out the Italian ambassador, Sergio Fenoaltea, to see if his government would object to having an American of Italian extraction as our envoy. Fenoaltea made his check quickly and reported to the president that my appointment would be received warmly. I reluctantly turned the president down. My reason for leaving was economic. I had run out of money, I had debts to pay, and I needed to earn more money for my family.

On April 25, 1966, I received a letter from the president acknowledging my departure:

April 25, 1966

Dear Jack:

This has been a very long day.

Your letter of resignation and the personal note just came in, and I wanted to acknowledge both before knocking off for the day.

You know how much I will miss your companionship, your good cheer, your brilliant mind, and your storehouse of information. You have been some very special something to me for a long time—first because of Mary Margaret, and then Courtenay, but really all the time—it was you yourself.

I guess I just didn't want to admit that a man should need another man quite so much. This move will be good for you and your family, and they must come first. They deserve anything you or I could do for them because all of them have already gone a long way with us.

You have served your country with devotion and distinction, and you can always be as proud, or prouder of that, as you are of your fifty-one missions. You served me, though, even more—and I thank you, and love you, and am very proud of you.

Sincerely,

LBJ

Hon. Jack J. Valenti
1694–31st Street, NW.
Washington, D.C. 20007

PART III

The
Press

Every day the press and the president meet as adversaries.

Hundreds of newsmen, monitoring the White House, sight along their barrel the vision of presidential ineptitude implanted in the cross hairs. And every day the president uneasily imagines himself in danger of ambush by nosy newsmen who ought to be praising him instead of criticizing him.

Puzzling though this may be to the general public, it is nonetheless true. There can no more be compatibility between president and newsmen than there can be jollity between mouse and cat. The press strains to know not merely what happened, but more intemperately, to the White House, why. The president intends that what he does should not be marred by suspicion, but the press is endlessly suspicious. The president expects his election by a majority of his peers to be justification enough for faith in his actions. The press distinguishes presidential election from presidential action only by a calendar frame; a distinction the president views neither as sensible nor deserved. It is in this persistent array of opposites that both the president and the press find themselves, like uneasy sentries on the alert, ceaselessly probing the outer edges of the other's camp. There is nothing unusual in all this. It is a matter of record that most presidents are not long in the White House before it is patently clear that the press gives them a royal pain in the ass. One may count on this as one counts on tomorrow.

Presidents handle the press differently. JFK charmed them, LBJ talked to them, Richard Nixon ignored them, and Gerald Ford pals with them. Toward the end of the Johnson presidency it was clear that LBJ's way didn't work the way he wanted it to.

But the story grows stranger; I would wager that Lyndon Johnson enjoyed press people more than any modern-day president, truly wanted them around, liked to chat with them, and in general counted the press the kind of folks he found persistently interesting. What went awry? Why did LBJ leave office totally convinced the press (as a generic group) was opposed to him, not objectively, but rudely, coarsely, malignantly opposed?

In the Johnson White House, the correspondents gathered each day in the West Lobby (the size of an extra-large living room, with a pit nearby called the press room where telephones, tiny alcoves, and high decibel noise levels lived in somewhat uneasy alliance). Off to one side was another small room where the broadcast commentators worked.

Twice a day, at 11 A.M. and 4 P.M., the press secretary called those in attendance to the press briefing where, in all my days in the White House, precious little was ever revealed. Indeed, there was enacted a drama as unvarying in its form as a Madrid bullring ritual. The press secretary put out what was described as news, and the assembled correspondents, like picadors harassing a bull, darted in and out with barbed questions aimed at tormenting a cautious press secretary into giving them the answers they wanted.

Pierre Salinger, George Reedy, Bill Moyers, and George Christian each developed his own style of saying enough but not too much, just enough to preserve credibility, just enough to satisfy the daily news nutrient requirement of the reporters. The press secretary had to be cautious because President Johnson viewed darkly the perversity of the press in insisting on answers they knew full well could not be forthcoming, while the press smelled cyanide in every crumb that dropped from the lips of the press briefer.

It is this conflict between leader and reporter, between the presidency and the commentator, that everyone in Washington is aware of, and on which opinion is freely laid, and from which judgments are made depending on which side one's vantage point happens to be.

What the public believes about the White House and its occupant is indispensable to the strength of the president. President Lincoln understood this and gave it clear meaning when he said: "In this and like communities, public sentiment is everything. With public sentiment nothing can fail; without it nothing can succeed. Consequently, he who molds public sentiment goes deeper than he who enacts statutes or pronounces decisions." There is some irony in the fact that Lincoln came to this unsettling conclusion before the advent of high-speed communications and television. If Lincoln was right in the 1860s, the certitude is binding and blinding today.

Surely no modern president can ignore what I consider to be a prickly truth: It is as important to be thought right as it is to be right. To achieve that truth demands a special skill from the White House.

There are probably a couple of thousand correspondents certified to cover the White House. But this is only a surface covering. Add to this the many famous columnists, commentators, and special interest reporters who write about the White House and the scrutiny becomes intense.

White House correspondents are first of all human beings, subject to the same disquiet and frustrations that afflict ordinary folks. They are, by and large, men and women of enlarged interests in *homo sapiens* as politician, and therefore they are sensitive and aware; they feel and judge by instinct as well as fact and it is in no way a critical stricture to describe them thus.

When you station highly intelligent people in a sealed capsule (which is, in many ways, what the White House is), then invest the environment with a strong-willed chief executive warily suspicious of reporters who don't applaud his motives (which the president *knows* to be right), and set in motion a number of occurrences which persuades the press they are being "had" by Machiavelli with a southern drawl, then perhaps the stage is set to ask (and try to answer) the big question: How did it come about that a president, elected by a significant majority of the voters of the land, seemingly at the height of his popularity and power, was to be attacked, it would appear, by a press united in its purpose to wound, bleed, and destroy him?

It had its origins, in my judgment, in two festering sores, each infecting the other: the first was the credibility gap, the second was Vietnam. The credibility gap came first, and it came, in my estimate, in a strange and obscure way.

The president had a continual dislike for revealing his schedule far in advance. He claimed, and there is much hard truth in the assertion, that it would curtail his options. "If I say I am going a certain place at a certain time, and if something comes up which demands my presence, and I cancel the original schedule, immediately there is a crisis in the press as to why. Is there tension somewhere?

Did a terrible problem develop? These are simply the kinds of trouble that occur when you pin down your every movement to a specific time."

True, to a large extent. Any change in presidential schedule calls for explanation, and behind the questions are always other questions, ever probing, never quite believing.

And yet in one particular event, which reoccurred with frequency, there was seeded all the emergent agony and vexation of both press and president. This was the president's visits to his ranch in Texas. The tableau was usually acted out in the following manner.

There would be a stirring in the press room that the president was going to the ranch next weekend. The press office would be queried. The answer would come back: "Off the record, there might be a movement to the ranch, so pack a bag, but this is not yet a fact."

"Off the record" is a cute little device honored more in the breach than in the acceptance. An administration uses it to let reporters know about a particular event or forthcoming operation so they won't be caught off guard (and thereby become vengeful), and sometimes to counter a charge made by someone else in which the off-the-record comment will become common knowledge soon, and thus take the heat off the administration. It is accepted by the press, sometimes grudgingly, so that they can gain information that might be fitted into other news puzzles where missing pieces are needed.

Off-the-record rules, though they stipulate no reporter present can use the information in the context in which it is given, have no restrictions on reporters who are not present, who pick up off-the-record information from someone who was present and print it. This all gets rather confusing at times.

Meanwhile back at the ranch . . .

With this off-the-record information, the White House correspondent now ponders what to tell his wife. Is he going to be away next weekend from home, or isn't he? Does she cancel the dinner she and her husband had planned with three other couples attending, or does she carry on? "Why can't the president tell you if he is going or if he is not going?" asks the perturbed wife. The disgruntled correspondent agrees; the discontent grows, the fury of this on-again, off-again procrastination increases, and the next morning a fiery reporter confronts the press secretary. Only now, he is not alone. Other reporters, equally lashed by questions from vexed wives, are ready to charge.

"When the hell are we going to find out about the ranch trip?" they implore the press office.

"As of now, nothing is set. There are no plans to definitely go to the ranch." That's the answer.

"Does that mean we are definitely not going?"

"No," says the press secretary, "that means as of now there is no definite decision to go and no definite decision not to go."

This creative conversation goes on for another twenty minutes, reporters increasingly enraged, press secretary increasingly harried.

Inside the president's office, the press secretary determines to find out what the final plans will be or else he will have a violent rebellion to quash.

The president engages his press secretary in conversation. No, he cannot give a final answer yet. Yes, he wants to go, but if a meeting develops with Secretaries Rusk and McNamara he may have to cancel. Therefore, he will not say one thing knowing that he may have to revise plans.

"Can we give them a possibility of going?" the press secretary wants to know. He describes the mood of the press. The president wants to know if the press or the president is running the country.

The press secretary has no answer for that. But he does respond by reminding the president that the press's anger will ventilate itself in petty assaults on the president and that ought to be avoided.

The president answers the phone; a cabinet officer is calling. The conversation with the press secretary is ended.

Back at the press office, the press is in an ugly mood. It is now Thursday, and the Saturday dinner plans are at the point of no return. It is either go or no go with the wife, and today is the deadline.

The sullen press briefing begins. The press secretary suggests that bags be packed just in case, but still no definite decision.

The questions now assume splenetic proportions. The reporters mutter ominously to each other as they straggle back into the press lobby. In the back of each reporter's mind is the notion that perhaps a story ought to be written about the mismanagement of the White House. Why not follow up on the *Time* magazine story about the president's driving too fast, and that beer can bit? Ought there not be some story filed very soon about the president saying one thing in New Hampshire about the war, and now doing the very opposite of his pledge? Yes, there are necessary and needed pieces to be written, perhaps this week.

Now it is Friday, and the air, as the novelist would say, is charged with emotion, or at least there is a rumbling that could be classified as either discontent or insurrection.

The press secretary fled his office early this morning to escape the hundred phone calls beckoning him. He is once more closeted with the president. "Yes," the president says, "I want to go to the ranch. I would like to leave this afternoon. But I am having a meeting with Rusk and Mc-Namara and it looks as if I cannot go."

An eager press secretary asks if he can relay this precious news. The president frowns. He understands the pressure on the press secretary, whose face is already twitching with the anxiety of facing the mob in the press office. "Yes," says the president, thoughtfully, "I suppose I cannot go, though I would like very much to go. I would like to get away for a day or two, but I suppose I'll wait till another time."

The press secretary flies from the presidential office on wings, if not of joy, perhaps of hope.

He tells the reporters, again off the record, the trip is off, though again there is not a definite no, he vouches for the 75–25 bet there will be no trip. It is now 11:10 A.M. The press, grousing ever so slightly less, heads for the telephones.

The clocks show 12:45 P.M. The president is calling the press secretary. I have just finished my meeting with the secretaries, he says, much earlier than I anticipated. I will be going to Texas after all. We ought to leave about 5:00 P.M.

The press secretary holds the phone which has turned to soft paste in his hand. He murmurs something inaudible and the connection goes click.

The press secretary bleakly orders his staff to begin calling the press, wherever they are. Tell them the press plane will be boarded at 4:00 P.M. and baggage will have to be in the press office at 3:00 P.M.

In a hundred different places, homes, bars, restaurants, and in the West Lobby itself, there are yowls heard that rend air and heart with equal fury.

And somewhere, perhaps at the National Press Club bar, perhaps in the Sans Souci or the Black Steer, or maybe in one of those heavy, green leather-covered chairs in the West Lobby, wherever it is, there is heard a voice that says: "Ye gods, there's a credibility gap in the White House!"

The press will probably deny this. Perhaps President

Johnson would have too. But from such historical insignif-
icance do large and turbulent events emerge. One must
remember that decisions and movements of the most towering and profound shaping are reported by human beings, and that even those who create the *grand designs* are
also mortal; so it is that those of us without divinity are
subject to habits and moods and even silly reactions quite
out of joint with the historian's readings of the *great event.*
The disruption of a reporter's home life, the jostling of his
rational good sense, a president's vexing discomfort at revealing his schedule, are the want of a nail whence a kingdom is lost.

From this first rupture in the president's rapport with
the press, the dikes began to sprout more holes until the
faraway thunder began to be louder and larger and finally
the dam shattered and crumbled and the floodtide of press
dissension with the administration swept across Washington.

Blame is difficult to fix. For some inexplicable reason
the president never accepted reporters' discomfort as cause
for either alarms or anxiety. Sometimes one had the dis-
tinct feeling the president was determined to prove that
the press was not going to be allowed to lead him around
by the nose, that the specific desires of White House reporters as to time and place of announcements were not to
be obsequiously followed.

This sparring, at first desultory, speeded up, until
within the space of a few months it had reached that level
where further acceleration was much easier to achieve, and
where braking had scant effect.

There have been numerous psychic probings as to the
why of this. Some press historians decided that the president's work habits as majority leader, where secretiveness
and maneuver were staple strategic weapons, hindered the
possibility of change once the leader became president.

Others, including some professors and intellectual observers, determined in some occult fashion that the president's humble origins and lack of an eastern education were so much a part of him that he was never able to be at ease with those who viewed him dispassionately, and whose duty it was to be critical. And then there were the psychologists—who sprout in Washington with all the fierce fertility of rabbits in an expanding warren—who found the president unlikable, who examined his aberrations from the norm (as they decided the norm) and determined that they stemmed from his own plaintive desire to be loved, and when that love was not forthcoming his moods evolved into the broodings of a lover unrequited—surly, bitter, vengeful.

That the president erred with the press is no longer a debatable subject.

The president never invoked Oscar Wilde's prescription that: "The greatest sin one human being can commit against another is the sin of indifference." The press knew the president read and cared about what he read. It follows that there is nothing more satisfying than the sure conviction that what one writes can get under the skin of the one written about.

The president surrounded himself with the apparatus of the news. As we have seen, he had news teleprinters in his office which made him privy to the news before most of Washington journalists were aware of it. He made visible, and audible, his outrage at stories, columns, and leaks. Yet he plainly wanted newsmen's approbation of his goals and plans.

The president, as incredible as it may sound, and as it seemed to me on occasion, was unable to accept a reporter's objectivity as part of the reporter's craft, or understand that that the great majority of correspondents reached for the story and the facts without being inter-

ested in venting their spleen. Unhappily, it was LBJ's unvarying view that all reporters had a tilt that showed all
too clearly. To LBJ the reporters were obstinate in the
face of reasonable persuasion and he found this unreasonable.

In midterm and later there were mounted in so many
papers, and over so many TV news shows what seemed to
be an avalanche of barbaric (as the president saw them) attacks, and as the criticism grew more virulent, LBJ saw an
odious conspiracy stalking him. I remember once I was
idly reciting some humorous anecdotes I had found in
Duff Cooper's biography of Talleyrand. I mentioned to
the president that during Talleyrand's time there lived a
notorious character not overburdened with scruples named
Montrond. He had a venomous tongue and he loved to
flay his friends and his enemies with unflattering word
portraits. It was said of Montrond, I related to the president, that he was a wit who lived on human flesh. The
president chuckled. "He is a first cousin to those piss-ant
writer friends of yours," he said.

I recall another time when I reminded the president of a
story told about Metternich, the cunning Austrian diplomatic magician who was the key figure in the Congress of
Vienna. Metternich was absolutely totally, unflinchingly
suspicious of everything and everybody. Once one of his
aides rushed into a meeting to whisper into Metternich's
ear, "The Russian ambassador has just dropped dead."
Metternich scowled and muttered, "I wonder what his
motivation could have been."

LBJ relished the story. I had the feeling that the president was silently saying, "Stout fellow, that Metternich."
But what LBJ did say when I recounted the story was: "If
that Austrian fellow had to deal with this Washington
press corps, he wouldn't have been wondering about any
motivations for their dropping dead. He would have sim-

ply believed it was one of God's better calls!" Then he
roared with laughter.

There were, at base, two torments that the president
simply could not abide. One was the dereliction of liberal
writers who, the president determined, ought to be laud-
ing him and defending him instead of poisoning him. He
was sufficiently pleased when I read him a letter I had
received from a psychiatrist friend of mine. He had written that the radicals and the liberals were furious with
Johnson because he had taken all their shibboleths and
slogans, causes and passions, and made them into law.
Now they had nothing left to get passionate about. If, said
my doctor friend, Johnson ever settles Vietnam this will
be the last, cruel blow to them and they will never forgive
Johnson for this rudeness.

The other was what LBJ believed to be mean, dirty,
personal attacks on him and his family. After Vietnam
became the central agony of our time, the writing took on
a sour tone and reporters began to investigate in print and
on the air the personal traits of the president: how he conducted himself at the dinner table, how he treated assistants, what he said to Lady Bird, how he drove a car, and
so forth.

In a review of Gay Talese's book *The Kingdom and the
Power*, Ben Bagdikian, a former Washington correspondent for the *Providence Journal*, chides Talese for his
too-often and too-personal insights into the *New York Times*
executives. This is what Bagdikian said:

> The men of the *Times* emerge not as godlike models of
> intrepid journalism, but as unique individuals who, in
> addition to other human traits, have trouble with their
> ambitions, alcohol, wives and analysts.
> But this is the book's weakness. It implies value in

professional newspapermen on the basis of personal id-
iosyncrasy. Individual tastes are important, but so is
man's perception of reality of issues, and of public
events, which, after all, are the substance of his trade. It
is interesting to learn the kind of woman and clothing
that turns on a particular editor, but there is more to
judgments of journalism than bedmates or haber-
dashers.

Mr. Bagdikian capsules what I would call the indictment of those who wrote so meanly of the president.
Their emphasis was on the personal Johnson: whether he
picked a dog up by the ears; whether or not he uttered a
foul word; his table manners; the kind of tongue lashing he
gave a staff member; the accent of his voice; the way he
drove his car; and endlessly on and on.

But the fact remains that had the president stood aloof
from the press, he would have fended off most of their
probings. LBJ's obsession to talk to the press, to have
them near, was a narcotic for him. He wanted their approbation. He wanted them to notice his strength, not his
inadequacies.

Yet, the irony in all the Johnson trauma is that he need
not have felt inadequate. In the latter part of his presidency, he held a press conference in the East Room, on
live TV; he discarded the mammoth rostrum, did away
with the usual mikes, and confronted his questioners with
only a small lavalier microphone pinned on his chest. He
was free, now, to be himself. He roamed the small enclosure before the press, he gestured, he was alternately
serious and mockingly humorous. In a word, he "wowed"
the audience, in the East Room and in the country. But he
never repeated the performance. Why? I don't know.

I believed, and still do, that if President Johnson had
spoken less from a script, but from notes, had stripped

himself bare of the teleprompters and stout rostrums, had done more of the extemporaneous speaking which he did so splendidly, he would have fared better in his communication with the public. He had the physical presence, immense height and frame, that is the big plus factor in crowd attraction.

The sad part of Lyndon Johnson's opposition to scheduled press conferences with live TV was the bitter (and to be honest, understandable) reaction of the press who were not physically aboard at hastily called Saturday morning press conferences in the West Wing when only the hardcore regular press corps was present and accounted for. Then, there were the "long march" press affairs, when the president walked briskly around the asphalt drive of the South Grounds, almost a half-mile lap, with hordes of newsmen in unmilitary ranks straining and straggling in his wake; the youngest ones picked up most of the presidential talk; the older ones, dog-trotting with hands cupped half-around aging ears, sometimes gave me the idea that a Geritol concession stand near the fountain would be good business.

As one irate newsman told me: "Dammit, I did this on the Burma Road, but I was twenty years younger!"

*   *   *

When I worked in the White House, one of my pet projects was how to construct some way for the president to leap over the barriers of difficult and hard-to-explain subjects (Vietnam, the economy, The Dominican Republic, the canker in the heart of the cities, white vs. black, the thin anti-missile system—my God, the list could go on forever), to interpose himself between the people and the press, so that he could tell his story, in his way, to the American people and tell it truthfully, simply, dramatically, and briefly.

This is part of the president's role, to be educator and communicator. There is no higher priority than the president's need to inform the American public, so they understand his motives, his actions, and the facts behind whatever it is the president has chosen to place before the people. For the modern truth exists, particularly in this day of instant communications, that no leader can lead when those whom he abjures to follow him are confused about "why," fearful about "how," and hesitant about "what."

He cannot fudge the facts. He cannot make a situation look one-sided, all on his side. I have always felt the American public would find favorable a leader who admits he does not know all the answers, but who gives the people a commonsense assessment of the problem. It is also my judgment that if the president admits an error, confesses he made a mistake, and owns up to it before the press takes up the omission, he comes out ahead with the voters.

President Johnson exhibited the trait that is found in almost all public officials: the inability to admit mistakes. Most men who rise to high public station are not enchanted with the possibility of error and even less attracted to the act of announcing it.

I besieged the president with my thoughts on his role as educator-communicator, and pressed upon him the various ideas I had. I suggested the following to President Johnson. First, go on TV at a time not earlier than 6:30 P.M. EST and not later than 10:00 P.M. EST with a series of ten-minute telecasts on Vietnam. The choice of hour and the limitation of time were both essential. The audience had to be potentially present, and the audience must know that whatever the president said would take no longer than ten minutes.

Second, I suggested that he break Vietnam down into four separate and different telecasts: (1) why are we there

and why it is important to our long-range national security; (2) how are we doing; (3) is it possible to peacefully
reconstruct Vietnam and are we doing it; (4) after the
fighting, the hope of lasting peace.

Third, I suggested he do the same with the other difficult problems confronting the president and the country.
The issue of pollution, and its evils, the injury to the
country in health and economic loss if pollution were allowed to consume all that was clean and fresh in the land,
all this demanded to be told in simple, understandable language to the people. Having been educated in this subject
by the president on TV, the funds and the commitment to
attack and defeat pollution would be forthcoming. The
other problems of crime, racial discrimination, the urban
sprawl, and indeed dozens of other mean issues could be
taken up one at a time by the president and after having
explained them, the inspiration, the incitement of public
indignation, and the enlistment of public support would
surely follow.

The thesis was this: The president needed to use national TV as a rostrum, editing out all needless words and
ideas, keeping what he had to say simple and clear. He
could not invade the TV screens too often else he debased
his appearances with frequency. There is a fine line dividing mystery and need. The more the leader visits the living room of American families, the less exotic and attentive become the thrill and the hospitality.

Moreover, the president must choose his subjects carefully. He must separate his "crisis" speeches (i.e., Cuban
missile crisis, the Dominican Republic intervention, etc.)
from his national and international problem speeches.

He must carefully judge impact and receptivity. It was
my judgment that appearances spaced shorter than six
weeks apart would be a mistake; and that there ought
never be an appearance because "we haven't been on the
tube in a long time."

And finally, though presidential TV speeches must be counted of high national value, they ought never lose sight of the American tendency to outrage when a favorite TV program has been pre-empted for the president. Hell hath no fury like a TV viewer blanked out.

If all this sounds commercial, even cynical, it is not, anymore than reality is founded in subterfuge.

The president listened to my suggestions, and did not shut me off, but he never took me up on these ideas. I never really understood why. I must confess I was never certain why he was so fearful (perhaps that is not the word) or uncertain about television.

I would say he recoiled from being compared with John F. Kennedy, as superb a television performer as ever inhabited the White House, Somewhere deep in LBJ there lingered some messy doubts about his TV image being measured against JFK's. But I really don't know.

One minor sidelight: sometime in 1964 or 1965, my notes don't indicate the date, I did make a breakthrough. I had been urging the president that we should get experts in to guide and counsel us on television. Finally, to my surprise, he said, "Okay, call Ed Weisl and ask him to locate some top people."

Edwin L. Weisl was probably the closest confidant of Lyndon Johnson, and surely one of the most trusted. He was also the most decent, intelligent, and wisest man I have ever known. He was a brilliant lawyer with the soothing qualities of a master negotiator, a senior partner of the law firm of Simpson, Thacher, & Bartlett in New York. He was introduced to the young congressman from Texas in the late thirties by Harry Hopkins, who told Ed Weisl, "Watch this Texan. He's going to high places." Weisl took the young congressman in hand and from that day forward no one held a more intimate grip on the president's affections and needs. Weisl was the chief counsel of LBJ's Senate investigation of the defense establishment (when LBJ was Senate leader) and his son, Edwin Weisl, Jr.—also a brilliant lawyer, and later an assistant attorney general during the Johnson administration—was his assistant in those investigations; as was another attorney from Weisl's firm, who was later to make his own international mark, Cyrus Vance. Ed Weisl was also one of the most eminently respected executives in the movie world, stemming from his being chairman of the executive committee of Paramount Pictures' board of directors. Thus he was knowledgeable about the visual entertainment arena.

I talked with Ed Weisl and he brought me Stuart Rosenberg, at that time considered to be the most skillful and successful of television directors. Later, Rosenberg went on to Hollywood to become an accomplished film director. One of his films was *Cool Hand Luke* which starred Paul Newman. I was overjoyed. Now, for the first time, we had a professional on the scene.

Rosenberg and an associate came to the White House to discuss the matter with me and the staff. I cautioned Rosenberg that the president was excessively sensitive about anything concerning this enterprise "leaking" to the press. Rosenberg understood. Mum was the word.

On the day that Rosenberg was to come back to the White House to meet and talk with the president about his new assignment, the damn fates hit me over the head with a claw hammer. I picked up the *Washington Post* and in some column there appeared an item about Stuart Rosenberg and his new task for the president.

Dreams shattered. The president was on the phone and he was very calm, very soft-voiced, the ice frosting up the receiver in my hand. "Cancel the meeting with your TV people."

"But, Mr. President," I said, "he is due at the northwest gate this minute. Let's go forward with our plan. Let's not let this newspaper item botch up what is a very good idea."

Again the voice was calm: "Cancel the meeting." Click went the phone.

One of the classic examples of reportorial alchemy at work was performed by a chap named Michael Davie of the London *Observer*.

Davie importuned me (as the president's appointments secretary) to get him a meeting with the president. I was easy prey for foreign correspondents for I held the view that the president ought to see as many of them as possible so they could make accurate accountings of the president's stewardship to a worldwide audience. But for the various reasons, mainly because of the press of business, I was never able to work Davie in.

Thus, Davie spent a week or so in Washington attending public functions where the president was present, but to my certain knowledge never came closer than twenty feet to the chief executive and surely never had any conversations, private or public, with him.

To my amazement he published a series of articles, later published in a small hardcover volume, about Lyndon Johnson. It was a highly personal account, in which Davie quoted directly presidential remarks seemingly overheard by Davie in private meetings in the Mansion, and quoted conversations between the president and the first lady as though he, Davie, curled up snugly under the couch or the bed, had written down verbatim the actual words that passed between them.

It was a total bag of flim-flam, and Davie scurried back to London basking in the afterglow of his "coup." I shook my head in disbelief when I tried to convince others in Washington that Davie's book was a joke, and failed.

I personally became incensed over some other books and articles I read about the president. From the perspective of a decade later, I am a bit embarrassed at my passion then. I suspect my friends in the press accounted me a snarling unpredictable fellow, jumping and snapping at them for doing what they obviously considered their duty and their job. I recall with some amusement (now) my assaults on Philip Geyelin, then the premier Washington correspondent for the *Wall Street Journal* (and now the chief of the *Washington Post* editorial page). Geyelin, a sophisticated, Yale-educated journalist, had written a book, *Lyndon Johnson and the World*, in which he traced the LBJ foreign policy role.

I read the book with increasing frustration, taking umbrage at paragraph after paragraph; indeed, I painted my discontent on almost every page with a yellow Hi-liter pen, scrawling hash marks across sentences and phrases I thought were just plain wrong.

I recall meeting with Geyelin, taking his book as my text, going over each page, with its yellow markings, venting my spleen on a smiling and bemused Geyelin. His parting comment to me was: "At least you convinced me you read the book. That's something."

Probably the bleakest and most incomprehensible conflict with the press came in a most unlikely manner. It began in secrecy, hooded by necessity and carried forward with a swift precision that James Bond himself might have admired.

On December 18, 1967, the day following the death of Harold Holt, prime minister of Australia, I received a call from the president in my Motion Picture Association office in Washington. Could I come to his office immediately? Yes, I answered, and within minutes I was ushered into the Oval Office.

The president, somber-faced, told me that he was going to the funeral of Harold Holt. "I want you to go with me, Jack, and at the same time handle a matter that I want only you to know about right now." I was pleased to accompany the president, I made that clear, and waited for my instructions.

"I am anxious to visit the pope. He may be able to help us in the prisoner of war problem." This weighed heavily on the president's mind. He fretted and worried about the POWs and his inability to extract them from their miserable confinement. He worried about their treatment. "Maybe, just maybe, the pope might be able to intercede. At any rate, it is worth a try. You get in touch with your contact at the Vatican and quietly, very quietly, set up the arrangement. Check with Jim Cross (he was the president's airplane pilot, an officer in the Air Force) and find out when we could get to Rome from Australia. Figure in a stop in Vietnam—and keep that quiet—as well as a refueling stop. Get back to me as soon as you firm it up."

I decided that I should not make the phone call from my office. I picked out a pay phone outside a service station near my home. Within an hour after leaving the president, I was huddled in the phone booth, my dime plinking down and my voice asking the operator to reach Monsignor Paul Marcinkus in the Vatican in Rome. Marcinkus, Chicago born, is a burly figure of a man, and it is clear that a sophisticated education has not totally shed him of his midwestern origins. With his bald head and massive shoulders, he is constructed along the lines of a Chicago Bear middle guard, bold, assertive, yet invariably genial, and intellectually alert. I suspected that when the need arose he was capable of being tougher than saddle leather. He is now a bishop in charge of Vatican finances, about as important a post as anyone can have in that tightly bound enclave of Vatican politics.

Surprisingly, I got Marcinkus on the phone within minutes.

VALENTI: "Monsignor, this is Jack Valenti in Washington."

MARCINKUS: "Wonderful to hear from you, Jack. How are you:"

VALENTI: "Fine, just fine. If you can hear me well, then listen for a moment." (I paused. He said he could hear me perfectly. I went on.) "My friend here is anxious to talk to your friend if you think that could be arranged."

MARCINKUS (without breaking stride, he knew instantly what I was saying): "I am sure that would be alright, but what time and date do you have in mind."

(I told him approximately when we would arrive, but cautioned him it might be a day or a half-day either way).

MARCINKUS: "Good. Let me talk to my friend and I will be back to you."

VALENTI: "No, let me call you. How about the same time tomorrow?"

MARCINKUS: "Yes, I think I could have a response by then. I will expect the call."

I hung up. Then I called the president and told him of the contact. He listened, said little, except to notify him as soon as the arrangements were pinned down. Then as an afterthought he said, "You might tell your man that if everything is alright, Jim Rowe will go to Rome to settle on the final details."

At exactly the same time the next day, I got Marcinkus on the phone.

MARCINKUS: "My friend says he will be delighted to see your friend. Now, how do we go about finalizing all this?"

VALENTI: "You will receive a call from the president's emissary, Jim Rowe. He will be in Rome in hours to see you and complete the plans."

MARCINKUS: "Should I call the embassy if I have any questions?"

VALENTI: "No, Rowe will be in touch and you and he can deal directly."

MARCINKUS: "Fine. See you in Rome. You will be coming won't you?"

VALENTI: "I'll be there. Goodbye."

On December 19, 1967, the same day, we took off from Andrews Air Force Base on what turned out to be an adventure without known parallel,* and an enterprise that split the press ranks, embittered a good many of them, and rankled the president to a greater extent than I ever saw before.

For the next four days we practically lived aboard Air Force One.** First to Canberra (where we slept in a hotel for the only time on the trip), and then Melbourne and a take-off for Korat in Thailand, where in the misty gloom of the early morning the president visited with American soldiers and fliers, thence to Cam Ranh Bay as the sun was struggling to rise. From there we flew on to Karachi to refuel. Here the president had an airport conference with President Ayub Khan.

It was also here that I had a short but impassioned

---

* We flew 28,210 miles in 59½ hours flying time, and were away from Washington a total of 112 hours. LBJ met with leaders of fourteen countries during the trip. We took off from Andrews Air Force Base outside Washington at 12:05 P.M., December 19. We stopped at Travis AFB, California; Honolulu; Pago Pago; Canberra, Melbourne, Darwin; Korat Air Force Base in Thailand; Cam Ranh Bay in South Vietnam; Karachi, Pakistan; Rome; Lajes Field in the Azores; and returned at 4:55 A.M. on December 24, 1967.

** Also accompanying the presidential party were Charles Engelhard, captain of the fabled Engelhard Industries and his graceful, intelligent wife, Jane. The Engelhards were longtime chums of the president and he liked to be with them. They were personal friends of Prime Minister Holt and ostensibly they were only to be with the president at Holt's funeral, no more. But abruptly, in Melbourne, the president insisted they go the full distance of the journey. The Engelhards, slightly overcome, assented. Charlie Engelhard (now deceased) was a bit of a genius, an expert on gold. He prepared on the trip several memoranda for the president on this arcane subject. But it was Jane who was the heroine of the journey. She became the president's hostess, managing him with a firm charm, never complaining, sleeping little, not fussing over hair-do or makeup and lending a bit of feminine softening to the hard days and longer nights.

argument with some of my best friends in the press corps. Standing on a hot tarmac a hundred yards from the enclosure where the two presidents were meeting alone, I engaged in a wild discussion with Hugh Sidey, one of the most respected of all Washington journalists and White House correspondent for *Time* magazine.

Sidey was clearly vexed. "This is a flying circus and you know it and the president knows it," he said to me, every word biting me in the ear. "The best damn thing you and the president can do is start up this airplane, turn it around and head back home right now, in the same direction we came from," Sidey continued.

I think I said something like, "You can take your opinion and stick it up . . ." or some other elegantly phrased suggestion.

Sidey eyed me venomously. "You're heading to Rome, aren't you?"

That was one trap I was not going to fall into. I gandy-danced around the question by hoisting a small grenade myself. "I find it damn short-sighted of the press to define the president's trip as grandstanding when none of you know what the hell you're talking about."

"It is Rome, isn't it?" Sidey pushed again.

I took refuge again in non-sequitur. "How the devil can you be better informed than the president of his intentions, his objective, and his reasons for them."

Sidey growled and I scowled and we surveyed each other like two bottled scorpions. Hugh Sidey is a temperate man, little given to bursts of outrage. Indeed, he is reflective and even his barbs are couched in eloquent civility, so his out-of-sorts frustration and anger were not in character; they bespoke the gaudy passions that raged inside him.

As I look back on this day, it seems quite clear that we were all tired. I had only a few hours sleep in the last thirty-six hours. The tension was stretching to the snapping point. We were all, staff and press, growling, grumbling, out of sorts. Patience was in pitiful short supply.

I harumphed, and turned on my heel, Sidey probably assessing my temper as indicative of the loosely disciplined trip (as Sidey viewed it). When the president came aboard, he, to my surprise, asked me, "What was going on between you and Sidey?"

I found out later that some member of his staff had overheard my *contretemps* with Sidey and passed it on to the president.

I thought it valorous on my part to downplay the whole thing. "Hugh and the press guys think the trip is grinding them down and they don't know where we are going next which puts them in bad humor."

The president grinned dryly. "As of now, I am running the president's airplane, not Sidey."

"But, Mr. President," I remonstrated, "we ought to give them advance notice of where we are going otherwise they probably have good reason to grouse at us."

The president glared at me. He reached into his pocket and pulled out a piece of paper. "You want me to advertise where we land and have an international crisis on our hands?"

I read the paper. It was a top secret message from Rome. The Secret Service recommended changing our landing location. Rumors of the president flying into Rome had infiltrated the Italian capital and large Communist mobs were planning a cheery welcome for the president when he put down.

"Now, if I explain to the press where we are going and when we get there, don't you suppose we would be helping enlarge our greeting when we get there?"

I couldn't argue with that logic. So I buttoned up and said no more. Little did I know the worst was yet to come.

At approximately 7:00 P.M., a day and a half before Christmas Eve, we landed at Ciampino Airport, on the outskirts of Rome. It was dark and the airport, which was not the international commercial landing spot, was cordoned off by security forces. The president, Walt Rostow, Frederick Reinhardt (ambassador to Italy), and I boarded a chopper at 7:08 P.M. and winged our way to Castelporziano, the hunting lodge retreat of the president of Italy. No press was allowed. Only one official U.S. photographer, one official Italian photographer, and one Italian TV photographer—from RAI, the official Italian government television authority—were allowed inside the grounds. We landed at this forest enclave at 7:20 P.M. By automobile we were taken to the inner courtyard of Castelporziano.

There, the president was greeted by President Saragat, his daughter and her two children, and we all proceeded to a large drawing room on the second floor of the old castle. Prime Minister Aldo Moro, Foreign Minister Fanfani, Ambassador Corrias, Ambassador Malfatti, Admiral Spigaj chatted with Marvin Watson, Ambassador Reinhardt, and me, while the two presidents gathered alone, with interpreters, in the adjoining room.

When finally all of the party moved into the same room, I stayed behind and put in a phone call to Monsignor Marcinkus. We talked briefly. I wanted to know if all was going well, and to inform him that we might be running as much as a half-hour late. Marcinkus understood and said that his end of the line was in good shape. I re-entered the meeting room, and after a long discussion, suggested to the president it was time to depart.

The president, Ambassador Reinhardt, and I, with two Secret Service men, clambered aboard the chopper and we were airborne again, this time to the Vatican. Once we were in the air, I found out from Rufus Youngblood, chief of the Secret Service detail, that we were going in blind to the Vatican. We were to land at night in one of the inner gardens, a tiny circumference at best, with a pilot who had never made a dry run. It was going to be a hairy experience, a virgin landing in the dark, putting down on the head of a pin! God!

I thought it best not to report that handsome piece of news to the president. Soon, we were above the Vatican and the pilot began to circle to get his bearings. We circled, once, twice, three times until the president pressed his mouth near my ear. "Does this pilot need a road map?" he asked. I wanted to blurt out that he needed a seeing-eye dog. But I merely said, "The pilot has to set down in a small location, sir, and he's getting himself set to float in. No problem."

Like hell. I thought, dear God, what a massive travesty of justice and divine belief would it be if the president crashed in the Vatican gardens just a few yards from the holy father. Well, at least I would have the best in the last rites. I remembered that beautiful retort of President Kennedy when he was asked by a reporter, when flying on Air Force One, what would happen if the aircraft crashed. President Kennedy smiled and said, "I'm sure of one thing, your name would be in the paper the next day, but in very small type."

Finally, the pilot must have screwed his courage to the sticking place (I didn't envy him at all) and began to flutter and float above what appeared to be a six-inch opening in the foliage below. The opening got larger and we began to drop ever so slowly, swaying a bit from side to side, and finally after what seemed like eternity, the chopper shook with a confident clatter as we touched down.

There to greet us was Archbishop Benelli, the assistant secretary of state of the Vatican, Monsignor Marcinkus, my old cloak-and-dagger friend, and Count Galeassi, the Vatican administrator.

Marcinkus squeezed my arm as we made our way to the president's limousine. "You made it the hard way, didn't you?"

I grinned. "Yes, but if we had crashed I could have said when I arrived at the pearly gates that the pope himself gave me extreme unction."

"No such luck," said Marcinkus, "I would have done it."

We arrived at what is known as Cortile San Damaso where our reception party consisted of Monsignor Nasalli Rocca, known as the *maestro di camera*, responsible for the pope's appointments. He spoke no English so he and the president nodded warily to each other. The other man was Monsignor Daniel Cronin, from Boston, who had met the president on his 1963 visit to the Vatican as vice-president.

The president beckoned to me. I came to his side. "I want you in the meeting with me," he said. "Perhaps we will have Rostow in later. And if you can, take notes of what we say."

I nodded. We entered the elevator and were lifted to the second floor and escorted to the papal antechambers to the pope's library. There we met the holy father.

He was of medium height. His features were benign, his smile warm and friendly. He was clad in white and he lifted his arm in a half-benediction as he greeted the president. The president shook his hand vigorously. He turned to me and I knelt to kiss his ring. Even as my lips touched the ring, his hands, firm and strong, were urging me up.

I cannot say whether or not non-Catholics experience on meeting and seeing the pope the same emotional impact that must surely come to Catholics, but an eerie, beatific, good feeling pervaded me. Suddenly I felt quite comfortable, serene, and I gazed into the holy father's eyes as he returned my obvious affection and delight. He smiled at me and said so very softly in English, "I am glad you are here. It is good to see you again." I silently commended good staff work by Marcinkus. I had met the pope in 1965 in New York City.

With the pope was Cardinal Cicognani, an impressive figure, with a thousand years of clerical wisdom mirrored in the wrinkles and folds of his chin and cheeks. He was apostolic delegate to the U.S. from 1933 to 1958, and thus was as knowledgeable as a veteran congressman about the crevices, chinks, and markings of the federal city. He was eighty-four years old.

The library of the pope was filled with an atmosphere of history. High-ceilinged, spacious, richly splendid, it had housed, heard, and been privy to the most private pleadings of counselors and popes. Within these opulent walls had gathered through the centuries the dominating captains of church and state, their jousts were the stuff from which a thousand volumes had been constructed— gossip, truth, fact, and fantasy, all of it inhabited this room. The pope gracefully motioned the president to a table around which were six chairs. It was an ancient claw-footed table, marble-topped with a gilt edge; it sat with ponderous grace near a fireplace. We moved to the chairs where we all sat down. The meeting began at 8:55 P.M.

To the pope's left sat Marcinkus. He would interpret. To the pope's near right was Cicognani, and to Cicognani's right was Archbishop Benelli. I sat to the president's right.

The president began by saying, "Sadness brings me on this trip (referring to the death of Prime Minister Holt), a very good man died in Australia." The pope nodded soberly and inquired as to the president's health.

The president told the pope he was pleased with the holy father's December statement and of his recent reply to the College of Cardinals. He recounted his visit to Australia and what he had discussed with the world leaders gathered there. He gave the pope a brief summary of the Vietnam war situation and how the American people felt about it. He pointed out that while he had to keep the pressure on, he was pleading to get negotiations started.

The pope listened quietly and said, in a friendly voice, that he was unhappy the North Vietnamese had not responded to U.S. peace moves. The president explained that problems in Vietnam must ultimately be settled by Vietnamese, but he asked the pope's help in getting talks started.

The pope responded by expressing his gratitude for the president's visit and his work on behalf of peace. "You went to South Vietnam to protect and defend a small country and now you are engaged in a great war." He pointed out that while he understood what the president was trying to do and he wanted to help, he could never give any indication that he could approve of war. The pope told of his several incursions into peace talks with other countries, and how he had failed. "We must," said the pope, "declare our position to the world as friends of peace and foes of war." The pope wondered if the war could change its character and become a defensive one instead of an offensive one. He hoped the bombing could cease. "Could I be an intermediary for you and say what I know to be true, that the U.S. truly wants peace?" the pope asked. The president quickly responded that he would be pleased to have the holy father as an intermediary.

Cardinal Cicognani interposed with a question of how Hanoi's reluctance to talk could be overcome. The president gravely stated in reply that the bombing in the North had been halted five times but to no avail. He said that the Russians had informed the U.S. if the bombing stopped talks would get started. We pressed them, said the president, to give us some word this would be the case, and we would be willing to stop the bombing, but no word came. "Continue your appeals," urged the pope, "for patience is needed. Everything you do for peace, I will support."

The president remarked that Hanoi is not going to the conference table simply because they think they will win the war in Washington. The president said he felt that we are ready to stop the fighting and the bombing but we can't stop half a war: we must stop it all. He remained convinced that the best avenue available is in the South, between Saigon and the Viet Cong. The pope eagerly agreed, and said he would encourage it.

The pope told the president he would like to convey the president's obvious passion for gaining peace to others who might help. (He intimated it was the Russians about whom he was talking.) The president recounted his own conversation with Kosygin and spoke of Kosygin's talks with Harold Wilson.

They talked more of Vietnam, the president exploring how the pope might bring differing factions together, and the pope eager to be of help if his help could be useful. Then the president asked the pope if he could send a representative to see American prisoners in the North. Hopefully, the president said, if the pope could call on both sides to accord just and humane treatment to prisoners and ask for permission to visit both sides, we would be willing to open our doors immediately.

Again the pope pleaded for patience and perseverance, and urged that the war take a defensive rather than offensive turn.

The president pressed the pope to encourage the Catholic leaders in Vietnam to sit down with their enemies to try to find a settlement. Here the president smiled and said, rather engagingly I thought, "I would hope the holy father would encourage them to talk just as he has encouraged me to pass my education bills. We are now spending nine billion dollars more on education in the United States and the pope can claim some credit for this." The pope seemed genuinely pleased. He raised his hands as if to clasp them in prayer, a gesture of modest pleasure.

Again the president pressed the point home that the peace needed to be made in South Vietnam. Then he reached for an analogy, a bit homely, but typically Johnson. He said: "In my home state in Texas a lot of Ford automobiles carry a sticker that says, 'Made in Texas by Texans.' I would like a slogan in Saigon that says, 'Peace in South Vietnam made by the Vietnamese.' "

The pope said he would try with all his heart to help. Then he asked if the Christmas truce could be extended.

The president responded by recounting what his military leaders had told him: that the North Vietnamese have trucks lined up bumper to bumper and as soon as the truce begins they will start them moving toward the South, filled with soldiers that kill Americans. He reviewed his past peace overtures and bombing halts. In the thirty-seven-day pause, the president said, the North built up a seven months supply of weaponry.

The pope asked where the Viet Cong was getting its men and material. The president replied that through terror the Viet Cong was recruiting in the South, sometimes impressing fourteen-year-old boys into their ranks and were using *kamikaze* tactics.

Again, the president turned to the prisoner problem, and papal assistance with the South Vietnamese Catholic leaders. "Can I assume you will help us on these points?" The pope smiled and nodded. He said he would do whatever is possible, that he would study the prisoner problem, and make the contacts desired. "This is a cause close to my heart," said the pope.

The pope and the president then looked over a presidential draft statement of a press release of the meeting. The pope nodded as the draft was read to him. He objected to one sentence which quoted the president as saying, "we will never surrender South Vietnam to aggression or attack." The holy father said that if this line were in the statement it would appear the pope was endorsing war. The president instantly struck it from the release.

Now we all stood. It was 10:17 P.M. (Rostow was now in the meeting. Midway, I had fetched him from the outer room, at the president's direction, and brought him in.)

The pope and the president shook hands warmly, each seeming to regret the meeting was ending. They were smiling as the room filled with aides and others who came in now to chat in the closing minutes of the conference.

Soon, we left. As I prepared to get in the president's limousine, I felt a firm hand on my shoulder. I turned. It was Marcinkus. He was grinning widely. He whispered, "Please tell your boss that my boss felt it was a wonderful meeting and he was so glad the president took time to visit him."

I laughed, waved, and got inside. I repeated the words of Marcinkus to the president. He was plainly pleased. "I thought it was a good meeting, too," he said. Both the president and I were grateful the conference had moved so smoothly, so full of evident goodwill. It was worth the long trip.

We landed in Washington in time for Christmas and I slept for what seemed like two days straight, weariness infecting every part of me.

Several days later, the roof fell in on the president and buried me in the debris.

Newsweek ran the following story about the president's trip:

ROME HAUL

From the moment he flew off in Air Force One two weeks ago on his round-the-world Christmas trip, Lyndon Johnson made news everywhere he went—from Australia to Vietnam to the Vatican. But it was not until he arrived back in Washington in the early hours of last week that word began to leak out of a story everyone had missed: the meeting between the President and the Pope had, in fact, been less than completely harmonious.

Reportedly, the meeting was sought by the White House in the first place primarily because of concern that there was a growing divergence of views between the two world leaders over how best to settle the Vietnamese war. Before Mr. Johnson left on his trip, he had been informed that Pope Paul VI "planned to do something very dramatic about Vietnam." Coming as it did only a month after the Pope had implicitly criticized the U.S. bombing campaign against North Vietnam, this news understandably filled the President with concern that the head of the Roman Catholic Church might take some action that would embarrass the U.S.

Audience: Mr. Johnson's concern was heightened when it began to seem that the Vatican was less than eager to grant him a papal audience. It was, in fact, only after the President's plane had left Karachi and was well on its way to Madrid that word was received from Rome that "protocol and logistics" problems had been cleared up and the visit to the Vatican was all set.

The meeting itself turned out to be a correct but impersonal encounter. According to diplomatic insiders, the President in folksy Texas fashion sought to bridge the gap by telling the Pope how pleased he was about his daughter Luci's conversion to Catholicism. But the Pope, who had a ten-page memo on the desk in front of him, immediately launched into a discussion on Vietnam.

Why, His Holiness wanted to know, couldn't the U.S. prolong the 24-hour Christmas truce and indefinitely suspend the bombing? The President sought to explain that so long as U.S. troops were fighting in Vietnam he was duty-bound to give them all the possible military support at his disposal. Visibly upset by this reply, the Pope sharply demanded: "*Perche* (Why?)"

At another point the President made it clear that he was not entirely happy with Vatican diplomats interfering with the U.S.'s own peace initiatives. (For some time, the Pope reportedly has been sending messages to the governments of North and South Vietnam through Hanoi's Archbishop Trin Nhu Khue and Saigon's Archbishop Nguyen Van Binh.) But the Pope was unimpressed by the President's argument.

After the meeting, a knowledgeable official in Rome reported: "Everyone left unhappy. The encounter ended as a frigid meeting between two diplomats." And in Washington, another source in a position to know admitted:

"I would be less than honest with you if I said there was a complete meeting of minds."

For the record, Washington put the best possible face on the meeting. Administration spokesmen insisted that the Pope had been "sympathetic and understanding." As proof that everything went smoothly, one senior official pointed out that, when LBJ expressed concern over the treatment of U.S. prisoners in North Vietnam, the Pope replied that he would take the problem "under advisement." And when it appeared last week that the

Pope was, in fact, considering sending a mission to Hanoi, the Administration chose to conclude that the mission would be primarily concerned with the POW problem. In Rome, however, the expectation was that if a papal mission does eventually materialize, the Vatican emissaries will spend more of their time discussing peace than prisoners. But whether they will find the North Vietnamese leaders *simpatico* is, of course, another question.

The president was on the phone to me the very day *Newsweek* came out. He was furious. Actually, that understates the case. Suffice to say, he was mad as hell.

"Get in touch with Kay Graham and find out how she tolerates such stupidity on her magazine. Any idiot that writes a story like that ought to be confined." That was only part of what he told me. When my ear, scorched from the heat of the president's tirade, detached itself from the receiver, I called Kay Graham.

Mrs. Philip Graham, Katherine Graham, is a totally feminine woman, pretty, clear-eyed, soft and endearing to her friends, and yet a woman who successfully directs one of the most powerful and influential communications establishments in all the country. She is a thorough-going professional who does her homework and knows her business. The *Washington Post*, brought to its Washington morning monopoly by her late, charismatic husband (a man whom my wife called one of the most electric personalities she had ever known) and *Newsweek*, are the linchpins of the Graham empire. They are manned and led by the ablest professionals in the field, and no politician would dare conclude that the *Post* is a toothless tiger for he would be labeled a fool. The *Post*, commanded daily by Ben Bradlee and Philip Geyelin casts its net over the federal scene and nothing escapes its brazened, tutored, relevant eye. *Newsweek*, fending weekly with *Time*, has caught up with the Luce giant and battles on equal terms with its once dominant competition.

Thus, the Graham kingdom is important to whomever lives in the White House. President Johnson earlier determined that Kay Graham was tuned to every slug of type that filled the printing drums of the *Post* and *Newsweek*, and he brought, or caused to be brought, to her attention every presidential flogging in both her publications. Kay suffered under this presidential scrutiny, for of course she didn't read every piece of copy before it was printed, but she wearily and dutifully endured the calls from White House aides crying "foul."

I called her and let her inspect my summary of affronts, concluding with the final summation that the Rome story in *Newsweek* was a lie, plain and simple. As usual, listening politely, and invested with a tinge of understanding, Kay suggested I call Osborn Elliott, editor in chief of *Newsweek*.

Mr. Elliott was next on my call list. In our first conversation which lasted about forty-five minutes, Oz Elliott and I sparred, parried, half-snarled (at least I did), and accomplished absolutely nothing.

The scenario went something like this: I told him his story was totally, 100 percent, from stem to stern, beginning to end, false. What *Newsweek* reported just didn't happen. I went over in some detail the conversation between the pope and the president, and offered to let him read my handwritten notes. Elliott responded by saying that *Newsweek*'s sources were excellent and he would go with the source and the story.

Are you saying, I exclaimed with some heat, that you refuse to believe the president of the United States and his aide and swallow whole the report of some source instead? That was more or less what he meant, said Mr. Elliott.

I told him I didn't know who was leaking but I damn

sure knew it wasn't the pope, and I couldn't believe that Benelli, Cicognani, or Marcinkus would lie. It would be a bit embarrassing to their vows, which, of course, *Newsweek* sources hadn't taken, or if they had would conveniently forget. A bit harsh on my part, responded Mr. Elliott, but the fact is *Newsweek* would stand by its story.

After some similarly charming talk in which we both divested ourselves of any credibility in the other's word, we hung up. I have to report Mr. Elliott was civil, calm-voiced, and persistently agreeable. He just didn't believe me.

I then called Marcinkus with my roll call of complaints and he said he intended to call in the *Newsweek* correspondent in Rome and chastise him.

I was determined to bring *Newsweek* to heel not because I thought that would be amusing, but because the president's fury had not abated. He considered the *Newsweek* story a black and invidious smear on his word and on the warmth of the meeting with the pope and he was going to do his damnedest to get a retraction. Needless to say he was not pleased with my handling of the situation. I reported little of my Elliott conversation because it would only inflame the president and would be of no worth to future talks.

I also brought my case to Mel Elfin, Washington bureau chief of *Newsweek*. Elfin, brainy and quick, with that marvelous news instinct that only the really great correspondents have in any substantive quantity, was sympathetic, but he had nothing to offer me in the way of substance since he was unaware of the facts. While this was a presidential story, which normally came within his ken, this particular story emerged from the Rome bureau and escaped his jurisdiction. I bemoaned privately Elfin's exclusion from the arena. He would have been receptive, I am sure, to what I was saying.

Meanwhile, I had learned from Rome that the source of

the *Newsweek* story was a stringer in the Vatican, a lady named Sullivan. So in my second conversation with Oz Elliott, I confronted him with this, and he confirmed that Ms. Sullivan had brought the story to them, though, he hastened to add, Ms. Sullivan's sources were impeccable, which, naturally, sent me up the wall.

Elliott told me that his magazine had four different sources in the Vatican from whom Ms. Sullivan collected her facts, two or more in the State Department, and what he called "one or two triangulating reports from correspondents in the field." To which I responded with some heat that I didn't care if he had resurrected Euclid to do *Newsweek*'s triangulating, whatever the hell that was, and had a whole battalion of sources, the story wasn't true.

Not so, said Elliott. *Newsweek* had, he said, taken special care with this story. He had a "reading from State from more than one person about a sour atmosphere." Indeed, he remonstrated that it was interesting that *Newsweek* had gotten such a fine degree of triangulation (there was that blasted word again) with precise fitting of all parts of the story.

I continued to press Elliott, what about my notes, how could there be a more prime source than the man who was actually taking down what the pope said, who the hell was this Sullivan dame and all those precise fittings and sources who weren't there. Unless Ms. Sullivan had that claw-footed table bugged, how could she be certain, and if she indeed had it bugged the truth would have come out, and if she didn't have the table bugged how could all these "impeccable sources" have printed out such dung as was in the *Newsweek* story. I was, as I think about it, neither charming nor diplomatic. Elliott, as usual quite calm, said he must rely on professional reporters. I replied that he was relying on shadows and rumor. This sort of logic and form pervaded our conversation.

Elliott listened with a disciplined urbanity and stood his

ground, such as it was. I was unable to bend or turn him. But I honestly believe I shook him. I have the feeling, to this hour, that Oz Elliott and the rest of the *Newsweek* hierarchy must have had some second thoughts about the story. It was inconceivable that the president and I could have pressed this point so passionately unless we were right and they were wrong. And we were there and they weren't. I suspect that in the private chambers of the magazine's editors, there was the torment of knowing something was amiss and being unable to do anything about it.

This episode sticks in my mind today, vivid, scarring, unforgettable, because it is a classic case of wrong information being published and because it spotlighted the president of the United States, with all his supposed vast and limitless powers, bogged down in discontent and ineffectual importunings.

To the day he died, the president never forgot it either. He was able to joke about it later and oftentimes, to needle me a bit, he would say something like: "How are you and Kay Graham getting along? Has she introduced you to any new Vatican stringers yet?" Or he would read something in the *Post* and grin at me, saying, "Here's another one of those pope and president stories, Jack," meaning he had read something that he considered to be nonsense. But the president always regarded Kay Graham with durable affection. He liked her as a human being. He admired her husband with a depth and intensity that I marveled at. Often he would mutter that if "Phil Graham were living, it would have been a different kind of presidency for me," supposedly meaning that Phil, with his strength and dominance, would have championed LBJ and leveled much of the press opposition to him.

Once at a dinner party at Kay's home (I believe he was no longer president then) LBJ sat with Don Graham, Kay's son, and Don's wife, and regaled them for a long time with stories about Don's father, and how much the president loved and respected him. It was a poignant evening, for both the president and Kay Graham.

When LBJ became president, he continued his easy and close relationship with Joe Alsop, as fascinating and unbelievable a figure as could be conceived by Charles Dickens or Charles Addams. He is sublimely, supremely, endlessly arrogant, which of course does limit the number of those who will swear undying love for Joe Alsop. But he is a professional and he works at his job.

There is also no question that Alsop is the last of a breed of correspondents whose specialized art form and fevered dazzle bring adventure to newsprint. We live in a more corrosive world where Alsop's brand of reporting, personal, righteous, intimate, and slightly overblown, is no longer in fashion with younger press tigers.* Alsop's younger brother, the late Stewart Alsop, was esteemed in Washington as one of the sanest, most rational, and respected of all columnists. The Alsop family quite obviously bears out President Johnson's keen sense of the value of heredity. "There is something in the stud," LBJ used to say when he wanted to compliment a family whose achievements were outstanding.

The president found Joe Alsop a sometimes ally, interesting and companionable, if not consistently right, as the president saw it. I remember clearly one evening, June 15, 1964, when the president had to dinner the Clark Cliffords, Joe and Susan Mary Alsop (Joe's wife, a wisp of a lady, charming beyond measure and a sweet and engaging dinner companion), and my wife and me.

After dinner, we four men took a walk. The night air

---

* For my part, I found, and find, the Alsop style fascinating. Any man who can, as Joe Alsop did, use the phrase "bottom-dwelling slug" to describe a political villain, has redeeming qualities.

was soft and the elements were comfortable. So we walked around the asphalt Ellipse of the South Grounds, some five times around, a total I would guess of about a mile and a quarter. The president was expertly needling Joe and I daresay Joe was unaware of the presidential jabs.

"Now, just what would you do in Vietnam, Joe? You are always full of alarm and urgency, but now I want to hear from you exactly what you would do," the president chided him. Alsop wound up and laid down a barrage of conversation in which he generalized about the situation. He uttered apothegms and maxims and then the president interposed: "Now, that's very fine, Joe, but what the hell would you do at 9:00 A.M. tomorrow morning? Every time I ask one of you experts who write knowledgeably about all the problems a president has—what you would do—you always blow generalities in my face. You tell me we ought to be firm, but you don't tell me how. You tell me we should apply sanctions, but you don't tell me what."

The president laughed, turned to Clark and me and said, "Joe reminds me of General De Gaulle. When De Gaulle talked about neutralization I said that is very fine. But when you asked him 'what's your plan, general,' De Gaulle would always wave his hand and say: 'Don't bother me, those are just details.' " The president, still laughing, saluted Joe in the manner of a French general. Joe wore a half smile, not quite sure whether the president was joshing him or what. Joe did something unaccountably strange. He shut up.

In fact, Joe Alsop represented a point of view that the president took care to listen to. He had always drearily concluded that his big problem in extricating himself from Vietnam stemmed not from the left, but from the right. He was sorely afraid that Republicans and conservative Democrats would maul him unmercifully if he detached from Vietnam without leaving behind a stable enterprise.

He was haunted by the thought of increasing pressures from this wing of political conviction which would damage his own leadership of his domestic legislative program.

Few editorial writers were recommending withdrawal. The Kennedy commitment was still intact among the influential news journals of the country, and their impact was felt in the Senate and House chambers. What Joe Alsop was reciting to the president was not merely his own stoutly held views. He was repeating what at the time was a majority opinion in the nation. Johnson knew this. Every instinct inside him was investing him with the alluring prospect of getting out now before we became mired down. But he was tugged at by the policies of three presidents and the currents that ran through most of the leadership opinion in the press and in the Congress.

The Alsop syndrome was the president's hairshirt. Its coarse covering could be felt by the president every time he ached to be rid of Vietnam; it intruded into every presidential desire to cut losses and get out. It was a fact of life and the president knew it.

Thus, Joe Alsop, the elegant gun, stood for and represented the hard hawks of the town and the nation. The president listened to him because LBJ never turned his ear away from any viewpoint. He wanted to know all about everything. The only way he could chart a course out of a labyrinth was to understand every curl and twist, no matter the source of the information. So he talked, and listened, and knew that if ever he reversed course, there were ambushes ready for him, to shoot him down in the press and in the Congress.

*   *   *

The president revealed himself with remarkable candor in many of his press interviews. I thought that he spoke with too much frankness and allowed the reporter to quote too much about him. These stories would race through Washington with the speed of light and add to the ever-growing lore about LBJ. I record now one of those early interviews in which my own notes were rather complete, as an example of numerous chats with reporters. This interview took place on July 25, 1964, before the election, and some eight months after LBJ acceded to the presidency. It is typical of the ones he gave to reporters at the time. Dan Rather, the CBS White House correspondent, and Bob Thompson, then the White House correspondent for the *Los Angeles Times*, were the two reporters. It began at 6:30 P.M. and lasted to 7:40 P.M.

The rules of the game were that this was a "backgrounder," which means that no direct quotes of the president were allowed but the story could be written that "the president is known to feel" and "the president regards," and so forth. The professionals in Washington, reading or hearing such a story in print or in broadcast, would know instantly that the reporter was giving an accurate and almost verbatim recounting of the president's words. The following is from notes taken at the interview:

QUESTION: The president was asked why he has been more successful than his predecessors in getting legislation through Congress.

PRESIDENT: Mr. Johnson said he hoped he had done better than his predecessors, and actually believes he has. But he predicted he will have problems later on, as all presidents do. For example, he recalled that President Roosevelt had great difficulty with Congress after the Supreme Court "packing" fight. The president pointed out that he currently is concerned because there is no one in Congress who really has the skill for "counting heads." He made some off-record remarks indicating that Bobby Baker—other issues aside—had a talent in this area which has not been duplicated.

Mr. Johnson went on to say that because there is no one in Congress at present with this skill, he anticipates delays and eventually trouble with his legislative program. The president explained that one of the major reasons for his success as a leader in Congress was that he learned early in the game to count heads, and to discern which way individual members were leaning. He added he thought he was successful also because "I don't wear out." He recalled the advice given him by a senior senator when he accepted the majority leadership. The advice was "You've got to be tough . . . you've got to stay with it . . . and you can't wear out." He said this advice was given to him when it was necessary for him to break a filibuster. He said he later used that same advice against the man who had given it to him. When he initially received the advice, Mr. Johnson said, he went to the Senate floor and announced: "We're going at least until midnight." He said he did that to give himself a lesson in being tough and not letting anyone "wear me out."

QUESTION: The president was asked particularly why he fared better than Presidents Kennedy or Eisenhower in getting legislation through the Congress.

PRESIDENT: Mr. Johnson pointed out that when he came to the presidency Congress had completely stopped Mr. Kennedy on the tax bill, education, civil rights, and other legislation. In explaining his attitude toward congressional relations, he recalled Speaker Rayburn's quote: "If General Marshall doesn't know more about the war than I do, then we've wasted a lot of money on West Point." Mr. Johnson went on to say that if, in his thirty-two years on Capitol Hill, he had not learned a great deal about legislative management, then he had wasted a lot of time.

The president explained he had learned a great deal during his twelve years in the House, twelve years in the Senate, and three years as vice-president. He said he likes to think he puts in more time in congressional relations than Eisenhower did, and perhaps shows more interest than Kennedy, who, he said, appeared many times to look upon congressional liaison with contempt.

QUESTION: The president was asked how involved he is in personal persuasion of members of Congress.

PRESIDENT: He said many of the stories about his using personal persuasion are misleading. He explained that you don't win a congressman just by calling him on the telephone and giving him the devil, or complimenting him. To the contrary, Mr. Johnson said, "You've got to know the man; he's got to know that you respect him, or at least think you do, and you've got to know a great deal about him."

The president pointed out that he and Mrs. Johnson have spent much of their lifetimes with members of Congress. He said they know most of them, and try to let congressmen realize that the Johnsons like and respect them. He recalled that one of his first acts was to invite all 531 members of Congress to a Christmas party. He said he and Mrs. Johnson decided that he would brief members of Congress on defense, foreign, and domestic matters, and that she would brief the wives on the White House. The president recalled that Mrs. Johnson took all the wives on a tour of the Mansion and gave them a full rundown on its operation. He said the Christmas party made everyone who attended feel that he was a part of the government, and a part of much of what the administration was trying to accomplish.

The president said a basic tenet of his dealings with Congress is to let members know that they are regarded as important in the White House. He recalled a telephone conversation he had just had with Senator Dirksen. He said he kidded Dirksen about his nominating speech for

Senator Goldwater and suggested to Dirksen that he spend much of his summer "looking after flowers" rather than campaigning for Goldwater. In response to Dirksen's request for a visit with the president, Mr. Johnson said he told the senator: "Come on down any day next week after 7 o'clock in the evening and I'll buy you a drink . . . and it won't be Sanka." The president laughingly recalled Senate speeches in which Dirksen chided Mr. Johnson for serving him Sanka.

Mr. Johnson said he is determined to pay a lot of attention to everyone who comes to the White House. He seemed particularly pleased with his luncheon for 264 businessmen, and said he anticipates that 200 of them may vote for him. He pointed out that he has had more business and labor leaders in the White House than any previous administration in history. He noted, for instance, that at his luncheon for labor leaders last week, he had at least one AFL-CIO official from every one of the fifty states. He said he wants these men to feel they are part of what his administration is doing. He said a president cannot delegate authority in this area . . . he must do it himself.

QUESTION: The president was asked to tell how he envisions a good vice-president operating.

PRESIDENT: The president said that a vice-president has an excellent opportunity for leadership as a cabinet director of independent agencies such as the AEC and NASA. He said a vice-president should provide inspiration and direction for these agencies. And, he added, the vice-president should offer better liaison with Congress.

He said that if he gets the man he wants this year (and he emphasized that for varying reasons he may not get the man he wants) he would have that man officed in the White House and make him "an executive operating vice-president." The president described this ideal vice-president as an "improved model of a Mac Bundy or Sherman Adams." Mr. Johnson said he considered Barkley and Garner excellent vice-presidents who operated well with Congress. He said he thought the vice-president should operate much as they did. In response to a direct question, the president said that Richard Nixon was not able to operate this way because he didn't get along well with most senators. The president told a story of how Nixon indirectly helped put him in the White House. He recalled that Speaker Rayburn finally advised him to accept second place on the Kennedy ticket because Mr. Rayburn was afraid Nixon might win if he did not. He said Mr. Rayburn was concerned that the Democrats might lose Texas and that could have been the difference in the outcome of the election. Mr. Johnson pointed out that Speaker Rayburn had never forgotten Nixon campaign remarks questioning the loyalty of the Democrats in the early 1950s.

QUESTION: The president was asked if the late President Kennedy had been sensitive to Mr. Johnson's feelings as vice-president.

PRESIDENT: The president said yes. He recalled that Mr. Kennedy once said, "I don't know how you're able to contain yourself," indicating that Mr. Kennedy knew the sense of frustration Mr. Johnson felt after so many years of leadership in Congress. The president confirmed that he had indeed experienced considerable frustration. The president said that he had tried to be extremely loyal to Mr. Kennedy. He said he wanted Mr. Kennedy to know, "I wouldn't let him down." He told the story of seeing Mrs. Kennedy at the White House just after the Bay of Pigs when Mrs. Kennedy said: "You'll never quit us will you, Lyndon?" The president said he replied: "No, I'm here for the duration." Mr. Johnson said that was the way he had wanted the Kennedys to think of him.

QUESTION: The president was asked about foreign policy, specifically differences between his approach and that of previous presidents. Latin America and the appointment of Ambassador Mann as assistant secretary of state were mentioned specifically.

PRESIDENT: The president said he first became aware of Mann during the early days of the Kennedy administration when Mann made appearances at high level White House meetings. Mr. Johnson said he liked and admired Mann then. He said he thought the Kennedy administration had too many idealists trying to implement too many ideas simultaneously in Latin America. He said he thought that after Mann went to Mexico during the Kennedy years there was no real take-charge person administering Latin American affairs. The president promised that now with Mann back Latin America will "get roads and schools instead of a lot of conversation." He said he thinks the Panama situation has improved because he sent a Spanish-speaking former Peace Corps official down there as ambassador rather than yielding to pressure to appoint a former congressman. The president said that it was not commonly known when he came into office that there were a great many problems fermenting in Latin America. One of these was the trouble in Panama; another was the Guantanamo water situation.

Concerning his personal involvement in foreign affairs, the president said he adhered to the idea that the better you know people the better you understand them. He said he felt the president should have as much personal contact as possible with foreign heads of state and their envoys. He pointed out that he has seen thirty heads of state in eight months compared with President Eisenhower's record of seeing only seventy in eight years.

He explained his role in the Cyprus dispute, comparing it with his involvement in the railroad strike. He acknowledged that he may not be as successful with Cyprus as he was in settling the railroad dispute. But, he said, he always feels obliged to get personally involved if there's a chance that it will help. He also said he tried to get the best brains available to help settle any problem. He pointed to Dean Acheson's role in trying to settle the Cyprus problem as an example. The president emphasized, however, that he likes to remain in personal control of most situations. He said, "We may go to hell in a hack and sink the ship tomorrow, but I'm going to be up there with the wheel in my hand. I'm going to be in the middle of things."

QUESTION: The president was asked what he had learned from each of the presidents he had served.

PRESIDENT: Mr. Johnson started with President Hoover, whom he greatly admires. He pointed out that when he came to Washington in 1931, Hoover was in the White House. The president said he likes Mr. Hoover and respects him. He said, "I thought Hoover was a victim of sadistic people and economic conditions over which he had no control. He was unusually equipped to be president." But, Mr. Johnson said off the record, he personally never wants to be guilty of "inaction."

Turning to President Roosevelt, Mr. Johnson remarked that Roosevelt is his "hero" of the five presidents he has served under. He said Roosevelt had a heart as compassionate as that of his own mother, and a mind as strategic as that of his father. He recalled that Roosevelt, like his father, "had a touch of the populist." The president pointed out that his father, a member of the Texas legislature, fought for railroad legislation, opposed the Ku Klux Klan, and was a champion of civil liberties. The president recalled that his father beat down a bill in the Texas legislature which directed the burning of books of German immigrants. The president said his father got that bill recommitted.

Mr. Johnson said Roosevelt was a great help to him and actually acted as a father to him. He told the story of Roosevelt's helping him get government financing for a hydroelectric project in his home district, even though the district's population density was about half the required amount for a loan. Mr. Johnson said Roosevelt told the man in charge, "If that's the only problem you have with it, just send the loan over here and I'll sign it, because those people breed fast down there."

The president said his concept of the need for full employment, the Great Society, and the abolition of poverty came from Roosevelt. Of President Truman, Mr. Johnson said, "He's going to really be one of our great presidents." Although he was not close to Mr. Truman during the Truman White House years, Mr. Johnson said he did play poker with the president and Senator Clint Anderson, the late Chief Justice Fred Vinson, Clark Clifford, and others. The president said Mr. Rayburn usually was present at these sessions, but did not play poker. Mr. Johnson remarked that Mr. Truman had guts and courage. When he recently faced the problem of sending U.S. planes over Laos, the president said, he asked himself what Truman would do. He said he decided that Truman would send them. Mr. Johnson said he had sent the planes on their mission, then stayed up until 3 A.M. until he received word they had returned.

Mr. Johnson described President Eisenhower as a fair and competent man, and one who was strongly bipartisan. The president said he tries to conduct himself toward the Republicans as Mr. Eisenhower "conducted himself toward me."

The president paused a long time before describing his views toward President Kennedy. He then said that Mr.

Kennedy was very just and good to him. But the president said he looked upon Mr. Kennedy differently than the other chief executives he had known. He pointed out that Mr. Kennedy was elected by only .08 of 1 percent of the total vote. He also noted Mr. Kennedy had served briefly in the two houses of Congress, not long enough to ever be in command of them. Mr. Johnson said he had wanted to help Mr. Kennedy, and had wanted Mr. Kennedy to think well of him. He said he admired President Kennedy's intellect and courage and felt President Kennedy had treated him well.

QUESTION: The president was asked what philosophy he brought into the White House about organization of the executive branch.

PRESIDENT: Mr. Johnson reported that he felt Mr. Kennedy had good men around him, and he feels fortunate he has been able to keep most of them. He said he thought the White House was well organized under President Kennedy. Mr. Johnson said he tries to see cabinet officers and other officials, singly or in groups, as often as possible. He pointed out he had invited cabinet officers to church with him and to dine at the White House. He said he has a standing engagement to have lunch every Tuesday with Secretaries Rusk and McNamara.

QUESTION: The president was asked to express some of his feelings at the time of President Kennedy's assassination.

PRESIDENT: Mr. Johnson, in reply to a direct question, said that he had thought, an international conspiracy might be underway to "flatten us out." Because of this concern, the president said, he ordered that Air Force One be moved at the airport. Then, he said, he decided to go directly to the plane from Parkland Hospital. Even beyond that point, the president said, he had grave doubts about the advisability of "sitting at the airport" for two hours, but he felt it imperative that President Kennedy's body be returned immediately to Washington.

* * *

I personally found the White House press corps a group of uncommon intelligence. I liked them, and liked to be around them, talking to them, listening to them. The president, somewhat amused by my own special interest in the press, was tolerant of my rapport with many of the White House correspondents. But on several occasions, he ordered that his staff was not to sit down and hold conferences with the press. That was the duty of the press secretary, and when Bill Moyers was press chief, the presidential order was that we inform Moyers of any contacts we had with the press so that Moyers would know what we were saying, which in the president's judgment ought to be damn little.

LBJ, as all presidents before and after him, regarded leaks as inexcusable, blunders of the first rank, and he exhibited toward leaks a Johnsonian wrath which began in frustration and ended in anger. He hoarded large decisions, shielding them from the view of all but a few staff members, depending on whom he considered to be the "leaker of the week." Sometimes he floated names of possible appointees around the staff to see what would be leaked. It was an axiom of the press that LBJ withdrew from nomination the names of some whose names had been flung to the press ahead of announcement. I honestly don't recall any specific instance of this, and it is possible that the press was not in visible error, since on several occasions it was a "floater" and not the person about to be named.

When the president determined to name Walter Washington as the first mayor of the nation's capital, Washington's name was emblazoned in headlines some days before LBJ was to announce him. In truth, I must state that LBJ was fit to crawl the walls of the White House so incensed did he become over the leak of the name. Along with others on the staff, I fretted lest the president withdraw the name of Washington, an able, energetic man of enormous talent. But the president, after some hours of ire-spilling went forward with the nomination, to the exhaling of relief on the part of the staff.

Perhaps the most intimate friend of the president's within the press corps was William S. White, the Pulitzer Prize–winning newsman, first with the *New York Times* and lately a widely read syndicated columnist. Bill White was one of those enduring friends who had first met Lyndon Johnson when the future president was a congressional secretary, living in the basement of the Dodge Hotel. He and Bill White spent many an evening together, Johnson, new to the capital, eager to make his mark, and White, a novice reporter just beginning to ply his craft. They knew each other in those dog days, when both were young and obscure, and from that relationship was created a binding friendship never to be breached or shattered.

Bill White, a literate, honest, iron-minded newsman, with an engaging prose style, and reporter's instinct, never in all the years of the Johnson presidency ever encroached on his intimate kinship with LBJ. I cannot remember ever having Bill call me to seek out any news, and his visits to the president were seldom in the Oval Office to ferret out information. They were invariably in the Mansion, in the evening, over drinks and dinner, or strolling together on the South Grounds, where, as old friends often do, they exchanged stories of long-ago days. The president gave Bill White total trust, for he knew nothing he said or any feelings he hinted at would find their way into print. Bill

White is a newsman of the old-school, respectful of the presidency, but independent of mind and habit, valuing his own integrity. Few presidents form this kind of relationship with a reporter but the Johnson-White friendship was durable enough to withstand almost anything.*

*   *   *

Like the blight of a disease that kills the crops, like the endless eternity of a drought parching and wrinkling the land, the Vietnam War pulled from the president all the laid-up goodwill and adulation that his unerasable human and social achievements had stored for him.

There was for him only a despairing notion that the more he tried, the sharper was the cut of the reporting press.

That is the way of the public man caught up in events he strove to avoid. It is a story often told in the history books, which, ironically is where President Johnson finally put his case.

"We'll just have to see how it comes out," he said.

Some time in the future, when the rains have come, when the crops are clean and growing, and the land is fresh again, we'll see how it came out.

---

* Charles Bartlett, the *Chicago Sun-Times* syndicated columnist, had that same relationship with President Kennedy. It was Bartlett and his charming, high-spirited wife, Martha, who introduced JFK to Jacqueline Bouvier, and JFK was godfather to one of their children. Bartlett was privy to the innermost JFK thoughts, but not once did Charlie Bartlett ever infringe on his affection and fidelity to President Kennedy by printing anything that fell from the president's lips.

PART IV

The War

How did Vietnam come about? How did it break the continuity of an administration? What was the decision-making process that conceived an intervention in Vietnam on a scale so huge that it broke the spine of public support? What were the ingredients that caused press, public, and Congress to gather enlarging forces of opposition that in time and with increasing fury attacked and wounded the chief executive? What turn of luck and events intruded themselves on a president who, though he had brought to fruition every liberal cause of the generation, finally—in order to begin the achievement of peace in Vietnam and to unify the nation—deliberately, and consciously renounced re-election?

There is no one person who can accurately report all the answers simply because, other than the president, there is no one person who was eyewitness or participant in every event that shaped a decision that in turn ordered another decision that in turn demanded still another decision. Every public act that commits to a public policy has a beginning. Every decision has an ancestor which beckons his progeny to precedent, and the slow involvement in a war which tormented and tortured the American spirit has its own sources. To isolate a decision of a magnitude and vastness (which Vietnam surely was) to a single moment of crisis is both unrealistic and untrue. The roots of Vietnam (as LBJ found them) were embedded in all that happened from the late forties to LBJ's presidency and to deny this, or to ignore it, is to lose both truth and understanding.

The first decision is the key decision; from it flows the next decision, hinged and entwined to the first; the decision after that is buckled to the previous one; until a body of fact and precedent and policy is so tightly locked together that to try to separate its parts is well nigh impossible. Each decision breeds a policy increasingly resistent to change. Disengagement then becomes complex and difficult, and the chief executive and his advisers are forced to feed into their own alternatives the decisions that came before them. In truth, in time, whenever a new decision is imminent, it is already girdled round with new factors, grown older and more inflexible by the time a brand new appraisal is called for.

If this retelling has any value, it is the realization that every decision is freighted with possibilities of disaster as well as triumph. No single movement by a great nation stands alone, disembodied from all that surrounds it.

In the summer of 1965, the thirty-sixth president was faced with more than the fearsome question of whether or not to commit even larger bodies of American troops than were then positioned in South Vietnam. It was a total decision to determine whether to pull out completely from Vietnam or to stay. The slow accumulation of public statements, presidential policies, and national intent were now weighing down on the available alternatives.

This is crucial. Lyndon Johnson was the only one of four presidents to be confronted with the leprous alternative: *get out* or *get in with more, much more.* All the previous presidents escaped, through circumstance or chance, an ugly confrontation with this decision.

Each previous president—Truman, Eisenhower, and Kennedy—had examined the situation and each had done what he thought to be right in the long-range best interests of the country whose future he swore by solemn oath to protect and defend. Each decision by each president narrowed the alternatives of his successor. It is difficult for critics to be dispassionate, that is, to set the scene exactly as it happened. The critic is fortified by hindsight, that which give him gifts of knowledge that at the time of the crucial decision were nowhere to be found.

In the hot summer of 1965, the curtain went up on the bullet-biting crisis of the Johnson administration.

Essentially, the military high command had examined the nature of the war at that moment in time and found that the entire bastion was crumbling. In their judgment the South Vietnamese armed forces were not capable of stemming the tide of reinforcements from the North; the war was going so badly, worsening so swiftly, that the joint chiefs had concluded everything was going down the tubes, and fast, unless the United Sates was prepared to commit large bodies of troops, *now.* The alternative was disaster for the Vietnamese and the prospect of evacuation of American forces immediately.

The unaskable question had now been asked.

It had to be answered.

At 10:40 A.M. on July 21, 1965, in the Cabinet Room of the White House, the first prime meeting took place, hours after the arrival from Vietnam of Secretary McNamara and General Wheeler.

When President Johnson looked squarely at the facts of the U.S. commitment and the U.S. involvement he probably looked at them with the same gaze President Kennedy might have fixed on the same questions. The same advisers who had counseled President Kennedy were now counseling President Johnson. It is fair to assume that their advice to him was what it would have been to President Kennedy.

The green draperies were drawn in the Cabinet Room in the West Wing of the White House, a spartan and sparsely furnished rectangle. Usually, the draperies were kept open during meetings, and one could see the Rose Garden, and beyond it the graceful white facade of the Mansion. Today, the Rose Garden was aglow with a profusion of colors, the gardeners having only recently planted new blooming flowers. The lawn had been cut the day previously, and the thick carpet of grass lay close to the soil, clipped and shorn of its shaggy edges.

Around the immense octagonal table sat fifteen men. The president had not yet joined the gathering. His highbacked, black leather chair was empty. In front of the vacant chair was a yellow foolscap pad, three sharpened pencils, and to the side of the pad was a carafe of water with two glasses.

These fifteen men were the president's closest advisers. He had plainly put his trust in their judgment over the previous months and whenever there was a crisis in Vietnam these were the men he summoned to take their counsel. Some of them were statutory members of the National Security Council. Some were not. Two of the men were special assistants to the president.

They were: Robert McNamara, secretary of defense; Dean Rusk, secretary of state; Cyrus Vance, deputy secretary of defense; McGeorge Bundy, special assistant to the president for national security affairs; General Wheeler, chairman of the joint chiefs of staff; George Ball, under secretary of state; William Bundy, assistant secretary of state and brother of Mac Bundy; Leonard Unger, assistant to Bundy; Richard Helms, deputy director of the CIA;

Admiral "Red" Raborn, director of the CIA; Henry Cabot Lodge, ambassador to Vietnam; Carl Rowan, head of the USIA; John McNaughton, assistant secretary of defense; Bill Moyers and Jack Valenti, special assistants to the president.

Now all of them were sitting, prepared to discuss what they all knew to be possibly the most troubling decision the president had yet faced. Each of them had read the top secret recommendation of the Defense Department; each knew he was to respond to presidential questions concerning that recommendation. Indeed, the subject of the meeting was, as everyone knew, to counsel the president on what course of action was to be taken. But the gristly question was still, *get in or get out;* most of the men around that table were aware that doing more of the same was no longer a suitable answer.

At precisely 10:40 A.M. the meeting began without the president.

The top secret memorandum of the Defense Department was read by everyone and carefully each copy was returned to McNamara. Not even the burn bags would be sufficient to clamp the lid on secrecy. Not one copy was allowed to be held by anyone.

McNamara, in his usual unvarnished prose, flat-accented, told the group that the paper was his own view of the situation. His specific recommendations had been concurred by Ambassador Lodge, Admiral Sharp, General Taylor, General Johnson, and General Westmoreland— but it was his own thinking in the paper.

Lodge frowned and raised his eyes to McNamara. Mc-Namara nodded. At this juncture in the meeting there was no chairman. What went on was a mingling of views, informal, marking time until the president made his appearance. Lodge, imperceptibly, sought McNamara's approval before he opened the discussion.

"If I thought a diplomatic move would be successful, I

would be for it. Now, it would harden the enemy. This is not the time to do it. Clarifying objectives is good for the world public, but not necessary for governments. They understand it," Lodge said.

McNamara, tracing with a pencil the document in front of him, said, "It seems to me that our call-up and the increase in budget is evidence that we are not taking over North Vietnam, nor do we want to."

"Our public utterances will make it clear that we are not trying to take over North Vietnam," Bundy put in.

(It should be noted that North Vietnam had launched a propaganda drive to convince public opinion the U.S. and South Vietnam were building toward a massive overland invasion of North Vietnam.)

McNamara took further note of this. "Our public actions must do this. We must show that we are not in accord with Ky's objective to invade North Vietnam. We are building such a force that the North might think that is what we are going to do."

Lodge scoffed, "Remember that this 'on to North Vietnam' movement is part of a propaganda move and nothing more."

Bundy turned to McNamara. "Are there divergences between the GVN * and the U.S. in troop use?"

McNamara answered, "GVN wants us to use troops in the highlands. This is unacceptable to us. While GVN originally recommended this, they are now in agreement with us."

"Bob, what is the capability of GVN to mobilize their own forces?" Rusk asked McNamara.

The secretary of defense replied, "They are trying to increase by 10,000 per month. Our country team is optimistic. But I am not. The desertion rate is high. They

---

* GVN is a shortened form for government of South Vietnam.

say it is lessening, but I don't agree. We did not find any threat of discontent among our own troops. U.S. morale is of the highest order. I am proud of their dedication and devotion. It refects the belief that they are doing something worthwhile."

Wheeler nodded. "I agree," he said. "Our advisors are pleased with the Vietnamese. They speak very highly of the Vietnamese foot soldier. The officer corps, however, is very different. Some officers are not of the highest quality. But this is not total. The big weakness in the GVN forces are lack of adequate officer material, in their training and their attitude. But they are getting better."

Rusk wanted to know if there were any summary of enemy trouble. "No," said McNamara, "nothing more than we already know. They are suffering heavy losses. They are well supplied with ammunition. I suspect much of the inflow of supplies is water-borne. The only part of our action that is unsatisfactory is our patrol of the seashore. But even if we did have tight control, it would make little difference in the next six to nine months."

Rusk pondered this a moment and asked, "What is the timing on how we should proceed?"

McNamara replied, "There ought to be a statement to the American people no later than a week, once the president's decision is reached." Bundy agreed and offered the thought that "it is quite possible the message to the Congress, once the president has determined our position, would be a message to the public."

There was more conversation, bearing on the details of how to convey a decision, no matter what its form, to the public. At precisely 11:30 A.M., the door to the Cabinet Room opened and the president entered. Everyone stood up and murmured greetings to the president. He was wearing a gray suit, with blue-flecked tie, a pale blue shirt with the usual high collar. He looked grave, even a little worn, but his stride was quick, forceful. He nodded to those around the table, sat quickly in his chair.

There was a moment's pause. He looked swiftly around the room, fixing each man's eyes on his own, then moving to the next man. His face was now a mask, neither smile nor frown, allowing only a slight nod to punctuate his inspection of these advisers.

He nodded to McNamara, and speaking very softly, addressed him, "Would you please begin, Bob."

McNamara was and remained a favorite counselor of the president. LBJ commended, I would think, President Kennedy's choice of the Ford president, former Harvard Business School professor, to become secretary of defense. When LBJ succeeded to the presidency his embrace of McNamara took on fuller and larger meaning. The precision of the McNamara mind invited the president's approval. LBJ for all his days enjoyed and appreciated the spacious dimension of intelligence coupled with a resolution capable of enduring (indeed, savoring) tedium and detail, knowing to the tiniest jot of accuracy, all that was possible to know of the problem or the issue involved. The president reveled in aides "doing their homework," to understand the nuances and shadows of what needed to be known and had to be done. McNamara was a "homework man," always knowledgeable, always informed. It was as if McNamara gulped down, in a full swallow, the indices, the numbers, the arithmetic, the circumference, and the grain of the problem, and with superb intellectual digestion absorbed it and poured it out in serried figures and action recordings. One could almost hear the clackety-clack of the McNamara brain sorting, cataloging, reinserting, and then, through some interlocking, sorting mechanism, the answers came forth in verbal printouts.

McNamara is one of the most unusual men I have ever encountered. Exact, measured, mercilessly logical, unremitting in his thrust toward deliverable solutions, with no nonsense, no cloudy metaphysical contortions to bar his way, this was McNamara at work. What Bagehot wrote of Lord Lyndhurst, one could also apply to McNamara: "There was no laxity in his intellect, everything there was braced and knit." Yet, beyond the periphery of the job, Bob McNamara was a companionable man, quick to laugh, eager to share in wit and gaiety, warmly sympathetic to another's problems. A puzzling aberration in the public view of McNamara was their lack of knowledge of his compassion, his sensitivity to human misery and deprivation. The reporter's view of McNamara centered on the McNamara mind and overlooked the McNamara heart, large, feeling, caring. Perhaps it was because there mixed within him equal portions of logic and warmth; the political observer or the technical critic tended to focus on the visible sharpness instead of the less visible softness.

His wife, Margy, melded with him so that they became almost one person. No man can say what stirred within his heart and mind, what nettlesome doubts may have seeped into those crannies of his brain where only McNamara was privy and where his innermost convictions lay hidden.

I am not sure that I "really knew" Bob McNamara. Perhaps none of us really knows the full and unrevealed parts of a superior human being, as he surely is. But I never found him false. I never saw evidence that he shaded truth or debased his opinions. He fed himself on facts; this is the bone and blood of his life. He never twisted what he believed. He never mauled the truth as he saw the truth. It is fair to say that as far as my observation was concerned, McNamara was (and is) a fair man, a just man, an honorable man. I would testify that I confirmed the president's unshaken confidence in McNamara's ability, his lacerating energy and the sure and honest harness with which he controlled every demand on his judgment so that it would be sound.

At the president's invitation, McNamara began his summary of his memorandum. He spoke without pause or hesitation. McNamara's last part of his summary concluded with a statement that to support 200,000 troops in Vietnam, by the first of the year the reserves in the U.S. should be reconstituted by a like amount. He recommended calling up the 235,000 reserves a year from now, replacing the reserves with regulars. In mid-1966, said McNamara, we would have approximately 600,000 additional men available.

When he had finished, the president, who had listened impassively, said nothing. He leaned back in his chair, with a yellow pencil in his hand. He pointed the pencil at McNamara and spoke, the voice husky and low, almost inaudible. "What I would like to know is what has happened in recent months that requires this kind of decision on my part. What are the alternatives? I want this discussed in full detail, from everyone around this table."

The men around the table listened intently. I leaned forward in my chair, seated just behind and to the right of the president. His hand, holding the pencil, was steady. He seemed perfectly calm, composed, and I recognized the mood and flex within the president. He had summoned his disciplines. He was examining with exhausting penetration this possible decision and like so many other similar occurrences, I knew he was beginning to circle the problem, approaching it from all sides, determined to find its soft spots, analyzing the chessboard, figuring with that rigorous intensity he brought to bear on any difficult problem what turns in the road would be permissible and how deep into uncharted territory he was prepared to go.

He continued: "Have we wrung every single soldier out of every country that we can? Who else can help us here? Are we the sole defenders in the world? Have we done all we can in this direction? What are the compelling reasons for this call-up? What results can we expect? Again, I ask you what are the alternatives? I don't want us to make snap judgments. I want us to consider all our options. We know we can tell the South Vietnamese we are coming home. Is that the option we should take? What would flow from that? The negotiations, the pause, all the other approaches we have explored, are these enough? Should we try others?"

I watched Rusk. He lit a cigarette carefully. He said nothing, holding the president in his fixed gaze. Seated to Rusk's right was Ball, in profile to me, unruffled, seemingly ready to speak, yet not quite ready to.

McNamara held up a chart for the president to see. It was a map of Vietnam, North and South. It was colored in red splotches, and white configurations. "This is our position now. It is estimated by our country team that the VC controls about 25 percent of these areas in red." A small pointer in his hand darted over the map, tapping the red areas. "The VC tactics are terror and sniping."

"It seems dangerous to put U.S. forces in those red areas," the president said.

"Yes, sir," said McNamara. "You are right. We are placing our people with their backs to the sea, for protection. Our mission would be to seek out the VC in large scale units."

General Wheeler spoke up. "The big problem, sir, is good combat intelligence in Vietnam. The VC is a creature of habit. By continuing to probe, we think we can make headway."

George Ball stirred in his chair. He raised his hand tentatively, and the president nodded to him. "Isn't it possible that the VC will do what they did against the French—stay away from confrontation and not accommodate us?" Ball asked.

The president seemed to agree. He turned to Wheeler

and the general responded, "Yes, that is possible, but by constantly harassing them, they will have to fight somewhere."

McNamara interposed at this point. "If the VC doesn't fight in large units, it will give the ARVN (the Army of South Vietnam) a chance to resecure hostile areas. We don't know what VC tactics will be when the VC is confronted by 175,000 Americans."

Raborn, newly appointed chief of the CIA was heard for the first time. "We agree. By 1965's end, we expect NVN (North Vietnam) to increase its forces. It will attempt to gain a substantial victory before our buildup is complete."

The president frowned. "Is anyone here of the opinion we should not do what the memorandum says? If so, I want to hear from them now, in detail."

Ball answered. "Mr. President, I can foresee a perilous voyage, very dangerous. I have great and grave apprehensions that we can win under these conditions." He paused, "But let me be clear. If the decision is to go ahead, I am committed."

The president sought to stir the discussion further. He turned his great bulk sideways in his chair to squarely face Ball. "But, George, is there another course in the national interest, some course that is better than the one McNamara proposes? We know it is dangerous and perilous, but the big question is, can it be avoided?"

Ball took up the challenge with some eagerness. "There is no course that will allow us to cut our losses. If we get bogged down, our cost might be substantially greater. The pressures to create a larger war would be irresistible. The qualifications I have are not due to the fact that I think we are in a bad moral position."

The president persisted. "Tell me then, what other road can I go?"

"Take what precautions we can, Mr. President. Take our losses, let their government fall apart, negotiate, discuss, knowing full well there will be a probable take-over by the Communists. This is disagreeable, I know."

The president nodded. "I can take disagreeable decisions. But I want to know can we make a case for your thoughts? Can you discuss it fully?"

"We have discussed it," said Ball. "I have had my day in court." Ball was obviously referring to his lengthy memos to the president importuning LBJ to his views.

"I don't think we have made any full commitment, George," the president said. "You have pointed out the danger, but you haven't really proposed an alternative course. We haven't always been right. We have no mortgage on victory. Right now, I am concerned that we have very little alternative to what we are doing." The president paused to let his words sink in. He went on, "I want another meeting, more meetings, before we take any definitive action. We must look at all other courses of possibility carefully. Right now I feel it would be more dangerous to lose this now, than endanger a greater number of troops. But I want this fully discussed."

Rusk now gathered the president's attention. "What we have done since 1954 to 1961 has not been good enough," he said. "We should have probably committed ourselves heavier in 1961."

Carl Rowan, the first black man to head the USIA, spoke up. "What bothers me most is the weakness of the Ky government. Unless we put the screws on the Ky government, 175,000 men will do us no good."

Lodge now intervened. This slim, elegantly clad Brahmin, inheritor of a continuous political tradition, confident of his identity, sure of his link to past greatness and a position in society too rooted to be shaken by politics or political parties, was a curious figure at the table. LBJ liked him, though I never really felt that he would hand Lodge the mace of authority. LBJ felt comfortable with this aristocrat sitting at his council table.

"There is not a tradition of a national government in Saigon," Lodge said. "There are no roots in the country. Not until there is tranquility can you have any stability. I don't think we ought to take this government seriously. There is simply no one who can do anything. We have to do what we think we ought to do regardless of what the Saigon government does. As we move ahead on a new phase, we have the right and the duty to do certain things with or without the government's approval."

The president listened, saying nothing. He leaned back again in his chair, as if savoring the Lodge comments. Then he turned to Ball. "George, do you think we have another course?"

Ball's answer was firm, his voice clear. "I would not recommend that you follow McNamara's course."

"Are you able to outline your doubts?" the president asked. "Can you offer another course of action? I think it's desirable to hear you out, truly hear you out, then I can determine if your suggestions are sound and ready to be followed, which I am prepared to do if I am convinced."

"Yes, Mr. President," Ball replied. "I think I can present to you the least bad of two courses. What I would present is a course that is costly, but can be limited to short-term costs."

The president seemed satisfied. "Alright, let's meet again at 2:30 this afternoon to discuss George's proposals. Meanwhile, let Bob tell us why we need to risk all these Americans' lives. I don't choose to do that casually."

McNamara and Wheeler proceeded to outline the reasons for more troops. Essentially, they said, 75,000 men are just enough to protect the bases. It would let us lose slowly instead of rapidly. The extra men, they insisted, would stabilize the situation, and then improve it. It also would give the ARVN a breathing space, they said. We would limit the incursion of more troops to 100,000 because it might not be possible to absorb more in South Vietnam at this time. Both McNamara and Wheeler declared there was no major risk of a catastrophe, meaning of course, the intrusion of Russian or Chinese troops into the fray.

The president was not convinced. He fiddled with his tie clasp, chin deep in his chest, the folds of flesh lapping over his collar. "It seems to me that you will lose a greater number of men. I don't like that."

"Not precisely true, Mr. President," Wheeler replied. "The more men we have there the greater the likelihood of smaller losses."

The president hunched forward, tapping his forefinger on the yellow pad in front of him. "Tell me this. What will happen if we put in 100,000 more men and then two, three years later you tell me you need 500,000 more? How would you expect me to respond to that? And what makes you think if we put in 100,000 men, Ho Chi Minh won't put in another 100,000, and match us every bit of the way?"

Wheeler smiled. "This means greater bodies of men from North Vietnam, which will allow us to cream them."

"But what are the chances of more North Vietnamese soldiers coming in?" asked the president.

"About a fifty-fifty chance," Wheeler answered. "The North would be foolhardy to put one-quarter of their forces in SVN. It would expose them too greatly in the North."

The president still was not convinced. He turned to Admiral Raborn and asked, "Do you have people in North Vietnam?"

Raborn ruminated a moment. "Not enough, Mr. President. But what we have we think are reliable."

"Why can't we improve our intelligence in North Vietnam?" pursued the president.

Raborn clipped his answer. "We have a task force working on this, Mr. President."

The president wearily, it seemed to me, leaned back in his chair. The answers, I felt, were not in the bullseye. They were glancing off the side, not fixed clearly where they ought to have been. The president, I felt certain, was entertaining the same thoughts as I. The president looked at his watch. It was just after 1:00 P.M.

I suddenly felt closed-in, a kind of strangling of space and air. I got up and pulled back the drapes to the rear of the president. The room seemed constricted and I felt the need of light. The heavy, blurred rumble of a jet plane overhead filtered through the window. The White House policeman standing alert at the west end of the walkway leading from the Mansion to the West Wing peered at his colleague slowly patrolling from the southwest gate to the guardhouse that sat on the edge of the circular asphalt drive. A cement walkway curled from the guardhouse to the president's office. The Rose Garden was bursting with color, yellows, reds, golds flinging their brilliance off the heavy green grass.

The president stood up, and the others at the table immediately got to their feet. "May I suggest," he said, "that we meet again at 2:30 this afternoon. I want to hear from George Ball and I know we all do."

He strode quickly to the door to his secretary's office; the others remained standing, pushing their chairs back, and when the president left the room, amid muffled tones of conversation, they all departed by the side door leading into the West Wing corridor. Everyone carefully removed all the papers in front of his chair before leaving. Within minutes, both a White House policeman and a Secret Service agent entered the Cabinet Room and retrieved the stray papers left. They very carefully tore off the first page of the memo pads before each chair and deposited the entire residue in the burnbags they brought with them.

Inside the president's office, a mess steward brought him a bowl of hot soup and a cold Fresca. He sat behind his desk, reading as he finished lunch.

At 2:30 P.M., the same fifteen men were gathered again in the Cabinet Room, and within minutes before 2:40 P.M., the president again entered, took his chair, and the meeting began again.

"Alright, George," said the president, nodding to Ball.

Ball crisply arranged some papers in front of him. From my seat I could barely see what was on them; neatly typed paragraphs with what appeared to be Ball's handwriting scrawled on the edges. Ball cleared his throat. He began.

"We cannot win, Mr. President. This war will be long and protracted. The most we can hope for is a messy conclusion. There remains a great danger of intrusion by the Chinese. But the biggest problem is the problem of the long war.

"The Korean experience was a galling one. The correlation between Korean casualties and public opinion showed support stabilized at 50 percent." Here Ball leaned over and put in front of the president a chart showing coordinates and lines which revealed the relationship between casualty figures and public support as disclosed in public opinion polls. He continued: "As casualties increase, the pressure to strike at the very jugular of North Vietnam will become very great.

"I am concerned about world opinion. If we could win in a year's time, and win decisively, world opinion would be alright. However, if the war is long and protracted, as I believe it will be, then we will suffer because the world's greatest power cannot defeat guerrillas.

"Then there is the problem of national politics. Every

great captain in history was not afraid to make a tactical withdrawal if conditions were unfavorable to him. The enemy cannot even be seen in Vietnam. He is indigenous to the country. I truly have serious doubt that an army of westerners can successfully fight orientals in an Asian jungle."

The president listened with obvious interest. Ball's last statement triggered a response. "This is important. Can westerners, in the absence of accurate intelligence, successfully fight Asians in jungle rice paddies? I want Mc-Namara and General Wheeler to seriously ponder this question." With that, the president again nodded to Ball and the undersecretary continued his exposition.

"I think we all have underestimated the seriousness of this situation. It is like giving cobalt treatment to a terminal cancer case. I think a long, protracted war will disclose our weakness, not our strength.

"The least harmful way to cut losses in SVN is to let the government decide it doesn't want us to stay there. Therefore, we should put such proposals to the GVN that they can't accept. Then, it would move to a neutralist position. I have no illusions that after we were asked to leave South Vietnam, that country would soon come under Hanoi control.

"What about Thailand? It would be our main problem. Thailand has proven a good ally so far, though history shows it has never been a staunch ally. If we wanted to make a stand in Thailand, we might be able to make it.

"Another problem would be South Korea. We have two divisions there now. There would be a problem with Taiwan, but as long as the Generalissimo is there, they have no place to go. Indonesia is a problem, as is Malaysia. Japan thinks we are propping up a lifeless government and are on a sticky wicket. Between a long war and cutting our losses, the Japanese would go for the latter. My information on Japan comes from Reischauer (the American ambassador to Japan)."

The president answered Ball. "But George, wouldn't all these countries say that Uncle Sam was a paper tiger, wouldn't we lose credibility breaking the word of three presidents, if we did as you have proposed? It would seem to be an irreparable blow. But I gather you don't think so."

"No, sir," responded Ball. "The worse blow would be that the mightiest power on earth is unable to defeat a handful of guerrillas."

"Then," said the president, "you are not basically troubled by what the world would say about our pulling out?"

"If we were actively helping a country with a stable viable government," Ball replied, "it would be a vastly different story. Western Europeans look upon us as if we got ourselves into an imprudent situation."

The president allowed himself a smile. "But I believe that these Vietnamese are trying to fight. They're like Republicans who try to stay in power, but don't stay there long." The president grinned, shrugged his shoulders, and said, amid the laughter that floated over the table, "Excuse me, Cabot." Lodge managed a smile.

Ball continued. "Thieu spoke the other day and said the Communists would win the election."

"I don't believe that," said the president. "Does anyone believe that?" His hand circled the table. McNamara, Lodge, Bill Bundy, Leonard Unger all expressed views contrary to Ball.

"Ky will fall soon," McNamara said. "He is weak. We can't have elections there until there is physical security, and even then there will be no elections because as Cabot said, there is no democratic tradition." Wheeler suggested that McNamara was right about Ky, but said, "I am very much impressed with Thieu."

The president hunched against the edge of the table. "There are two basic troublings within me. First, that westerners can ever win a war in Asia. Second, I don't see how you can fight a war under direction of other people whose government changes every month. Now, go ahead, George and make your other points."

Ball continued. "The costs, as well as our western European allies, are not relevant to their (European) situation. What they are concerned about is their own security, that is, troops in Berlin have real meaning, troops in Vietnam have none."

"Are you saying," said the president, "that pulling out of Korea would be akin to pulling out of Vietnam?"

McGeorge Bundy spoke up. "It is not analogous. We had a status quo in Korea. It would not be that way in Vietnam."

Ball objected. "We will pay a higher cost in Vietnam. This is a decision one makes against an alternative. On one hand, a long, protracted war, costly, very costly, with North Vietnam digging in for the long-term. This is their life and driving force. The Chinese are taking the long term view by ordering blood plasma from Japan. On the other hand, there are short-term losses if we pull out. On balance, we come out ahead of the McNamara plan. Of course, it is distasteful either way."

Mac Bundy thrust himself forward in his chair. "These are truly important questions that you raise. The difficulty I have with accepting George's argument is it would be a radical switch in policy without visible evidence that it should be done. George's whole analytical argument gives no weight to losses suffered by the other side. A great many elements in George's arguments are correct though. We need to make it clear that this is a somber matter, that it will not be quick, and that no single action will bring quick victory."

"Yes," said Ball, "but my problem is not that we don't

get thrown out, but that we get bogged down and don't win."

Bundy nodded and said, "Let me sum up. The world, the country, and the Vietnamese people would have alarming reactions if we got out." Dean Rusk now joined the conversation.

The secretary of state is one of the most enigmatic men I encountered in Washington. He had a commitment to decency and honor that he vigilantly guarded, steeling himself against visible passions and intemperate conversation. He rarely made long speeches in meetings, almost always sitting quietly until prodded by the president into a statement or an opinion. He reserved himself for private talks with the president, and thus the public Rusk, the conference Rusk, remained unrevealed, unexplorable, inviolate to prying minds and tongues. It could have been written about Rusk as it was once written about Elizabeth's faithful counselor, William Cecil: "Yet what Cecil thought, few could discover. Heart and soul a servant of the state, this was a man wholly discreet; one of those who have no windows in their breasts." I found him a congenial man, always courteous, possibly affectionate to me, and yet I have often thought, after my White House tenure, that I knew Dean Rusk as little the last time I saw him as I did the first time I met him.

He was tall, taller than first glance might measure, a grey, bald stone mountain, impervious to the crunch and heavy breathing of inquisitive climbers. The fact remains Dean Rusk, this man of prodigious intelligence and energy, stood self-shielded against press and colleagues.

Some say he molded himself after his hero, General George Marshall. Possibly. If Marshall indeed bred those qualities of a hugely platformed sense of duty which even his critics could not deny resided within Dean Rusk, then the similarity has merit.

I recall several times he asked me to come to his office

on the seventh floor of the State Department to talk privately about matters. Once he called me to discuss the possibility of the U.S. reinstituting its ambassador to the Vatican. He wanted my judgment, as a Catholic, on the issue. We sat, the two of us in the enormous office domain of the secretary, he behind his smallish desk, out of proportion in the vast room, and I in a chair facing him. He ordered a Scotch from his mess, and I had one with him. Sipping our drinks, and each of us eating a sandwich (which was the Rusk dinner we shared), we talked; Rusk speaking easily and knowledgeably about the Vatican issue. He was obviously well-informed as to the past history of our relations with the Vatican. I remember this evening well, for it was one of the few times the secretary seemed to relax. He was amiable, humorous, and yet there remained the view of the battlements, that detachment from camaraderie which set him apart from his fellows.

The president had immense respect for Rusk, mainly because he considered him to be totally selfless in the performance of his chores, proffering advice and counsel unmixed with anything except the hard flavor of truth, as Rusk saw it. Whenever the president had a briefing at the White House for businessmen, educators, labor leaders, academics, or friends, it was Rusk among the Johnson high command who impressed his audience, speaking as he always did without notes.

The war disfigured his image to the outer world to which he went when he left his office. But Dean Rusk in private life is of the same stern piece he was in public life, no excuses, no whining, no call for pity or revision. He did what he thought was right, without hoisting any fingers to test the winds of public favor.

In this Cabinet Room meeting, the secretary of state said: "If the Communist world finds out we will not pursue our commitment to the end, I don't know where they will stay their hand. I have to say I am more optimistic than some of my colleagues. I don't believe the VC have made large advances among the Vietnamese people. It is difficult to worry about massive casualties when we say we can't find the enemy. I feel strongly that one man dead is a massive casualty, but in the sense that we are talking, I don't see large casualties unless the Chinese come in."

Here Lodge interposed. "I feel there is a greater threat to start World War III if we don't go in. Can't we see the similarity to our own indolence at Munich? I simply can't be as pessimistic as Ball. We have great seaports in Vietnam. We don't need to fight on roads. We have the sea. Let us visualize meeting the VC on our own terms. We don't have to spend all our time in the jungles. If we can secure our bases, the Vietnamese can secure, in time, a political movement to, one, apprehend the terrorist, and two, give intelligence to the government. The procedures for this are known. I agree the Japanese agitators don't like what we are doing, but Sato is totally in agreement with our actions. The Vietnamese have been dealt more casualties than, per capita, we suffered in the Civil War. The Vietnamese soldier is an uncomplaining soldier. He has ideas he will die for."

Leonard Unger spoke up. "I agree this is what we have to do. We have spotted some things we want to pay attention to."

The president was grave and somber. "How can we get everybody to compete with McNamara in the press?" he asked. "We are trying to do many other things with our economic and health projects. Can't we constantly remind the people that we are doing something besides bombing?"

Unger nodded, "We have taken this question up with Barry Zorthian and the press people."

There was spirited talk around the table, more or less going over the same ground. The president stirred fitfully.

"I think we have said enough today. Let us adjourn for now. I am calling a meeting for tomorrow at noon, to hear in person from the joint chiefs. I want them to tell me personally what they think, and I want to tell them what I think."

The next day, July 22, 1965, at noon, sharp, the meeting got underway. Present were the president; McNamara; Vance; General Wheeler; General Harold K. Johnson, chief of staff of the Army; General John P. McConnell, chief of staff of the Air Force; Admiral D. L. McDonald, chief of Naval Operations; General Wallace M. Greene, Jr., commandant of the Marine Corps; Secretary of the Air Force Harold Brown; Secretary of the Navy Paul Nitze; Secretary of the Army Stanley Resor; McGeorge Bundy; Jack Valenti; and present at the request of the president was Clark Clifford.

The president began. "I asked Secretary McNamara to invite you here to counsel with you on these problems and the ways to meet them. I want you to hear from the chiefs the alternatives open to you and then recommendations on those alternatives from a military point of view.

"The options open to us are: one, leave the country, with as little loss as possible; two, maintain present force and lose slowly; three, add 100,000 men, recognizing that may not be enough and adding more next year. The disadvantages of number three option are the risk of escalation, casualties high, and the prospect of a long war without victory. I would like you to start out by stating our present position as you see it, and where we can go."

Admiral McDonald, the brilliant chief of Naval Operations, spoke up. "Sending in the Marines has improved the situation. I agree with McNamara that we are committed to the extent that we can't move out. If we continue the way we are now, it will be a slow, sure victory for the other side. By putting more men in it will turn the tide and let us know what further we need to do. I wish we had done this long before."

The president, his face grim and somber, asked, "But you don't know if 100,000 men will be enough. What makes you conclude that if you don't know where we are going—and what will happen—we shouldn't pause and find this out?"

(Some minutes before this meeting began, the president and I had been alone in his office. He had said to me: "All these recommendations seem to be built on a pretty soft bottom. Everything blurs when you get almost to the gate." LBJ felt bound by President Kennedy's actions and the prospect of unhinging the linchpin of the Kennedy commitment was dismally disturbing to him. And yet there was that queasy tremor of doubt that kept skittering through his thoughts, though of course no man can be certain what a president is truly thinking. Now in this meeting with the military brass the president was unleashing those skeptical ruminations which he had kept under wraps.)

Admiral McDonald responded to the president. "Sooner or later we will force them to the conference table."

"But," persisted the president, "if we put in 100,000 men won't they put in an equal number, and then where will we be?"

"No," said Admiral McDonald. "If we step up our bombing . . ."

The president interrupted with some acerbity. "Is this a chance we want to take?"

"Yes, sir, when I view the alternatives. Get out now or pour in more men."

"Is that all?" the president asked.

"Well," said McDonald, "I think our allies will lose faith in us."

The president managed a tight smile. "We have few allies really helping us now."

McDonald continued. "Take Thailand for example. If we walk out of Vietnam, the whole world will question our word. We don't have much choice."

The president turned to the secretary of the Navy, a tough-minded intellectual. "Paul, what's your view?"

"In that area not occupied by U.S. forces, it is worse, as I observed on my trip out there. We have two alternatives, Mr. President. Support the Vietnamese throughout their country or stick to the secure positions we do have. We need to make it clear to the populace that we are on their side. Then gradually turn the tide of losses by aiding the ARVN at certain points."

"What are our chances of success?" asked the president.

"If we want to turn the tide, by putting in more men, it would be about sixty-forty," said Nitze.

"If we gave Westmoreland all he asked for what are our chances? I don't agree that the North Vietnamese and China won't come in."

"Expand the area we could maintain. In the Philippines and Greece it was shown that guerrillas can lose."

"Would you send in more forces than Westmoreland requests?" asked the president.

"Yes, sir. It depends on how quickly they . . ."

The president cut in. "How many? Two hundred thousand instead of 100,000?"

"We would need another 100,000 in January," said Nitze.

"Can you do that?" the president queried.

"Yes, sir," said Nitze.

McNamara spoke up. "The current plan is to introduce 100,000 men with the possibility of a second 100,000 by the first of the year."

The president frowned. "What reaction is this going to produce?" he asked.

General Wheeler replied. "Since we are not proposing an invasion of the North, the Soviets will step up materiel and propaganda, and the same with the Chicoms. The North Vietnamese might introduce more regular troops."

The president wasn't satisfied. "Why wouldn't North Vietnam pour in more men? Also, why wouldn't they call on volunteers from China and Russia?"

Wheeler answered the president. "First, they may decide they can't win by putting in force they can't afford. At most they would put in two more divisions. Beyond that, they strip their country and invite a countermove on our part.

"Second, on volunteers—the one thing all North Vietnam fears is the Chinese. For them to invite Chinese volunteers is to invite China taking over North Vietnam. The weight of judgment is that North Vietnam may reinforce their troops, but they can't match us on a buildup. From a military viewpoint, we can handle, if we are determined to do so, China and North Vietnam."

"Don't you anticipate retaliation by the Soviets in the Berlin area?" the president asked.

"You may have some flare-up but the lines are so tightly drawn in Berlin, that it raises the risk of escalation too quickly. Lemnitzer thinks there will be no flare-up in Berlin. In Korea, if the Soviets undertook operations, it would be dangerous."

The president nodded and addressed McDonald, "Admiral, would you summarize what you think we ought to do?"

McDonald flashed a brief smile. "Yes, sir. First, supply the forces Westmoreland has asked for. Second, prepare to furnish more men, 100,000, in 1966. Third, commence building in air and naval forces, and step up air attacks on North Vietnam. Fourth, bring in needed reserves and draft calls."

"Do you have any ideas of what this will cost?" queried the president.

McNamara with his usual precision and unhesitating grasp of numbers said, "Yes, sir, twelve billion dollars in 1966."

"Do you have any idea what effect this will have on our economy?" asked the president.

McNamara answered quickly. "It would not require wage and price controls in my judgment. The price index ought not go up more than one point or two."

General McConnell spoke. "If you put in these requested forces and increase air and sea effort, we can at least turn the tide to where we are not losing anymore. We need to be sure we get the best we can out of the South Vietnamese. We need to bomb all military targets available to us in North Vietnam. As to whether we can come to a satisfactory solution with these forces, I don't know. With these forces properly employed, and cutting off the VC supplies, we can surely do better than we are doing."

The president scribbled something on the pad of paper in front of him. "Do we have results of bombing actions and have they, in your judgment, been as fruitful and productive as we anticipated?" he asked.

"No, sir, they haven't been," McConnell replied. "They have been productive in South Vietnam, but not as productive in the North because we are not striking the targets that hurt them."

The president faced McConnell, fixed him in his gaze and spoke very slowly. "Are you seriously concerned when we change targets we escalate the war? They might send more fighters down. Can you be certain it won't escalate efforts on the ground? Would it hurt our chances at a conference if we killed civilians in this bombing, though of course we will take utmost precautions not to?"

"We need to minimize all we can the killing of civilians."

"Would you go beyond Westmoreland's recommendations?" asked the president.

"No, sir."

"How many planes have we lost thus far?"

"About 106 of all types. This is a small percentage of our total."

"How many do we have out there?"

"One hundred and forty-six combat. We have lost 54 combat."

"How many Navy planes have we lost?"

"It's in the thirties. We have about 125 Navy combat planes," McDonald answered.

The president was silent a moment. Then he asked, "Doesn't it really mean that if we follow Westmoreland's requests we are in a new war? Isn't this going off the diving board?"

"If we carry forward all these recommendations, it would be a change in our policy. We have relied on the South to carry the brunt. Now we would be responsible for satisfactory military outcome," McNamara said.

"Would we be in agreement," said the president, "that we would rather be out of there and make our stand somewhere else?"

"The least desirable alternative is getting out," General Johnson replied. "The second least is doing what we are doing. The best alternative is to get in and get the job done."

The president's voice hardened. "But I don't know how we are going to get the job done. There are millions of Chinese. I think they are going to put their stack in. Is this the best place to do it? We don't have the allies we had in

Korea. Can we get our allies to cut off supplying the North?"

"No, sir," replied McNamara, "we can't prevent Japan, Britain, and the others from chartering ships to Haiphong."

"Have we done anything to stop them?"

"No," said McNamara, "we haven't put the pressure on them as we did in Cuba. But even if we did, it wouldn't stop the shipping."

Secretary of the Air Force Brown spoke. "It seems that all of our alternatives are dark. I find myself in agreement with the others."

"Is there anything to argument that the South government will fail, and we will be asked to leave?" asked the president. "If we try to match the enemy we will be bogged down in a protracted war and won't the government ask us to leave?"

There was silence. Then Brown spoke up. "Our lines of communication are very long, sir."

"How long?" asked the president.

"About 7,000 miles from the west coast, but not too much greater than China's. The biggest weakness of the political situation is the lack of security they can offer their people."

The president spoke very slowly. "Are we starting something that in two or three years we simply can't finish?" He was zeroing in on the key question and the men around that table knew it.

"It is costly to us to strangle slowly. But the chances of losing are less if we move in," Brown said.

The president persisted. "Suppose we told Ky of the requirements we need, and he turns them down. And then we have to get out and make our stand in Thailand."

"The Thais will go with the winner."

"Well," said the president, "if we don't stop in Thailand, where would we stop?"

"Laos, Cambodia, Thailand, Burma surely affect Malaysia," McNamara said. "In two to three years the Communist domination would stop there, but ripple effect would be great, in Japan, in India. We would have to give up some bases. Ayub would move closer to China. Greece, Turkey would move to neutralist positions. Communist agitation would increase in Africa."

General Greene, stiff-backed, every inch a Marine, spoke. "Situation is as tough as when it started. But not as bad as it could be. Marines in the first corp areas are an example of the benefits that come to us.

"Here are the stakes as I see them. One, the national security stake; it is a matter of time before we would have to go in some place else. Two, there is the pledge we have made. Three, there is our prestige before the world.

"If you accept these stakes, there are two courses of action. One, get out. Two, stay in and win.

"Now, how to win in the North and in the South? The enclave concept will work. I would like to introduce enough Marines to do this. Two Marine divisions and one air wing. We have 28,000 out there now. We need an additional 72,000."

McNamara said, "Mr. President, General Greene suggests these men over and above the Westmoreland request."

"Then you are saying you will need 80,000 more Marines to carry this out?" the president asked.

"Yes," Greene replied, "I am convinced we are making progress with the South Vietnamese, in food and construction. We are getting evidence of intelligence from the South Vietnamese. In the North, we haven't been hitting the right targets. We should hit pol (petroleum) storage, which is essential to their transportation. Also, we must destroy their airfields, their MIGS and their IL28s."

"What would they do?" asked the president.

"Nothing. We can test it by attacking pol storage. Then

we should attack the industrial complex in the North. Also, they can be told by pamphlet drop why we are doing this. Then we ought to blockade Cambodia, and stop supplies from coming through there. How long would it take? Five years, plus 500,000 troops. I think the American people would back you."

"How would you tell the American people what the stakes are?" the president asked Greene.

"The place where they will stick by you is the national security stake."

General Johnson spoke. "We are in a face-down. The solution, unfortunately, is long-term. Once the military problem is solved the problem of political solution will be more difficult."

The president leaned forward and said, "If we come in with hundreds of thousands of men and billions of dollars, won't this cause China and Russia to come in? No one has given me a satisfactory answer to that."

"No, sir," General Johnson said, "I don't think they will."

The president smiled wanly. "MacArthur didn't think they would come in either."

"Yes, sir, but this is not comparable to Korea," said General Johnson.

Time and again the president returned to his haunting fear, that by pushing in with large numbers of troops we would be igniting World War III or some unholy version of it. He never unfastened himself from the notion that China and Russia would not stand idly by and allow us to engulf Southeast Asia. This fear never left him.

The president continued, "But China has plenty of divisions to move in, don't they?"

"Yes, they do," replied General Johnson.

The president leaned forward. "Then what would we do?"

There was a long silence. The room was absolutely still. General Johnson finally said, "If so, we have another ball game."

"But I have to take into account they will," said the president.

"I would increase the buildup near North Vietnam, and increase action in Korea," said General Johnson.

"If they move in thirty-one divisions, what does it take on our part?" the president asked.

McNamara broke in to answer. "Under favorable conditions they could sustain thirty-one divisions and assuming the Thais contributed forces, it would take 300,000 plus what we need to combat the VC."

The president wasn't satisfied. "But remember they are going to write stories about this like they did in the Bay of Pigs. Stories about me and my advisers. That is why I want you to think carefully, very, very carefully about alternatives and plans."

The president turned to General Johnson. "Looking back on the Dominican Republic, General, would you have done anything differently?"

"I would have cleaned out part of the city and gone in, with the same numbers."

"Aren't you concerned about Chinese forces moving into North Vietnam?" the president asked.

"Sir, there is no evidence of forces, only terms involved in logistics. It could be they are investigating areas which they could control later."

The president leaned back in his chair. "What is your reaction to Ho's statement he is ready to fight for twenty years?"

"I believe it," General Johnson replied.

"What would you describe as Ho's problems?" asked the president.

"His biggest problem is doubt about what our next

move will be. He's walking a tightrope between the Reds and the Chicoms. Also, he is worrying about the loss of caches of arms in the South."

The president asked whether or not we were being careful about civilian casualties. He had laid down strict instructions that civilian targets and civilian areas were not to be touched. "Are we killing civilians in these Viet Cong areas?" he asked.

General Wheeler answered, "Certain civilians accompanying the Viet Cong are being killed. It can't be helped."

Stanley Resor, secretary of the Army, now spoke up. "Of the three courses the one we should follow is the McNamara plan. We simply can't go back on our commitment. Our allies are watching carefully."

"Do all of you think the Congress and the people will go along with 600,000 people and billions of dollars being spent 10,000 miles away?" the president asked.

Resor said evenly, "The Gallup poll shows people are basically behind our commitment."

"But," said the president, "if you make a commitment to jump off a building and you find out how high it is, you may want to withdraw that commitment."

There was no answer from those in the room, silence answered the president. He sighed. "I judge though that the big problem is one of national security. Is that right?"

There was murmured assent from those at the meeting. "Well, then," said the president, "what about our intelligence. How do they (the VC) know what we are doing before we do it? What about the B-52 raid; weren't the Viet Cong gone before we got there?"

McNamara answered, "They get it from infiltration in the South Vietnamese forces."

"Are we getting good intelligence out of the North?" the president asked.

"Only reconnaissance and technical soundings," said McNamara, "we have none from combat intelligence."

The president leaned back in his chair, looking at each man in the room. Before the meeting he had instructed McGeorge Bundy to prepare a paper on how we got to where we were. And to cite the tough questions that needed to be asked. "Some congressmen and senators," the president said, "think we are to be the most discredited people in the world. What Bundy will now tell you is not his opinion nor mine, but what we hear. I think you ought to face up to this too."

Bundy read from a paper in front of him. "The argument we will face is, one, for ten years every step we have taken has been based on a previous failure. All we have done has failed and caused us to take another step which failed. As we get further into the bag, we get deeply bruised. Also we have made excessive claims we haven't been able to realize.

"Two, also after twenty years of warning about war in Asia, we are now doing what MacArthur and others have warned us about. We are about to fight a war we can't fight and win as the country we are trying to help is quitting.

"Three, there is a failure on our own to fully realize what guerrilla war is like. We are sending conventional troops to do an unconventional job.

"Four, how long—how much? Can we take casualties over five years—aren't we talking about a military solution when the solution is really political. Why can't we interdict better? Why are our bombings so fruitless? Why can't we blockade the coast? Why can't we improve our intelligence? Why can't we find the VC?"

The president spoke. "Not only that, but now Gerald Ford has demanded the president testify before the Congress and tell why we are compelled to call up the reserves. The indications are he will oppose calling up the reserves."

McNamara, pointed to Bundy's paper, "I think we can answer most of the questions posed."

Clark Clifford now interposed. "If the military plan is carried out, what is the ultimate result if we are successful?"

"The political objective is to maintain SVN as free and independent," General Wheeler replied. "If we follow the course of action, we can carry out this objective. Probably after success, we would withdraw most of our forces, international or otherwise, though some would have to stay on. If we can secure the military situation it seems likely that we can get some kind of stable government."

With the president admonishing those present to ponder the questions posed by Bundy, the meeting adjourned. Later meetings were held morning, afternoon, and night. Even at Camp David.

In the next five days, hundreds of hours were consumed in the talks that went on. The president strained to extract every differing view he could find in the government and bring it to the table to be examined, to be put under scrutiny.

The options available, now that the gauntlet had been flung down in Vietnam were the following (as the president described them at one of the meetings):

1. We can bring the enemy to his knees by using our SAC and other Air Force. I don't think our citizens would want us to do this. I sure wouldn't. Though there are some who want to.

2. Another group thinks we ought to pack up and go home. I don't think too many of our people want us to do this. Ike, John Kennedy, and I have given commitments.

3. We could stay there as we are, suffer consequences and continue to lose territory and take casualties. You wouldn't want your boy out there, crying for help and not getting it.

4. Go to Congress and ask for great sums of money, call up the reserves and increase the draft. To go on a war footing, declare a state of emergency. There is a good deal of feeling that ought to be done. We have considered this. If we make a land war in Asia, then the North would go to its friends, China and Russia, and ask them to give help. They would be forced into increasing aid. For that reason I don't want to be dramatic and cause tension. I think we can get our people to support us without having to be provocative.

5. Give our commanders the men they say they need, out of forces in this country. Get such money as we need and must have. Use our transfer authority to get money we need until January.

Say to the South that they must get their military to get to work and make what gains we can. Meanwhile we will explore ways to find peace, explore them every day.

It became clear as the days wore on that options four and five were the ones looming up as the alternatives. There was much unease. Crystal balls were clouding up all over the government and "through a glass darkly" was the mood of the moment.

I have inspected my own thoughts a thousand times and I come to the conclusion that, given the moorings to which the commitments by earlier presidents clung, the hard difficulties of withdrawing if we tried to, the thunder on the right that was sure to reverberate throughout the nation, the president's choices had indeed narrowed down. He came to these options reluctantly, stubbornly resisting all the way. He had no illusions about a war. He had no great faith in the predictions of the military, but he had no sound countervailing arguments.

(Some weeks later I passed to the president a paragraph from Walter Bagehot about William Pitt, the younger, a wartime prime minister of England. It seemed to me to be so applicable to President Johnson in these July 1965 meetings, some 104 years after Bagehot's words were first published: "He [speaking of Pitt] was by inclination and by temperament opposed to all war; he was very humane and all war is inhumane. He postponed a French war as long as he could; he consented to it with reluctance and continued it from necessity." The president read my note, gave it back to me, managed a smile, and said, "I think I can understand Mr. Pitt's problem.")

He had one final meeting on Vietnam. It was with the congressional leadership. It convened on Tuesday, July 27, 1965, at 6:35 P.M. In the Cabinet Room were the president and his advisers: Bob McNamara, Dean Rusk, General Wheeler, Ambassador Lodge, Admiral Raborn, Bill Moyers, Douglass Cater, Larry O'Brien, Horace Busby, Richard Goodwin, Joe Califano, and myself. From the congressional leadership were: Senator Mansfield, the majority leader of the Senate; Senator Dirksen, the minority leader of the Senate; Speaker McCormack; Gerald Ford, minority leader of the House; Carl Albert, majority leader of the House; and other members of Congress: Senators Smathers of Florida, Long of Louisiana, Hickenlooper of Iowa, Kuchel of California; Congressman Boggs of Louisiana, Democratic whip; Congressman Arends, Republican whip.

The president outlined what he chose to do. There was spirited questioning on the part of the leadership, but no one opposed the move, except Mike Mansfield, who was silent through most of the discussion. As the meeting neared its end, Mansfield, puffing on his pipe, spoke. "I could not be true to myself if I didn't speak," he said. "This position has a certain inevitability. Whatever pledge we had was to assist SVN in its own defense. Since then there has been no government of legitimacy. We owe this government nothing, no pledge of any kind. We are going deeper into war. Even total victory would be vastly costly. Best hope we have for salvation is a quick stalemate and negotiations. We cannot expect our people to support a war for three-to-five years. What we are about to get is an anti-Communist crusade, on and on. Remember, escalation begets escalation."

But patriot that he is, this patient, thoughtful, decent, scholarly senator said, that as majority leader he would support his president in whatever difficulty or whatever crisis. Mike Mansfield represents that breed of public man who is devoid of personal ambition, committed to his country's better angels, unwilling to be courtier to either president or public; who always speaks his mind when he believes that his voice will give substantive measure to the debate; is always objective, without rancor or recrimination; the kind of man who extends his hand to a fallen foe. No man in the Senate doubts Mansfield's rock-like integrity or his wisdom. Indeed, it is fair to say that no senator, on either side of the aisle, suspects Mansfield of anything except total fidelity to what is right.

The president nodded to Senator Mansfield, his old colleague and friend, possibly feeling as I did, that this nation has managed to withstand the bloody assaults which threaten its survival because of men like Mansfield.

Mansfield's discontent was remarkably prophetic. The majority leader never wavered in his assessment of Vietnam and its deadly impact on the nation. What might have happened if the president had listened to Mike Mansfield and given his views more weight in his (LBJ's) own mind? Mansfield's assay of Indochina was probably closer to the mark than other public men, with the possible exception of George Ball.

I have often thought what a great president Mansfield could have been if this country were in the mood to elect as their leader a quiet, untroubled man, with neither charisma nor electric charm; a man so clear in his purpose that he never hesitated in the pursuit of his duty, and who saw with a dry, unclouded eye what needed to be done, and what ought not to be done. He would have attached himself to the first with dispatch and he would never have become doubtful about the latter. Mike Mansfield of Montana is an honest man, with himself and with the public.

With Mansfield's comments to the president, the meeting had come to its end. The die was cast. The decision taken.

At 12:30 P.M. on Wednesday, July 28, 1965, the president held a televised news conference in the East Room of the White House.

He informed the nation of what the nation intended to do, and in his remarks he outlined the decision that was taken:

WHAT ARE OUR GOALS
IN THAT WAR-STAINED LAND?

First: We intend to convince the Communists that we cannot be defeated by force of arms or by superior power. They are not easily convinced. In recent months they have greatly increased their fighting forces, their attacks, and the number of incidents. I have asked the commanding general, General Westmoreland, what more he needs to meet this mounting aggression. He has told me. We will meet his needs.

I have today ordered to Vietnam the Air Mobile Division and certain other forces which will raise our fighting strength from 75,000 to 125,000 men almost imme-

diately. Additional forces will be needed later, and they
will be sent as requested. This will make it necessary to
increase our active fighting forces by raising the
monthly draft call from 17,000 over a period of time, to
35,000 per month, and stepping up our campaign for
voluntary enlistments.

After this past week of deliberations, I have concluded that it is not essential to order reserve units into
service now. If that necessity should later be indicated,
I will give the matter most careful consideration. And I
will give the country adequate notice before taking such
action, but only after full preparations.

We have also discussed with the government of South
Vietnam lately, the steps that they will take to substantially increase their own effort—both on the battlefield
and toward reform and progress in the villages. Ambassador Lodge is now formulating a new program to be
tested upon his return to that area.

I have directed Secretary Rusk and Secretary Mc-
Namara to be available immediately to the Congress to
review with the appropriate congressional committees
our plan in these areas. I have asked them to be available to answer the questions of any member of Congress.

Secretary McNamara, in addition, will ask the Senate
Appropriations Committee to add a limited amount to
present legislation to help meet part of this new cost
until a supplemental measure is ready and hearings can
be held when the Congress assembles in January.

In the meantime, we will use the authority contained
in the present defense appropriations bill now to
transfer funds, in addition to the additional money that
we will request.

These steps, like our actions in the past, are carefully
measured to do what must be done to bring an end to

aggression and a peaceful settlement. We do not want an expanding struggle with consequences that no one can foresee. Nor will we bluster or bully or flaunt our power.

But we will not surrender. And we will not retreat.

Those who sat in on all the meetings over the week-long torment know that Lyndon Johnson had listened carefully to every viewpoint; he never hurried or seemed frustrated by the need for meetings and more meetings. It was as if he were determined to dredge up every piece of information that might have even the barest relevancy to the decision.

The men around the president's table who advised him in the decision were men of honor and decency. There was no meanness in their thoughts or decisions. They cared very much about their nation, and had spent, most of them, a good portion of their working lives serving their countrymen, at modest or great sacrifice. They had applied to this problem all the rigor their minds and consciences could bring to bear and they knew the enormity of the counsel and advice they had offered to the president, for they understood the dimensions of the decision that had been taken.

Every one of the advisers concurred in the final decision. (I have recorded the reservations made during the discussions, notably those of Mike Mansfield and George Ball.) Opinions may have changed later but at the time of decision in 1965, there were no staff dissents.

(I remember at a dinner party in early 1968, Arthur Schlesinger, Jr., lamented to my wife that LBJ had not listened to the war advice of Bill Moyers when he was a presidential aide. "But, Arthur," I remonstrated, "Bill held no such view, at least not before midyear 1966. He was as much in favor of massive intervention as the Pentagon. If he wasn't, he never let anyone know his true feelings. The president made it clear to me many times that with the exception of George Ball, no higher official in the government was opposed to our position and that includes *every* White House aide.")

From the first decision to give aid to Indochina in April 1950, to the summer-1965 decisions, the hoops of commitments bound the U.S. tighter and tighter. Every president, as the record so clearly shows, found it a fact of life to regard Southeast Asia as essential to the security of the free world. Once you let Southeast Asia fall to Communist domination, went the prevailing official opinion, the unravelling of that part of the world, insofar as it concerned our own security, would begin.

This view was staunchly held by every American administration since 1950. It was reinforced by President Kennedy when on September 9, 1963, two and a half months before his death, he was interviewed on NBC by David Brinkley, and the following exchange occurred:

BRINKLEY: Mr. President, have you had any reason to doubt this so-called "domino theory" that if South Vietnam falls, the rest of Southeast Asia will go behind it?

THE PRESIDENT: No, I believe it. I believe it. I think that the struggle is close enough. China is so large, looms so high just beyond the frontiers, that if South Vietnam went, it would not only give them an improved geographic position for a guerrilla assault on Malaya, but would also give the impression that the wave of the future in Southeast Asia was China and the Communists. So I believe it.

Thus, the domino theory riding high in the water. It would be some years later before its edges became frayed.

But in mid-1965, the moorings of the domino theory were still tautly held and LBJ felt its pull.

Of course, there was risk in going in further in Vietnam, but, reasoned the president and his advisers, what of the larger and even more crippling risk of total U.S. incredibility in Asia? How do we justify all that was said and done, not by one president, but by three and counting Johnson, four presidents, if we suddenly shifted gears and left the South Vietnamese alone to fend for themselves? Moreover, could an American president have withstood the fury of criticism beating in on him the day that Southeast Asia was indeed Communist encircled? No matter if the interment of democratic government there was either good or bad; no matter, for the critics would have justly argued that we fled when we didn't have to. What would have happened if there were thousands of Vietnamese massacred by a vengeful Ho Chi Minh? (That Ho would be capable of this was aptly proved by the murders he committed in his own domain as well as the Hue massacre.) Is it possible for an administration in the face of this bitter indictment, this careless neglect of a word firmly given, of a pledge solemnly offered, is it possible for such an administration to find afterward any promise or purpose it pursues worthy of belief?

Every public man knows he cannot take refuge in what might have been. He has to stand or fall on what happens. President Kennedy's bleak assessment of the Bay of Pigs— "Success has a thousand fathers, but failure is an orphan"—is a very accurate accounting.

All this weighed heavily on the group around the table in the Cabinet Room. Each man at the meetings probably toyed with the thought of defeat in South Vietnam. Imagine a president saying to the people of the nation, after massacres in South Vietnam, after the toppling of every government in Southeast Asia and the installation of a Communist apparatus, imagine an American president saying: "If we had not allowed this to happen, we would have suffered a terrible defeat in a war in South Vietnam." There would have been no proof of this. How would a president explain the desertion of friends, the loss of allies, the fall of governments, and the murder of innocents when his own act of abandonment was the cause.

What really happened around the cabinet table in the summer of 1965 was a commitment without the remedial benefits of hindsight. The clearest, most unobstructed view a human can have is the one which allows him to see what *has already happened*. It is what Edmund Burke called "retrospective wisdom." It does make wise men of us all.

Every piece of evidence placed before the participants in all the meetings on Vietnam made it inescapable that no decision other than the one taken would be approved. I believe it is a fair and just statement that to every man in the meetings, with the exception of Senator Mansfield and Under Secretary of State George Ball, the final decisions taken in 1965 on Vietnam were right and sensible, and worthy of the risk involved, and, indeed, the only course possible under the circumstances. Once that initial, crunching decision had been ordered, then a number of subsequent decisions, obviously, flowed automatically. Once the commitment was weighed and studied, and commanded to be kept on course, our choices in Vietnam narrowed so sharply that ultimately we had no choices.

To the counsel of those who urged the president to go all out in bombing the North, mining the harbors of Haiphong, invading Cambodia and even the North, the president always listened but never followed. He was haunted by the ceaseless fear of Russian or Chinese entry into the war. He agonized over "the start of World War III." He knew his course was a cautious one, at variance with the stern importunings of the generals, admirals, and hawks in the Congress, and he knew too that he risked the frustration of the American public (which when it came, came in avalanches), but the vision of a "wider war" was more powerful than the dazzle of military victory prophecies. He hung back from the brink. "Some damn fool will drop some TNT down the smokestack of a Russian freighter in Haiphong, or some plane will get lost and dump its bombs over China, and we're in World War III. I just can't risk it," was his response to the urgings of those who said seductive things to him about getting it over quick.

What went wrong?

In the more than a decade that has gone by, the readiest narrative and the most accessible prose have testified to the bitter tragedy of Vietnam. But it may be that de Tocqueville had the answer when he wrote (about the French Revolution), "the people grow tired of a confusion whose end is not in sight."

If one believes it was wrong, clearly wrong, for any American president to commit forces to a distant part of the world for any reason, then even the proffering of economic or other aid was a mistake, because that was the beginning.

But if you believe that the U.S.A. was right in trying to help a small country defend itself against aggression, then de Tocqueville's sour commentary has a special warrant. The struggle was too long, the drain on our resources endless, the enemy too diffused, the objectives too obscure. Under those conditions it is difficult to ask any people, particularly those with no stomach for dreary victory-less conflicts, to fasten their resolve to the sticking place. If World War II had gone on for four more years, or five more years, would we have been ready to seek a negotiated peace in Europe and Asia? Who really knows?

In the long, lamentable catalogue of Vietnam, of only one fact can I be certain. It is this: What Lyndon Johnson did, he did because he believed the long-range security of the nation he had sworn to protect and defend was best served by his actions. That was the only reason for his decisions. If he was terribly wrong, then history will have to make that accounting. He always believed that history would prove him right.

PART V

Later

I

t was the Vietnam War that cut the arteries of the LBJ administration. A stupefied nation listened as President Johnson, on March 31, 1968, announced he would not be a candidate for re-election. Only a handful really believed that LBJ would give up the power of the White House for any reason other than defeat at the polls.

Other than Mrs. Johnson, and possibly Arthur Krim,* I

---

* Arthur Krim is one of those unique men who come to counsel a president, but whose presence and influence goes completely neglected by the press. Krim, the chairman of United Artists, a successful film company, is the complete antithesis of the movie mogul. He graduated first in his law class at Columbia University Law School, with a scholastic record never equaled since, and immediately joined the firm of famed courtroom attorney Louis Nizer. With his law partner, Robert Benjamin, he took over in 1951 the collapsing corporate entity of United Artists, then the undernourished business-child of Mary Pickford and Charles Chaplin. Within a year, Krim and his associates turned UA around, brought it into the black, and within a few more years lifted United Artists to the level of a major film company.

He became friendly with John Kennedy, and in turn JFK leaned on him for fund-raising organizing leadership. Krim never felt com-

doubt that any others were privy to LBJ's private thoughts before he made his surprising announcement. I wasn't.

Those who disbelieved the intent of the president did not take into account a little-known trait of LBJ. Very seldom did he allow fantasy or self-imposed optimism to make his decisions. He had an ability to look down the road with a hard, clear eye. All his life he relied on facts and information to guide him. A lot of people believed President Johnson shot from the hip and roared unthinking into situations where he had no business. But he very rarely acted on anything without having all the facts he could assemble; when they proved insufficient he brought his instinct into play. But it was never instinct without some foresight. Neither the press nor the public really understood this element in the LBJ character. And it was this aspect of his political judgment that was the inner

---

fortable as a fund-raiser; it offended his own sense of purpose and though he continued to serve JFK in this manner, he yearned to spend his talent in other areas to serve his president. When LBJ became chief executive Krim wanted to retire from the political arena; he did not know the new president and felt LBJ would want to command his own men. But the new president urged him to stay on, with the prodding of Ed Weisl, Sr., LBJ's close friend.

As the years passed, the president and Krim grew closer. In the last two years of the LBJ presidency, it would seem that no man in the country had the total confidence of the president to the degree of intimacy and respect as did Arthur Krim. The president offered him various cabinet posts, as well as ambassador to the United Nations. Krim turned them all down. He preferred to serve the president without an official position and Johnson turned to him for advice across the board—foreign policy and political strategy.

I was always a bit amused that the press never really focused on Krim as a presidential adviser. Possibly it was because they still referred to him as "fund-raiser," and never understood the confidant-adviser-counselor role he was in truth playing. If the president needed advice, LBJ would sit with Arthur Krim and talk out the problem with him first. Yet, the press never zeroed in on this relationship. Krim never talked, never sought publicity, and no inkling of his influential role in the White House ever surfaced.

voice he listened to in making his greatest political decision.

After his retirement he talked to me often about that March 31 speech. He told me that he felt the country had lost its faith in his captaincy. The nation was polarized, seething with frustration and anger. LBJ knew this, and he understood it. He told me he believed he could have been renominated and would have won the election. Since Vice-President Humphrey lost by a bare one-half of one percent it is a fair assumption on the president's part. But he was concerned about what the re-election campaign would do to the country, and so, having objectively assessed the public doubts and the loss of confidence in him as a leader, he was ready to reject renomination. By stepping down, he told me, he would allow fresh leadership to come to the Oval Office and give the nation time and reason to compose itself.

Moreover, he told me that he was absolutely convinced that he must dispel any notions within the North Vietnamese leadership that he was using the peace talks as a political ploy. If he called for peace talks, and in the same breath foreswore renomination, Hanoi would have sufficient reason to believe that his pleas for peace were earnest and not politically motivated. Thus, it was that both war *and* peace were at the heart of the Johnson decision to give up the presidency.

He had changed the social face of America, forever. The blacks, the sick, the old, the poor, the young who wanted an education, would in a calmer time remember him and be grateful to him. The war, however, was too near, too fiery, to ignore. And so having done what he could, right or wrong, he decided he would no longer be president.

It was generally concluded that when Lyndon Johnson left the White House to go into retirement he would find it impossible to live without power. The pundits had it that the former president would be restless and impatient, and intrude on matters of state in Washington. In all honesty, I had my own doubts that this volatile and dominant man would be able to find peace and serenity out of office. We were all wrong.

LBJ returned to Texas—to his ranch and his land—and there went about the business of being a rancher: monitoring the rainfall, supervising his foreman and hands, inspecting his irrigation and his grass, buying and selling cattle, and of course, plunging into the matter of his library on the campus of the University of Texas.

Those of us who visited him and tried to engage him in political talk got only a smile and silence. The former president never voiced any opinions, except about his Herefords; and while he enjoyed conversation, it was usually centered around humor and a nostalgia for a hundred events, many of which had no impress on history, but recorded something warm and funny.

My wife and I spent vacations with LBJ in Acapulco at the seaside residence of the former president of Mexico, Miguel Aleman. There for a month or so (we usually joined him for a week) he and Mrs. Johnson would invite close friends to share their holiday. He loved the sun and the sea, and oftentimes in the late afternoon we would sit on the tiled veranda, a dozen or more of LBJ's friends, and watch the sun disappear over the blue water of the Bay of Acapulco. He joked, laughed, reminisced, and would find one or two of us to rib.

I heard all those famous LBJ stories, again and again. He would embellish them each time, adding some new twist, editing out a few lines and moving in some others, enhancing each delivery with that splendid gift of mimicry that enlivened all his stories.

But it was generally conceded by all in attendance that

hard political talk was *verboten*. It was not that the president resented the entry of politics into the conversation; he
simply let others carry on the discussion. Every now and
then, he would turn to me and say: "Are you still sleeping
good these days, Jack?" But he did want to know "the
news." He would enjoy hearing others talk about Washington, about what they heard and what they thought.

I never heard him criticize President Nixon or his administration. But then, I never heard him criticize any
president. When he was vice-president, the greatest sin
one could commit in his presence would be a critical comment about President Kennedy. I remember so well an
evening in 1962 when I was a guest at the LBJ Ranch.
The vice-president was entertaining some male guests, all
of whom (with the exception of myself) were millionaire
Texans; while supporters of LBJ, these men were not exactly fans of President Kennedy. One man, whose al-
legiance to LBJ went back many years, began to inveigh
against President Kennedy. LBJ fixed him with a stern
gaze, and as the tirade continued, the vice-president finally leaned forward over the table and said in a raspy
voice: "Either you quit your talk about the president or
you leave this table." The speaker was shocked, and the
others around the table made visible their own discomfort.
Then the man who was doing the talking said in a low
voice: "I am sorry, Lyndon, I didn't mean to offend you."
LBJ, still raging, replied, "Well, goddamnit, you did, and
you better stop it now."

That was the end of that conversation.

So, it was a natural thing with President Johnson to find
tough criticism of the incumbent president unacceptable to
him. I have no doubts that he had considerable faults to
find with what President Nixon was doing on the domestic scene, though he backed strongly Nixon's efforts on the
world canvas. But he never was publicly or privately criti-

cal of President Nixon. There were two negative incidents concerning President Nixon, though LBJ gave no public notice of any discomfort.

One occurred just after the election in November 1968. It had to do with a possible visit by LBJ to the Soviet Union in December. As has been disclosed in the press, President Johnson had almost put the finishing seal to an official visit to Moscow in mid-1968 when Soviet tanks and troops marched into Czechoslovakia, shattering the proposed plans.

One evening at his ranch, several months before he died, he chatted with me about what subsequently happened. We walked down to the river's edge. The night was washed clear and fine, with just enough clouds to promise some rain, the open sky had turned that shiny blue so much admired by Texas ranchers. LBJ spun some dry grass in his hands and told me the story. Very quietly the Russians had let President Johnson know, after the 1968 election, that they would welcome him warmly if he chose to go to Moscow, a visit he deeply wanted to undertake. But elated though the president was, he recognized that a visit by the lame duck president to Russia without the newly elected president might leave some bitter aftertaste.

LBJ sent word to the president-elect to suggest that they both go to Russia and in that unique combination perhaps a way could be found to really open up a détente with the Soviets. LBJ was fascinated with the prospect for he felt this kind of bipartisan journey, with both presidents locked arm in arm in negotiations with the Russians, would yield positive results. But from the Nixon camp came only silence. Then the response was forthcoming and it came not from the president-elect, but from his interim foreign policy adviser, Robert Murphy. The answer was "no."

The president was obviously disappointed. But he understood the Nixon decision. "He was coming in and I was going out, and he had the big decisions over the next four years. He saw it one way and I saw it another way. But he had to push the levers, I didn't and so I said no more about it except to decline to the Russians. But I think it would have been a good trip. I think it could have paid off for this country. Never before had two presidents, one in office and one about to go in office, ever joined in common cause for the good of the nation. It was one helluva idea"; LBJ's eyes were fired up, that engine inside him churning away. That was the only time he brought up this subject as if he wanted to let it run through him once more, and he let it spill away, not to be talked about again, at least with me.

The other incident had more of a cutting edge. The president spoke about it to me several times after he left office, but he first broached it to me in a luncheon at the White House on November 10, 1968. Mrs. Johnson had called Mary Margaret and me and asked us to lunch and the four of us dined in the family dining room in the living quarters of the Mansion. First we watched Walt Rostow on "Issues and Answers" and then went in to lunch.

The president told us he had had a bad previous six weeks. Beginning in early October he felt that all signs pointed to a break in the Paris peace talks. Hanoi began to show a willingness to go forward. We were in a delicate time, and all intelligence coming to the president, as well as direct conversations with the North and South, clearly portended a definite break for the better.

Just when it appeared that the gut issues separating both sides had begun to soften—the South willing to take part in the peace negotiations, with the proviso that the bombing would stop though parts of the agreement would not be made public at the time—and both President Thieu and President Johnson had definitely agreed on a joint statement of concord, something came unglued. Suddenly the South turned bafflingly stubborn, delaying, backing and filling, turning skittery at every importuning from the U.S. side.

The president said that hard information had come to him that representatives of Nixon reached President Thieu and urged him not to accept this arrangement. They intimated to Thieu that it would not be in his best interests, more than intimating that if Nixon won, the South would get a better deal. Moreover, the representatives of Nixon cited to Thieu speeches by the vice-president and by McGeorge Bundy, then president of the Ford Foundation, as evidence that the U.S. would sell out Saigon as soon as Humphrey took office. This information reaching the president told him that the Nixon campaign managers were terrified of a total bombing halt because they believed this would undercut Nixon's lead and would redound to his disfavor.

President Johnson said that he had kept both Nixon and Humphrey informed of every turn in the negotiations, and both Nixon and Humphrey said they would back LBJ in his every move. But the president said it was clear to him that the Nixon aides were nervous and fidgety over the prospect of a full bombing halt and the inclusion of the South in the talks.

The president knew every move made by the Nixon representatives with the Saigon government and it instilled in him a cold fury. It occurred to him that Nixon may not have known precisely what was going on and so the Johnsonian wrath was visited on Nixon aides rather than the candidate himself.

"I thought about going public with this information," said the president to me. "I never understood that kind of under-the-table maneuvering when the end of the war was at stake. Either you are for peace or you are not. To keep this war going when we could have stopped it was a damned shame."

Both Dean Rusk and Clark Clifford urged the president not to go public with the information. They felt it would fracture the society. LBJ, still furious, hesitated, but finally decided to keep this crucial information to himself.

At this same luncheon, the president also sketched out his philosophy about what his presidency was all about. He said that he was at odds with men like James Reston and Walter Lippmann. "They have no faith in the brown man and no faith in the Asian people," he said. He believed that Reston and Lippmann felt the great thrust of the future to be China and the Red Chinese Communist system. "I totally disagree.", said the president. "I place my bet against Communism and on the Asians. If it develops that stabilized governments in Asia are unable to carve out their own destiny, then I will be wrong." But he went on to say that he saw nothing in the present or the future to indicate that the Communist system will be the way of the future and indeed the direction in which Asian governments ought to go. He said he thought history would have to be the judge of this, but he was convinced that he was right and the Lippmann-Reston adherents were wrong. He said that he personally liked Scotty Reston and Walter Lippmann: "I enjoy talking to them. They are interesting and imaginative men." But he concluded he saw things in the world so different from them.

* * *

LBJ watched with interest and approbation the Nixon moves for détente with the Red Chinese. I suspect this was an opening he would have been pleased to make himself and he was full of praise of the Nixon Asian political adventure. "Republican presidents can do things with Communist governments for which Democratic presidents would be lynched," he said.

But he did have misgivings about the Great Society programs systematically razed by his successor. And I think it surely pained him to see what he considered back-pedaling in civil rights and education. I think one of the main reasons why he opened the educational papers and the civil rights papers in the LBJ Library to public inspection was to show his concern for what he thought to be dismantling of these LBJ programs.

On December 11, 1972, the day of the Civil Rights Symposium in Austin, in the LBJ Library, the former president was ailing. That was plain. His face was drawn. The flesh hung loosely from his jaw. But he was there and he determined that nothing short of a fatal heart attack would keep him from the auditorium. He stayed for the entire two days. There, surrounding him, were all his old allies in his historical struggle to free the black man in America. There were new ones there too: the immensely tall Vernon Jordon, smooth-faced, assured, articulate, head of the Urban League since the death of Whitney Young; Julian Bond, who curiously was an attacker of LBJ on the war, and now came to Austin to join this celebration of a great human rights victory; and Barbara Jordan, wise, confident, the new congresswoman from Texas, whose fund-raiser during the campaign LBJ attended, to show his support of and his affection for her. Roy Wilkins came, the longest-in-years friend of the president, to whom LBJ had turned for counsel, when the fighting in the Congress had been bitter and protracted. And Clarence Mitchell of Maryland was there, a stalwart who loved LBJ and who was in turn deeply loved by the president.

And there in the auditorium President Johnson rose to make what was to be his last public address on civil rights. The fire came slowly, for he ached with pain; in full view of the audience at one point he popped a nitroglycerin pill into his mouth. But as he spoke, the fuel of a thousand nights and days in a cause he made his own began to fill his veins. He came alive again, the gestures were vigorous, the chin and jaw thrust forward, the face was gleaming with righteous confidence. Roy Wilkins leaned forward in his chair, and his eyes grew misty. Clarence Mitchell throbbed with excitement; his president was on the rostrum again, and the cause of the black man was not alien anymore, it was front and center and the champion was in the ring once more. When the president descended the stage, anguish filled that auditorium for the giant was clearly not so strong as once he was. His steps were short and studied. He came down to his seat slowly, as if every step was a planned excursion. But he came down with applause roaring through the hall, bursting around the president like confetti filling an avenue. He smiled and gestured, and then he sat down.

It was the final act in a tableau which began in 1957 when Senate Majority Leader Lyndon Johnson masterminded the first civil rights bill to pass Congress in a hundred years, and absorbed the nation's attention as one after another the barriers fell, with LBJ wielding the axe and leading the way, pulling Congress and the nation with him.

It was Clarence Mitchell who supplied the ending line when he stood up to rebut an unscheduled black speaker who made some insubstantial remarks which, in essence, derided the work of President Johnson. Mitchell rose and roared: "If Lyndon Johnson had the courage to denounce white demagogues, then I have the courage to denounce black demagogues." LBJ smiled at this. It was the kind of talk he understood.

LBJ kept his own communication lines continually open to former Presidents Truman and Eisenhower. He admired them both, in different ways, and sought their counsel frequently.

I recall one poignant conversation between Harry Truman and Lyndon Johnson in, I believe, late 1965. LBJ had been taking a pounding in the press that particular week. Things were going badly for him and he was a bit testy one evening as we sat together in his bedroom in the Mansion. Abruptly he picked up the phone and told the White House operator, "Get President Truman on the phone."

When the call came through I picked up the extension in the bathroom to make sure they both got on the wire. I confess I held onto the receiver a little longer than I should have. When Mr. Truman came on the phone, the president said, "This is Lyndon Johnson. How are you, Mr. President?" I heard Truman's voice, surprisingly strong, obviously full of delight: "You are mighty nice to call me, Mr. President. I'm feeling pretty good, with no regrets."

After some "family" talk about their wives, LBJ began to summarize a number of his problems, and at the end of a brief recounting, he said: "What do you think I ought to do?"

President Truman replied with vigor: "You're doing damn well, Mr. President. You just keep up what you're doing because you are right on course. You are doing what is right for this country and I support you every inch of the way. Don't you let any of those goddamn critics get you down. The country is with you, and so am I."

I quietly put the phone down and came in the president's bedroom. He was holding the receiver close to his ear, his mouth widening in a big grin. It struck me again that presidents are human. Presidents like to hear somebody they respect applaud their actions. They continued to chat, LBJ unfolding his catalogue of lament, and HST, with gusto, reviving LBJ's spirit.

LBJ finally said, "I can't thank you enough for your words and your support. They mean more to me than you may know. Bird and I send love to Mrs. Truman. And don't forget to let me know whenever you want to come see me. You know you have a plane at your disposal at any time." * When the talk had ended, it was as if LBJ had taken a strong tonic. He was refreshed.

I learned a good deal about the need for presidents to "go to the country" when their spirits were low. LBJ would tour the nation with unflagging energy and while his aides would collapse in exhaustion from twenty-hour days, LBJ would remain energetic, full of enthusiasm. The reason is quite simple. To go among the people, to feel their affection, to see their outstretched arms, holding up their children to see the president, to hear their voices claiming love and loyalty, is to receive the equivalent of a ton of vitamin B-12. The press (and the staff) and critics may complain that a president travels too much, but to the chief executive hearing and receiving the rousements and the aroma of the people's affection is a tonic. Most presidents need it, and seek it, and rejoice in it. Never underestimate the power of public applause to a beleaguered public man.

Often, I would call General Schulz, military aide to President Eisenhower, to pass along an LBJ request to see

---

* LBJ had issued an order that former presidents, which at that time included Truman and Eisenhower, would have military jets at their command, complete with steward, military aides, pilots, etc., to transport them wherever they wished to go. Previous to that order former presidents travelled on a catch-as-catch-can basis, by commercial air or whatever. When LBJ opened the World's Fair in New York in 1965, President Truman was present. When I went forward to shake his hand, he poked a sturdy forefinger in my chest and said smilingly, "Son, you tell President Johnson I sure am grateful to him for the use of a plane. He's been so damn nice to me and I want him to know how much I appreciate it."

Eisenhower. On several occasions, in order to avoid press talk, Ike would be transported by Jetstar from Gettysburg to Andrews Air Force Base, outside Washington. President Johnson and I would travel by car or chopper to Andrews and in the cabin of the Jetstar the two men would meet, the former president and the current president. General Schulz and I would discreetly keep our distance in the small cabin, while Ike and LBJ chatted.

President Johnson put great store in these presidential counselings. He wanted to hear firsthand from each of the former chief executives what they felt, how they judged a particular issue, and what their advice would be. I don't believe he ever took any specific action in Vietnam that he didn't check with Ike to seek his counsel.

*   *   *

How did LBJ feel about the cloak of silence that high chieftains of the Democratic party seemed to have wrapped around him, cocooning him off from the political pit? Did he feel hurt or bitterness? Did he care? Yes, I think he did.

When the Democratic Convention of 1972 began, I watched the proceedings on television. This was the first convention I had not attended in twelve years. That first night I trembled with anger when I saw what was going on in the hall. Pictures of all past Democratic presidents—FDR, Truman, Kennedy—plus Adlai Stevenson, were hung in a grand sweep over the speaker's rostrum. But nowhere was LBJ's portrait to be found. Finally, when the camera gazed on the rear of the auditorium, one might pick up LBJ's picture alongside congressional leaders of past and present. No offense meant to these good and courageous men who led the party in the Congress, but it was an absurd malignant cut at President

Johnson, and I raged inside. I thought, God, what must the president think? Speaker after speaker rose to invoke all the past glories of the party, and not once did anyone mention Lyndon Johnson by name. It was not until Senator Ted Kennedy rose, late in the convention, that anyone dared to speak LBJ's name. Senator Kennedy was gracious and grateful to the president. It was almost an act of courage on his part.

I wrote a piece which Philip Geyelin, editor of the *Washington Post*'s editorial page, published in the Op-Ed section of the *Post:*

. . . But "Dejohnsonization" Made LBJ a Non-Person
By Jack Valenti

As I watched the Democratic telethon, and then the convention that followed I kept waiting for someone to acknowledge that Lyndon Johnson was a Democratic President. But as the week ended it became clear that as far as the telethon and the convention were concerned (except for a late Thursday night speech by Senator Kennedy) President Johnson was a non-person, expunged from the Democratic Party with the same kind of scouring effectiveness that Marxist revisionists use to rewrite Communist history. As a final petty insult, the managers of the convention made sure LBJ's picture was absent among the portraits of FDR, Truman, Stevenson and JFK.

It seemed odd that the party, so firmly fixed in its zeal to bring justice and hope to all Americans, turned its back on President Johnson, who more than any President in all U.S. history accomplished what had eluded all his predecessors in the area of human rights, education, health care, aid to the poor, conservation, and just plain caring about the powerless, the forgotten, and the uninvited.

It was an act of discourtesy, not to mention memory gone sour.

I cannot but believe that black people throughout this land understand with a fervor born of too much neglect that it was a President from the Southwest, of all places, who did more to lift the level of their living and to secure their pride than any other man. The first black on the Supreme Court, the first black in the Cabinet, the first black Assistant Attorney General. Have we forgotten? The Civil Rights Act of 1964, the Voting Rights Act of 1965, the Equal Housing Act of 1968 have fastened in conscience and legislation rights that belong to all U.S. citizens. But before Johnson these rights existed only in rhetoric. Lyndon Johnson gave human rights the covenant of national law.

Ever since Lincoln, Presidents have made the motions and gone through the ritual of putting human rights on the agenda. But not until Johnson came to command did aspirations transform into achievement. Charles Evers and every black elected official in the South know better than any of us that it was the Johnson human rights action that gave the vote to the black man, and with that vote he could now govern.

But in the convention no one wanted to remember, and no one seemed to care.

For years the Democratic Party talked and talked about bringing education to the masses, but federal aid to this educational advance always foundered and faltered and never happened. It was the Elementary and Secondary Education Act in the Johnson administration that burst the opposition and for the first time the poorest child in the bleakest ghetto or on the most remote rural farm now has a chance to get an adequate education. That Johnson legislative achievement was the beginning, the essential beginning, and all that now has taken place owes its life to that source-bed of educational aid. But in the convention, they all forgot.

To the aged and the sick, this blotting out of Johnson must have produced a peculiar torment. How long has the Democratic Party put Medicare in its platform? But that is where it always stayed, in the platform, words without substance, promises undelivered, pledges without redemption. Medicare and all that it has meant to those to whom lingering sickness was a family financial disaster didn't just happen. It was the result of the Johnson determination that help for the poor sick aged was a right that had to be fulfilled and it was. This was an achievement worthy of hall-bursting applause. But in the convention, there was only a shameless silence.

The list of advances in human justice is endless, almost a hundred landmark pieces of legislation that aimed at caring about those who had many partisans and shouters but few achievers.

It was all very strange, a dimly lit Orwellian adventure in which nonspeak and nonmemory paraded the telethon and the convention like some ravaged ghosts.

There is an old French maxim which declares that if we were without faults we would not take so much pleasure in finding them in others. Perhaps it is possible, for those who suddenly found hindsight a splendid luxury, to erase their Vietnam guilts by devouring their former leader. Perhaps.

It was written of Lord Burleigh, advisor to English monarchs, that "he never deserted his friends till it was very inconvenient to stand by them."

There was a lot of inconvenience on display over TV last week.

Two days after its publication, I received a phone call from President Johnson. His voice was light and warm: "I thank you, Jack, for that very nice piece you wrote for the *Post*. But I don't want you to do anything like that again. I am afraid it might hurt you, and cause you problems." I told him I did that on my own and I fully intended to do it again, if the occasion called for it.

Some weeks later I visited him at his ranch. The president was in a ruminating mood and for the first time since his retirement he brought up politics in my presence. He thanked me again for the *Post* article, and said, "I guess I might be a kind of a handicap but I don't really think so. But then, a man (referring to elected officials) has to do what he thinks is best for him right now and maybe putting an arm around me is not exactly politic right now."

We drove on a little further over the pastures adjoining the ranch airstrip. "I have gotten a lot of letters about your article. It must have been reprinted in a number of newspapers. They were all kind letters, rather nice to me. Not a one was a bad letter or an angry letter except on my behalf." He smiled slightly as if embarrassed, then stopped the car to talk with his ranch foreman about an irrigation pipe that was leaking. That was the end of that subject with him. He mentioned it not once again.

He did not lose interest in the affairs of the nation and the Democratic party. He was peeved when so many of his former colleagues and close friends joined Democrats for Nixon. He did not banish his affection and friendship for John Connally for leading this movement, for he knew for some time that Connally, an immensely able man, reeking of an animal charisma so attractive to voters, who resembled so much the young Lyndon Johnson in mannerism and sheer ability, would choose to cut his moorings to the Democratic party. Connally, at heart more conservative than LBJ and visibly uncomfortable with the loose ideological abandon of the McGovern groupings, had long made it clear that he would find a presidency under Nixon infinitely more palatable than under McGovern. LBJ understood Connally and his incompatability with the liberal-left element in the party. But the president felt that his own people, particularly those who had served him in his administration ought not make a public display of their irritation with McGovern.

He called me some days after it was announced that several former LBJ aides had joined the Democrats for Nixon movement. "You're going to stay hitched, aren't you?" he asked. "I'm not taking any public stands because of my movie industry responsibilities, Mr. President," I said. "That's good," he said, and he said no more about it.

He offered no reference at all to the fact that George McGovern had made only faint, and intermediary, attempts to talk with him. When McGovern finally contacted the president and requested an appointment to see him in Texas, the president assented, agreeably. He became a bit annoyed when it was announced in the newspapers that McGovern had been "invited to Texas by the president." Within hours that disparity with the facts had been straightened out; LBJ also stipulated that only McGovern and Sargent Shriver were to come to the ranch, without the press. The president told me he didn't want to make a big spectacle out of this visit. He was respectful of the McGovern candidacy and if the nominee chose to talk to the former president, McGovern would be received with courtesy and attentiveness.

Several weeks after George McGovern and Sargent Shriver had been to the ranch, I visited with the president. I queried him about what was said. He merely smiled at first, and later in the day as we sat in the stone-walled living room of his ranch house, he began to talk about the visit.

I asked him if he gave any advice to McGovern. "Yes,"

he said, "I did. I told George that, first, he should put a blanket over talk about cutting the defense budget by thirty billion dollars and all the specifics about cutting the carrier fleet from sixteen to six. Whenever you make an issue out of dismantling the Sixth Fleet, for in practical terms that is what would happen, you scare the hell out of every Jewish voter in the country, and you damn near frighten the devil out of almost everyone else. When you tell the American people you are ready to slice the air wings in half, scuttle the carrier fleet, and pretty much shrink the defense posture, you put everything in doubt. Tell the people that you are dead set on cutting fat and waste in the defense budget, about ten billion dollars worth of waste each year. Everybody is in favor of slicing fat, but they get mighty frightened when you say you are going to disarm the nation. And second, I told George that whoever thought up that $1,000 a person dole ought to be fired today. I told George that in all my years in politics I never heard of anybody elected to office on a platform of raising taxes. Everybody who makes over $12,000 a year is ready to run to the hills to vote for Nixon when they hear their taxes are going to be raised in order to give away $1,000 per person per year. It is a damn fool idea and probably is the best asset that Nixon has. And finally, I told George that he ought to surround himself with some working politicians, and throw out the amateurs who would ruin him long before he got to election day. Amateurs make speeches and make loud noises about how right they are, but they can't count, and they lose elections."

All of this was said with zest, with the mobile Johnson face transporting a listener to where it was all happening. The president spoke with ease and affection about George McGovern and Shriver. LBJ had never been close to McGovern when he was president, and it was not easy to erase years of McGovern saber-slashing LBJ on the war. I daresay McGovern felt something less than warm comfort sitting there with the former president whom he had flagellated and besieged over the past five years.

But the president did not criticize McGovern in his conversation with me. Indeed, his talk was without bitterness or rancor. "George McGovern is a good, decent man. His problem is he's running a bad campaign. Too many blunders."

"I'll show you something," he said, "that you will find interesting." He picked up the phone, buzzed his secretary: "Bring me the McGovern letter." When she came in, she gave him a letter which he passed to me. "Read this," he said.

My dear Mr. President and Mrs. Johnson:

Thank you, thank you, thank you for the one of the most interesting, informative, cordial and fascinating discussions I have ever experienced. There will be no more important discussion that Sargent Shriver and I will have in this campaign than our visit with you wise and dear people. I cannot properly tell you the thoughts that raced through my mind as we talked.

Mr. President, your greatness as a man, your vision of this country, our burning patriotism—all of these things shine through unmistakably. It is the mark of a really big man that in spite of my years of criticism of your policy in Southeast Asia, you not only received me with kindness, but with genuine concern about my responsibility as the standard-bearer of our Party in 1972. There isn't the slightest doubt in my mind that we not only share a common heritage, but that on nearly all of the great concerns of American life, we stand together.

I came to a new appreciation of both the remarkable force of your personality and your grasp of what is enduring in American life. Your endorsement means more

to me than I can adequately express. I only hope that I
will be worthy of your confidence . . .

> With deep admiration and affection
> I remain, sincerely yours,

> George

He knew he was sick. But never once did I ever see him
or hear him morbid about his future. He knew he would
die soon. He did what a man does when he has to—he got
his affairs in order. With deliberate planning he began to
sell the family holdings. He negotiated a sale of the family
television station.* One by one, he and his wife put the
stray pieces of the Johnson estate in place so that his family would not have to unravel complex business matters.
They would have few problems when finally he left.

His relations with his family were lovely to watch in
these afteryears. He adored his grandchildren and he
played with them joyously. He admired his sons-in-law,
former Marine Major Chuck Robb, married to Lynda
Bird, and handsome Pat Nugent, husband of Luci.
He told me so many times he was a lucky man to have
young men of such character and integrity.

With Mrs. Johnson, there was always that special kind
of oneness. She ministered to him, and he needed her with
a largeness that all of us close to the both of them saw and

---

* Like a political warhorse still squirming with nostalgic energy, LBJ
pawed the ground in delight when he encountered brains and ability
in a man or woman. The chief negotiator for the Times Mirror Corporation in its sessions to buy the Johnson family TV station was a
Harvard Business School classmate of mine, Albert V. ("Al") Casey,
then president of the corporation, and now president and chief executive officer of American Airlines. Casey absolutely fascinated the
president with his Irish gusto and shrewd intellect. "Why the hell
didn't you tell me about Al Casey before this," LBJ demanded to
know of me. "I could have used him in the White House."

understood. I just don't believe LBJ could have navigated the future if Mrs. Johnson had died first. He would have decayed, quickly, terminally. Without her, the juice of life would have fled, and he would not have had any incentive to keep going.

I worried about him, but I must confess I was victim to the LBJ durability syndrome. I could not conceive of his being unable to beat back any attacks on himself, from whatever source. I could see him aging. I could see the walk slower, the sitting down become more prevalent, the long rides in the car to inspect the cattle becoming briefer. And yet, I did not truly think he was dying. Did I refuse to think this, or was it a real conviction? I don't know.

But what I did know was that the president *knew.*

At 6:45 A.M. on Sunday morning, January 21, 1973, the phone in my Washington home rang. I was up, getting dressed to play an early morning tennis game. I answered the ring. It was the president. His voice was spirited, and full of humor. "I called you," he said, "because I told Bird you would be the only friend of mine who would be up at this hour." He laughed.

"How are you feeling, Mr. President?" I asked him.

"Well," he said, "I feel fine now. I always feel good in the mornings. But around noontime, I get these angina pains and they hurt like hell. I try to lie down to feel better."

Then he said he had called to tell me that he and Mrs. Johnson had decided to go to Acapulco again this year. They had debated it for some time since his illness, but he had determined he would go.

"Maybe the sun will do you good, Mr. President," I said.

"Yes, I think it will. Acapulco is at sea level so the altitude won't bother me. So, I decided we will go. We want you and Mary Margaret to join us. When can you get away?" We worked out a schedule as to when I could leave and then he said: "I thought you were going to send me that David Halberstam letter to you."

When Halberstam's book *The Best and the Brightest* came out I read it immediately. I was unhappy over Halberstam's portrayal of McGeorge Bundy and Bob McNamara. I thought he had treated these two public servants cruelly. I was also incensed over Halberstam's stories about me, all of which were factually inaccurate. Most of all, I was disturbed over the LBJ section in the book. So I wrote Halberstam a long letter spelling out my discontent. Some time went by and then I received a handwritten six-page letter in response from the author. It was surprisingly gentle. In the letter, he explained his own admiration for LBJ and said he considered him to be the only man "of juice" on the Washington scene. He praised the president as a man and leader and quarrelled only with Vietnam.

This is what Halberstam wrote me on the last two pages of his letter:

> My portrait of Johnson. Well, you may be right, perhaps no man can get him down on paper. He is the elemental leader. And yet, by God, I tried, and I think this portrait of a very great man caught in a terrible turn of history is accurate, fair and in a curious way, not unloving and not unsympathetic. He is, I think, the most human figure in the entire book. He reeks of human juices. You complain about my use of his vulgarities. I used them, not to titillate; I used them because they were, as comparable vulgarities of Andrew Johnson were, an important part of the man. And when I write that we will not see his like again, I do so, with very great regret.

It was such a turnabout limning of Johnson which I never expected that I told the president about Halberstam's letter. He had not read Halberstam's book, but I did whet his appetite; he wanted to read Halberstam's letter.

"I sent the letter down to the ranch, Mr. President. I sent it to Dorothy Territo." (Dorothy Territo was the chief custodian of the president's papers.)

"Dammit, why didn't you send it to me? Dorothy Territo didn't ask you for it, I did." I glowed, for this was the old LBJ scratching and churning and impatient with delay.

"I'll call Dorothy and have her send it out with the rest of the mail today," he said. (The letter from Halberstam to me was in the last mail pouch sent to the president. It arrived at the ranch some minutes after he died. The president never had a chance to read the letter.)

Then he asked: "What's new in Washington?"

It was almost as if time had not passed. This was the usual question and I answered it in the usual way, citing the people whom I had talked to, what the pulse-beat was in the capital; in general I spoke all that I had observed since our last conversation, a week before.

He chided me in that laughing way about my asking that if the Acapulco trip were on, we would be delighted if Mollie Parnis, the dress designer and a dear, close friend of both the president and Mrs. Johnson as well as my wife and me, would be in the visiting group to Mexico the same time we were there.

"Why do you want me to share Mollie with you? Lady Bird had told me you and Mary Margaret wanted Mollie down with you. I think I will ask you down when I have some boring men and not charming ladies like Mollie." But it was settled that Mollie Parnis would be at the Aleman place the same time the Valentis were.

Some forty-five minutes after we began, the conversation ended. It ended on a high note, the president laughing about our last golf game in Acapulco, in which he accused me of moving my ball in the rough. I denied the story indignantly. He insisted it was true. "I told the Secret Service to put you under heavy surveillance when we play. I am going to get the proof on you this time."

Swearing my innocence, we hung up. It was the last time I spoke with him, and it was the last phone call he made to Washington.

Some thirty-four hours later, death stalked the thirty-sixth president of the United States in his bedroom, on the ranch he loved so much. He died alone, gasping for breath, seconds after he had called for aid from the Secret Service.

I was in Palo Alto, California, at the home of Douglass and Libby Cater, my close friends since the days when Doug was a colleague of mine and special assistant to the president on educational matters. Doug and I sat on the patio of his home minutes before I was to leave for the Stanford University campus where I would be addressing a group of students.

We talked about the president, relaxing, remembering, trading stories about this man who had invaded our lives and changed them. The phone rang. It was my secretary calling from Washington. Did I know that President Johnson had just died?

The phone hung limply in my hand, and I placed it back on its cradle. I wept. Doug and Libby and I wept together. I cancelled my speaking engagement and flew home to Washington that night.

The next night, David Brinkley called me. Would I join him on the NBC special telecast of the return of the president's body to Washington and its ride to the Rotunda of the Capitol? I demurred. "I'm sorry, David, my place is in the Rotunda with the president," I told him. Brinkley's voice was understanding, "Jack, you can do a lot more good for the president talking to twenty-five million people about him than you can standing in the Rotunda."

I reflected and I thought he was right. I did try to explain to NBC viewers just who this man was, and the kind of man he was. Watching the monitors in the studio, I saw my life pass by, the years of loving and serving, and the day it ended. The next day, my wife and I boarded Air Force One, offered by President Nixon to Mrs. Johnson to take the president's body back to Texas and the ranch.

When we were airborne, I walked to the aft of the plane and stood by the flag-draped coffin. Suddenly it struck me. This was the same plane, number 26000 on its tail, the very same plane that had flown the new president from Dallas to Washington on November 22, 1963. I had seen in this very same spot another flag-draped coffin, that one bearing the lifeless body of John Kennedy. Now I stood beside a coffin with Lyndon Johnson inside.

I marveled that any box could contain this avalanche of a man. Perhaps, I thought, it was only temporary and he would come roaring out of that coffin, taking charge of the funeral to see that it was done with efficiency and dispatch. I still didn't believe it was possible to finally grab hold of that immense heart and force it to stop beating.

On that November day in 1963, Mrs. Johnson had been by his side, as she was now. He spoke to her on that flight from Dallas, he spoke to her to gain strength himself, and she responded to him quietly with that inborn grace that has no genetic certainty, that sweet firmness that is connected to no formulas. Now she sat in dry-teared grief, still stunned by an event she had contemplated, surely, but whose presence now was folded inside her heart.

Liz Carpenter had been on the Dallas flight. She was

aboard Air Force One now. Liz, so full of life, unable to resist a comic line or jest, slumped heavily in her seat—no laughter, no funny lines, just stillness. Marie Fehmer, the president's secretary, who had been so unflappable on that Dallas flight, now sat gazing out at the sameness of the thin blue horizon line, gazing out but seeing nothing.

And so we flew on that day. We had been with him at the very beginning, we had been at his side when he needed us, and now we were riding with him to the very end, to be with him when they put him in the Texas soil he loved so much.

* * *

What is President Johnson's epitaph? What would he have wanted on his tombstone? How would he have wanted to have been remembered?

On January 13, 1969, there gathered in New York in one of the great hotels a turnout of LBJ friends, colleagues, sometime-enemies, and sometime-allies to pay tribute to the thirty-sixth president. In seven days Lyndon Johnson would leave his office to retire to private life and this overflowing hall had one concern: to tell the president of the love and respect and admiration they felt for him. There were printed in the program that evening, essays from political observers, academicians, cabinet officers, and others of national stature. One essay was on the presidency. It was written by James MacGregor Burns, the internationally renowned historian. One paragraph said:

> Students of government, like myself, will remember Lyndon Johnson for a further and special reason. He was the first President to recognize fully that our basic social ills are so rooted in encrusted attitudes and stubborn social structures that no single solution or dramatic

crusade will solve them; the first President to see clearly that only a total attack across the widest front, with every possible weapon, would bring a breakthrough; and the first President to propose basic institutional changes to make a total attack possible.

Ralph Ellison, the famous author who wrote that unforgettable book *Invisible Man*, may have made a better assay. Ellison considered the Johnson presidency, with all its fury and all its flaws, and he wrote:

> When all of the returns are in, perhaps President Johnson will have to settle for being recognized as the greatest American President for the poor and for the Negroes, but that, as I see it, is a very great honor indeed.

But for me I remember most and best a meeting in the Cabinet Room shortly after the passage of the Voting Rights Act of 1965. In the room with the president were Roy Wilkins, Martin Luther King, Philip Randolph, Clarence Mitchell, and all the other black leaders of the nation. There was a religiosity about the meeting, which was warm with emotion—a final celebration of an event so long desired and so long in achieving. When the meeting had ended, I walked out with Roy Wilkins. He put his arm around me, and said softly, "You know, Jack, God does move in strange and wondrous ways. It is a fact and a truth that the bravest, most compassionate, and most effective friend the Negro in America has ever had is a southern president."

Index